CELEBRATING CHRISTMAS

CELEBRATING CHRISTMAS

An Anthology

Edited by Carl Seaburg

Illustrations by John Langan
Musical Arrangements by Leo Collins

Unitarian Universalist Ministers Association

Boston: 1983

The generous support of the Unitarian Universalist Ministers Association in making this book possible is gratefully acknowledged.

This book is dedicated to four who have
greatly enriched our common worship:
        Alfred S. Cole
        Kenneth L. Patton
        Vincent B. Silliman
        Jacob Trapp

CONTENTS

Foreword

When a UUMA "exec" member or two questioned why such a book as this, our President quickly asked around the group, "How many of you do *not* celebrate Christmas in your congregations?" The answer was, of course, unanimous, and I noticed one of those raising the question has some material included here.

Christmas is the Christian celebration we enjoy; Easter always leaves us a little uneasy. Charles Stephen says those of us who have the touch of the heathen about us can find good meaning in this season while Clarke Wells claims that it fits our metaphysics and that is why we like Christmas.

Whatever the reason, it is obvious we celebrate it and produce pages and pages, and more pages, about it. One critic has noted that the material here is unequal in quality; so are we all. You will discover contradictions and displays of ignorance of historical and mythical fact, always well-intentioned, in the spirit of the season. Our "learned" ministry is not always so, nor am I sure it should be. You may quarrel with the organization. The fact that an item is in one section in no way means we intended any limitation of its use to that; so many things could just as easily have fit in more than one section. We encourage you to adapt, just as we have been doing through the centuries with this celebration. (eg. many of the items not designated as responsive readings would be excellent if adapted for that use.)

Being involved in this project has pushed me through — in and out — many a holiday depression — in the midst of summer — as I aided in editing, which I discovered is mainly a matter of commas. Carl tells me that I am definitely a product of The University of Chicago which has discarded his cherished "Harvard comma." If you discern an inconsistency in commas in these pages, neither of us consistently prevailed on this issue.

I've learned much by virtue of my involvement with CELE-BRATING CHRISTMAS. Good will has no hyphen; it can be one

ix

word or two, but not hyphenated. I now know that there are almost as many ways to spell Hanukah as there are days in its observance, and that there are two types of menorah: the one we know as the Hanukkah lights with nine candles, and another with seven (in observance of the creation). I've found out, much to my surprise, that Twelfth Night is *not* January 6, as I've always assumed, but January 5. I have learned that I am much more of a traditionalist than I ever realized (and no more need be said about that!)

I hope that this volume will cause you, as it has me, to confront Christmas — examine its meaning and manner of celebration. Whatever faults you find as you work your way through it, may you discover that this is much more than a working book, one that ministers to you through some of its pages, and may you come to appreciate, as I have, the marvel of some of our colleagues to use words in ways that touch us — universally, communally, individually.

I want to express my special appreciation for the support I received from the members of the UUMA Board who voted this volume into existence, not once, but again, and yet again, and were more than patient during its ''long time coming:'' W. Edward Harris, President; Denise Tracy, Vice President; Alan Egly, Treasurer; John Cummins, William DeWolfe, Paul Johnson and Robert Reed; Bob Cratchit's ''A Merry Christmas to us all, my dears.''

Patricia Bowen
Sherborn, Massachusetts

September, 1983

PREFACE

What we call Christmas is one of the oldest and most enduring of human celebrations. It is built into the physical nature of our ride around the sun. The planet slants in, light loses, darkness and coldness gain, then the oscillation back to warmth and renewal. Always a happy ending!

Christmas is older than any one religious tradition. Every cult — and they are all cults — has adapted itself to the great mid-winter celebration. Way before there were Christians there was "Christmas" — by another name. Each temporary faith grafts its customs and meanings onto the celebration that is there and will outlast them.

Those who come to Christmas from a liberal religious tradition have more to celebrate than those approaching it from any single limited perspective. We join in this ancient festival with full appreciation for its deep roots in the human psyche. Celebrating Christmas we link up — we touch in — with our whole human tribe far back into its prehistory and far forward into any future.

It was not always so. In the early days of our particular Universalist and Unitarian traditions there were marked differences in attitudes. Unitarians — holding to older Puritan beliefs — rejected this celebration as a "Popish superstition." Universalists, however, were Christmas-oriented from the beginning, reflecting John Murray's Anglican and Methodist upbringing.

At a service in his Boston church in 1789 where "the Birth of our Saviour will be celebrated" they even included a special Christmas hymn written by the Rev. George Richards. The last stanza went:

> *He comes! He comes! The Saviour God!*
> *Goodwill, peace, joy for men:*
> *Glad tidings shout to all abroad,*
> *Amen! Amen! Amen!*

Six exclamation points for twenty-one words at least indicates

xi

Richards' fervor — but a collected edition of his poetry has never been demanded.

Certainly his ranting poetry would never convert Unitarians to celebrating Christmas. The Rev. Wm. Bentley up in Salem, Mass. could quietly jubilate in a diary entry for Tuesday, December 25, 1810 that "Christmas has a public service in the morning for English Episcopalians and in the evening from the Universalists. Our Congregational churches stands fast as they were from the beginning." That is — conspicuously — ignoring the day.

There is a record of William Ellery Channing, the great Unitarian, celebrating Christmas. Certainly his friendship with Charles Follen made him aware of how important the festival was to Follen. As a recent German immigrant, Follen brought with him the tradition of the Christmas tree and introduced it to his Lexington, Mass. congregation. New Englanders generally adopted it from there, although Pennsylvania Dutch folk had included the tree in their celebrations of the season a hundred years earlier.

By the middle of the nineteenth century, however, Unitarians were climbing onto the Christmas sleigh, and adding their decorations to the festival. It is claimed that Charles Dickens, after hearing the minister of the Little Portland Street chapel in London preach a Christmas sermon, was inspired to write his most popular work, "A Christmas Carol." We can all be grateful for that anonymous preacher's sermon. Would that all our sermons were as effective!

And that most popular Christmas song, "Jingle Bells" was written in 1854 in Medford, Mass., by James Pierpont, son of the local Unitarian minister. Clearly, as a Medford resident, I was "fated" to compile this anthology!

The collection of material that follows is an outgrowth of more than 150 years of liberal religious attention to the Christmas festival. Without question it is our most popular religious holiday as the abundance and richness of material offered for inclusion in this book would indicate.

The material gathered here is essentially the contribution of this generation and the one just past. Other voices yet to speak will be adding their contributions to the ongoing universal celebration of Christmas. This is ours. It begins with a bit of history, the rationale for a liberal celebration, and then contains a smorgasbord of service material: opening and closing words, responsive readings, poetry, prayers, readings, reflections and reminiscences, seven sections of special services, thirteen new carols, and concludes with additional resources.

Such a collection as this represents would have been impossible without the generous cooperation of the authors of the pieces used. Space precluded using all available items. The selection tried to be as broadly varied as possible to meet the many and diverse tastes and viewpoints within the denomination. If you don't find what you like — adapt! It's an old family custom in this denomination!

In fact, so many of us have "gathered, stolen, revised, and borrowed" from each other (and then forgotten the original authors) that there may be a few inadvertent mis-assignments of proper credit. I give them as they came to me. Of the anonymous attributions here, a fair number are pieces so much changed and altered by various hands as not to be honestly attributed to anyone. Others are of authorship unknown to the editor at this time. If you discover a piece which is "indubitably" yours, please let the editor know so that proper credit can be given in a future edition.

A good number of these pieces may be familiar to readers in a slightly different version. For this collection all but a handful of historical pieces have been made gender inclusive (with the permission of the original authors where possible). This is both a personal and denominational commitment. Once you move your mind into this larger, friendlier realm of inclusiveness, you'll never want to return to the old narrow prison of partiality. Ours is an including faith not an excluding one — and this great universal festival of Christmas is the most inclusive holiday of all.

I am grateful to my religious colleagues for their contributions that made this book possible and to the Unitarian Universalist Ministers Association who have so generously supported its publication. I thank John Langan for his "just right" illustrations, and Leo Collins for his caring attention to the music.

A number of my colleagues have also shared their extensive collections of Christmas material with me most generously and I am most appreciative for this privilege. The editorial assistance of the Rev. Patricia Bowen is particularly appreciated. It made an impressive difference.

I appreciate also the work done by Ann Bailey, Tom Hittle, and Eric Pohl in helping to assemble this collection.

In the dedication I have singled out four remarkable people who have greatly contributed over their lives to the enhancement of our common worship. We are all much in their debt. There remains but one person to thank — unfortunately posthumously — and that is Tracy Pullman, long minister of our church in Detroit, Michigan.

After his death I was given access to his files by his family. He had a full file drawer crammed with Christmas material collected over many years. A good number of items in this collection first came to my attention from his files, so I feel a real debt to him.

I last saw him about a week before Christmas 1980 shopping in a store on Charles Street in Boston with Alice Harrison. She looked like a jolly leprechaun in a bright red coat and he in brilliant red pants — like a slim beardless Father Christmas. The geniality and joy of Christmas were beaming from both.

A few months later and he was gone. But his love of our Christmas celebration lives in this book. May it live on in you as well. And though I write these lines on a July day when it is over ninety in the shade — let me wish you in my father's ancestral Swedish "God Jul" — and in my mother's ancestral Scotch --- "Merrie — hang on to your kilt or ye'll blow into the loch — Christmas and a Happy — May you eat oatmeal every morning for breakfast — New Year."

Carl Seaburg

Green River, Vermont
July, 1983

CELEBRATING CHRISTMAS

I. Christmas is coming

Christmas is coming,
The geese are getting fat.
Please to put a penny
In the old man's hat.

If you haven't got a penny,
a ha'penny will do;
If you haven't got a ha'penny,
God bless you.

Old English Carol

THE HISTORY OF THE FESTIVAL

Is Christmas a universal festival? A brief look at its evolution gives the answer.

From the dimmest dawnings of history, the days around the winter solstice, which under the old Julian calendar fell precisely on December 25, were regarded as a time of very special significance. The great midwinter festival was observed by people who had no more than the rudiments of civilization, but who had learned to become acute observers of the natural world around them. It is not difficult to picture their feelings as summer gave place to harvest, as the leaves began to fall from the trees, as the first snows of winter began to sprinkle the earth. They knew that winter would in the same way eventually yield to spring. At least, it had always done so in the past. But in the absence of exact knowledge as to why the seasons changed as they did, there was always some room for doubt. Perhaps it wouldn't happen this time. Perhaps the days would go on getting shorter and shorter, colder and colder, until the world was swallowed up in a perpetual Arctic night.

So the approach of the winter solstice was marked with growing apprehension. Elaborate ceremonies took place. As the critical moment approached, huge fires were kindled on the hilltops to imitate the light and warmth of the retreating sun, and to lure it back again by magical means. When it began to be apparent that the magic was succeeding, that the days were lengthening instead of shortening, that the sun was returning, the feelings of relief and rejoicing were expressed in the greatest celebration of the year. All normal business came to an end, wars were suspended by common consent, there was dancing and feasting and singing. Kings and peasants, lords and serfs even exchanged places for a day as all rejoiced in the rebirth of the year.

The period of festivities among most early people in the northern hemisphere lasted from December 25 to January 6, and it is no coincidence that these dates mark the traditional "Twelve Days of Christmas." The ancient Celtic and Germanic tribes celebrate these days as far back as their history can be traced; the Norsemen too believed that their gods were in some special sense present among them on earth at this time. A mysterious and awe-inspiring significance thus attached itself to the twelve days, as well as the air of rejoicing. Shakespeare echoed this ancient spirit when he wrote:

> "And then . . . no spirit dares stir abroad; The nights are wholesome; then no planets strike, no fairy takes, nor witch hath power to charm, so hallowed and so gracious is the time."

In most parts of northern Europe the houses were decorated with greenery during this season. The symbolism here is the same as that of the fire of the Yulelog. Just as the light and heat were supposed to attract the sun back, so the display of evergreens was designed to encourage the rebirth of the rest of nature, now lying stark in the chill of apparent death. In Britain, long before the earliest Christian missionaries arrived, the Angli celebrated December 25 as the beginning of the New Year. It was known to them as "Mother's Night." In ancient Babylon this season was the feast of Zagmuk; in the earliest days of Rome it was the Saturnalia.

But the most significant date in the emergence of Christmas as we know it now was 46 B.C. when Julius Caesar introduced the Babylonian calendar into Rome, making it the so-called Julian calendar. "From that day onward," writes Arnold Toynbee, "December 25 was *Natalis Invicti,* 'the birthday of the Unconquered God' for all the inhabitants of the Roman world; and the festival already had, for them, part of the meaning it has today for Christians." The Unconquered God was generally identified with Mithra, a being both human and divine who came originally from Persia. His festival at the darkest season of the year marked the crowning triumph in a great cosmic drama. In the midst of seeming defeat, suddenly there came victory; in the place of darkness, light. The powers of darkness and evil had seemed to be in the ascendancy; no mortal force could throw them back; but now through some miraculous and fearfully potent means salvation had been wrought, the battle had been won, and the path to the renewal of the world had begun.

The symbol of the Unconquered God, naturally enough, was the sun itself, the giver of life to all on earth. It was portrayed as a flaming disc, sometimes with human features inscribed upon it. For several centuries this symbol and the festival of *Natalis Invicti* continued to play a very great part in the life of the Roman Empire. It was not until the fourth century of our era that there came the first attempt to put

4

Christ into Christmas. The first mention of a celebration of the birth of Christ on December 25 dates from the year A.D. 336.

The Birth of Christ

In the earliest Christian church there had been no concern, at all, over the date of Jesus' birth. No one knew when it had taken place, but this was not the main reason that deterred people from deciding upon a date. The fact was that the celebration of birthdays — all birthdays — was looked upon as a pagan and undesirable custom. The great Christian leader Origen pointed out that only the bad characters in the Bible, like Pharaoh and Herod, celebrated their birthdays.

It was not until this attitude faded that Christians felt any compulsion to do the same as the other people among whom they lived; that is, to celebrate the birthday of him whom they worshipped. But, in due course the need was felt, and then there arose the necessity of fixing a date. In determining it, they depended mostly upon numerology and astrology, again following the usual practice of their time. March 28, April 2, April 19, May 20 were all dates which found their supporters during this early period, partly at least because the rebirth of nature in the spring seemed to provide an appropriate setting for the coming of him who would redeem the world. A spring season was also, it would seem, in the mind of the person who first set down the story of the shepherds and the angels. In the area around Bethlehem the shepherds are in the fields keeping watch over their flocks by night from about mid-March to mid-November. They are never out during the cold midwinter season.

But later tradition began to transfer the birth of Christ to the winter. The date now decided upon was January 6. A number of causes appear to have been at work in producing this change. The feast of Dionysus, observed in Greece as part of the celebration of the lengthening of the days, was held on January 6; so too in Alexandria was the birth of Aeon to the virgin Kore. References in ancient writings suggest that there were festivities elsewhere associated with other deities as well; at any rate, the date was one which already had a special significance for the people of the eastern Mediterranean, and it was therefore appropriately seized upon and accepted as a Christian festival.

In taking over an already established occasion in this way, the Christian leaders showed a fine perception of the way in which the human mind works. Revolutions, whether political, social or religious, never destroy the past entirely. Old ways of thought and practice inevitably find their way back. The wisest innovators have always tried to preserve as much continuity as they could consistently do without impairing their own purposes.

5

The choice of January 6 was therefore a natural one so far as the eastern part of the Roman Empire was concerned. But when Christianity became the official religion of the empire its most important centre inevitably became Rome itself. And so the Roman observances rather than the Greek ones came to weigh heaviest in the minds of those who were setting the dates for the Christian festivals. Another change was called for. What could provide a more auspicious setting for the celebration of the birth of Christ than the great Roman festival of *Natalis Invicti* on December 25? The devotion of the people could be transferred without too much protest from the sun itself to him who was symbolically called the Sun of Righteousness. Sir James Frazer uncovered the words of a Syrian Christian of the time who explained the reasons for the change thus:

> "The reason why the fathers transferred the celebration of the sixth of January to the twenty-fifth of December was this. It was a custom of the heathen to celebrate on the same twenty-fifth of December the birthday of the Sun, at which they kindled lights in token of festivity. In these solemnities and festivities and Christians also took part. Accordingly when the doctors of the Church perceived that the Christians had a leaning to this festival, they took counsel and resolved that the true Nativity should be solemnized on that day and the festival of the Epiphany on the sixth of January. Accordingly, along with this custom, the practice has prevailed of kindling fires till the sixth."

So the festival was moved, and before long Augustine was summoning the people not to worship the sun on December 25, but rather him who created the sun; in the same way, Pope Leo the Great rebuked those who still celebrated Christmas as the birthday of the sun rather than the birthday of Christ.

The Christian Battle Against Christmas

But many people in the churches were as resistant to change then as at any later period. Most of the eastern churches fought stubbornly against the efforts from Rome to move Christmas Day to December 25. It took fifty years for Constantinople to accept the change, and another fifty after that to convince Egypt. In Jerusalem opposition was even stiffer, since the Christians there, living in the same country as Jesus himself, supposed themselves to be a better authority on when he was born than the imperial power in Rome. It took two hundred years for them to yield. But the church even farther east, the Armenian church, was never converted at all, and it continues to this day to celebrate Christmas on January 6. The western Christians eventually gave up trying to win them over contenting themselves with calling the Armenians "men with hardened heads and stiff necks."

6

But throughout the west the festival of *Natalis Invicti,* the rebirth of the Unconquered Sun on December 25, became Christmas Day. It retained many of the features of the earlier festivals: the lights, the giving of presents (which had been a prominent feature of the Saturnalia) and the decorating of houses and churches with greenery. The process went ahead very successfully. The origins of the old pagan customs were largely forgotten, and they were all given a new Christian interpretation. Wherever Christianity spread the same process was encouraged. So Pope Gregory wrote to Augustine of Canterbury after the conversion of England, advising him to allow the new Christians to continue their former custom of killing and roasting large numbers of oxen at this season of the year, "to the glory of God" rather than, as before, "to the Devil." The traditional midwinter festivities of all parts of Europe were incorporated into the Christian observances, and some, such as the various ceremonies associated in many places with the Yule log, continue to this day.

But the battle by Christians against Christmas was not over. The Armenians were not the only nonconformists. After the Reformation a great many Protestants, who were well aware of the pagan origins of the occasion, tried to abolish Christmas. Religion was for them a very serious affair, not to be associated with popular festivities. They tried to reintroduce the term "Lord's Day" in place of "Sunday," because Sunday means the day of the Sun-god, and Sunday, like Christmas, had originally been devoted to his worship. In England the Puritans denounced Christmas as a "wanton Bacchanalian feast," and celebrations were at one time forbidden by an Act of Parliament. The same happened in the early days in New England. The first pilgrims, with all their stern insistence on the keeping of the Sabbath, worked as usual on Christmas Day, neglecting it completely. Later in the century the General Court of Massachusetts passed a law which ran as follows: ". . . anybody who is found observing, by abstinence from labour, feasting or any other way, any such days as Christmas Day, shall pay for every such offence five shillings."

This non-observance of Christmas was turned to good account during the Revolutionary wars. In 1776 Washington's army crossed the Delaware river on the night of December 25 to surprise and rout the Hessian troops, who in blissful ignorance of local custom had supposed that there could be no fighting on Christmas Day and had given themselves over to revelry.

Some Traditional Symbols

But in spite of this opposition on the part of many Christians, Christmas continued to grow in popularity as a midwinter festival. By the time Clement Moore wrote *The Night Before Christmas* and Charles Dickens wrote his *Christmas Carol* the full tide of popular support was swinging back to the old observances. Many of the

7

ancient customs, songs, and symbols which had been half-forgotten were now rediscovered, prominent among them the Christmas tree and Santa Claus. Both have a history running back through many centuries, but have only come into their own in English-speaking countries during the past hundred years.

There can be little doubt that the Christmas tree itself is simply a form of the ancient *Yggdrasil,* the World Tree which figures so prominently in the Norse Eddas, though it is to be found in various forms throughout the world. It is a symbol of life itself, and appears appropriately enough at the season of the beginning of life's renewal out of apparently triumphing death. Individuals may come and go, but life goes on. The decorations on the tree represent its fruits, and are intended as a symbol of the endless variety of the gifts of life. Significantly, many of these decorations are themselves presents.

In line with their attitude towards Christmas as a whole, the Puritans of the sixteenth and seventeenth centuries denounced the Christmas tree without mincing words. A German church leader of that period spoke scornfully of what he called "the Christmas or fir tree which people set up in their houses, hang with dolls and sweets, and afterwards shake and deflower. Whence comes the custom," he added, "I know not. It is child's play. Far better were it to point the children to the spiritual cedartree, Jesus Christ."

But the more general attitude has been to incorporate the tree, like other ancient symbols, into new Christian observances. The World Tree was already well known from the creation story in the book of Genesis. Another significance was also obvious. In the early legends from the northland Odin had been portrayed as hanging for nine days from the World Tree, pierced with a spear, offering himself to himself as he sought the victory which would enable him to enter upon his divine powers. Frequently enough in the hymns and rituals of Christianity the Holy Rood or Cross was figured under the form of a tree, only here its fruit was the God who would die and rise again, bringing new life to all. This fitted exactly into the place prepared for it by existing ideas and practices, which are still today very thinly veiled in some places. In the popular religion of tribes in some remote areas of Mexico the Cross still retains its original character as a sacred Tree, festooned with gifts from the people at the beginning of the year to implore a good harvest and thereby the renewal of their own lives during the days to come.

Little of this history may be in the minds of those who buy evergreen trees to place in their homes today. Yet deep within them stirs the same response to the renewal of life that took the dwellers in the northern forests out from time immemorial at the season of the winter solstice to bring in the coniferous boughs to set amid their blazing fires and festive tables.

As for Santa Claus, he too has appeared in many forms during his long life. Originally he was an historical personage, Nicholas, bishop of Myra in Asia Minor during the fourth century. No one knows very much about him, except that he became a saint in due course and for some reason or other, became more and more popular as the patron saint of children, of travellers and eventually of Russia under the imperial regime. Presumably it was his Russian associations that have made him so much a figure from the frozen north, for his original home was certainly far removed from Arctic snows and reindeer. And his association with children brought him his reputation as the bearer of gifts, which were distributed at the time of his feast on December 6, as they still are in some European countries.

The same process as led Christmas to draw into itself all the other features of winter festivals was at work here too. The Saturnalia had long since made Christmas the time for giving of presents, so it was only natural that the feast of Nicholas should be drawn into the general festivities, that good saint's name changing from its original Sanctus Nicolaus to the New York Dutch corruption of Santaklaus. His enormous present-day popularity dates from the publication in 1823 of Clement Moore's *The Night Before Christmas*. The visual image of today's roly-poly Santa Claus was pretty much fixed by the series of drawings by Thomas Nast published each year in *Harper's Weekly* from 1863 to Nast's death in 1902.

These are only some of the components of the richly varied mid-winter celebration. They belong to the season as completely as does the legend of the Christ-child and the theology which has grown up around that legend. With this wide range of meanings in mind, it is now possible to place the specifically Christian interpretations of Christmas in a true perspective.

The Christian Story

It is here that Unitarian Universalists begin to feel uneasy, because of the influence of a theology which we cannot share. Yet even the theology of Christmas, in its essential nature, is not as foreign to us as it might at first sight appear.

Once again it is necessary to appeal to history for an understanding of the real situation. We go back to an age when the real and the fabulous were not as sharply separated as they are today, at least in the more sophisticated parts of the world.

The people among whom Christianity arose would certainly have understood the way in which William Blake expressed himself:

*"What," it will be Question'd, "When the Sun arises, do
you not see a round disc of fire somewhere like a Guinea?"
O no, no, I see an Innumerable company of the Heavenly
host crying, "Holy, Holy, Holy is the Lord God
Almighty."*

This power of imagination was more frequently found in the
ancient world than in Blake's day or our own. It gave rise spontaneously to myths and legends, which attached themselves to the figures
of those who made an impact upon the lives of their fellows. Today we
find miracles an obstacle to our acceptance of a story; in the ancient
world, before the birth of science, the reverse was true. There were
plenty of people who could testify to first-hand experiences of miracles,
just as there are in simpler cultures today.

Early Christianity, it has also to be remembered, was persecuted
and on the defensive — conditions which were psychologically right
for fantasy and wishful inventiveness. The credentials of Jesus as
Messiah and Saviour had to be established. They had to be established
first in the eyes of Jews whose idea of a Messiah was that he would be
a mighty ruler of the house and lineage of David, not a carpenter's son
from the unpromising territory of Galilee.

The logic of the day could easily meet the situation, Christians
argued this: Jesus was the promised Messiah. The Messiah, it had
been foretold, was to be a descendant of David. Therefore Jesus was a
descendant of David (the ancestry was traced through his father, for
this was before the idea of a virgin birth arose). The Messiah, it had
been foretold, would be born in the city of David, Bethlehem.
Therefore Jesus was born in Bethlehem. No factual evidence was
necessary: it was proved by pure logic. But to convince the skeptical,
more and more detail came to be added to the study, until it gave a
colourful picture of the way Jesus' parents had to go from Nazareth to
Bethlehem for a census, and gave a complete family tree of Jesus'
descent from David. (Two of these family trees are recorded, one in
the *Gospel of Luke* and the other in the *Gospel of Matthew*. They are
quite different.)

Again, it had been foretold by the prophets that the Messiah would
come out of Egypt. So the infant Jesus was taken to Egypt. The legend
continued to grow.

But it was not only Jewish logic that had to be satisfied. Christianity
came to birth in a world dominated by Greek thought. The one whom
Christians worshipped could not be inferior to those worshipped by
other religions. The heroes and saviours of the mystery religions of
the day had all been supernaturally born as descendents of the gods.
Even Plato, who was no saviour but only a philosopher, was reputed
to have been born of a virgin.

10

So again imagination began to work. After all, no one knew that Jesus had *not* been supernaturally born. He may well have been. Once again they looked at what the prophets had said about the Messiah. There was a passage in Isaiah which read, "A young woman shall conceive and bear a son." as the context shows, (*Isaiah,* chapter 7) this referred to something which was taking place in the prophet's own time, but in popular interpretation it had come to be applied to a future Messiah. Furthermore, the Greek translation of the original Hebrew had narrowed the interpretation of "young woman" to "virgin." What more was needed? The Messiah would be born of a virgin. Jesus was the Messiah. Therefore Jesus had been born of a virgin.

The Development of Myths

We do not have to stand in condemnation of those who proceeded to spell out the story in detail. Even today there are those who write history in terms of "this is the way it must surely have been." Miraculous births were a commonplace among stories of great men in the ancient world. Several of the Roman Emperors were hailed as sons of a God. So were figures in the history of Greece, Egypt, and the Middle East. Among the greatest names in the history of religion, Confucius, Zoroaster, and the Buddha were all said to have been miraculously born.

The historical Jesus dropped out of sight very rapidly as this process continued. The attempt to remember him at Christmas and to celebrate his birthday is a modern development on the part of liberal Protestants. Some Unitarian Universalists have adopted this interpretation of the season, but there is a lot to be said for taking stock of the teachings and permanent significance of Jesus at some time of the year when there is less pressure to confuse fact with fiction, history with myth. The life and teachings of Jesus are worthy of study in a different atmosphere altogether.

The disappearance of Jesus from the celebration of Christmas was masked by the fact that for orthodox Christians Jesus was swallowed up in Christ as one composite being, Jesus-Christ, both man and in some sense God. Jesus is a figure of history, Christ a figure of myth, and the two are really quite different, although they have been fused in Christian theology.

What is myth? It is a product of the imagination. It is poetry or drama in which those who tell or portray the story themselves participate. Its function is to uncover in symbolic terms and deeper levels of human life and give us new insights into ourselves and our condition. It brings up the archetypal figures of the mother and child, shepherds and angels and kings following a star across the desert. In the Christian myth is celebrated the coming of Christ.

11

And what is the Christ? Essentially a spirit or influence, personified over and over again in human form, an influence to help save humanity from lower levels of being and raise it higher. The Christian interpretation of this spirit has usually been exclusive. According to this interpretation, this spirit became incarnate in only one man, Jesus Christ. But there has been and is a broader tradition, which sees this as the spirit of all who are "helpers and friends of humanity."

Surely, this expresses a real insight which Unitarian Universalists too can share. Some people's lives do exude a spirit which helps their fellows rise higher in wisdom and love. It can be called the Christ-spirit or the Buddha-spirit, or the Krishna-spirit, or by any other name. The label is not important, but the reality remains.

Incarnation

It is of this reality summed up in the traditional term INCARNATION, that Christmas stands as a symbol. The great Hindu scripture, the Bhagavad-Gita, puts its thus:

> *"When goodness grows weak,*
> *When evil increases,*
> *I make myself a body.*
> *In every age I come back*
> *To deliver the holy,*
> *To destroy the sin of the sinner,*
> *To establish righteousness."*

The same theme occurs in the Buddhist Scriptures:

> *"Know that from time to time a Tathagata is born into the world, a fully Enlightened One, blessed and worthy, abounding in wisdom and goodness, happy, with knowledge of the world, unsurpassed as a guide to erring mortals, a teacher of gods and men, a blessed Buddha. The truth doth he proclaim both in its letter and in its spirit, lovely in its origin, lovely in its progress, lovely in its consummation. The higher life doth he make known, in all its purity and in all its perfectness."*
>
> *(Tevigga Sutra)*

Nor is such an idea entirely unheard-of in the west. In the words of E. G. Cheyne:

> *"Some despise saviours, and are content with themselves and with things as they are. Some adore the saviours of the past, and ignore those of the present. Many will not heed the saviours of the present, but look to the saviours of the future. Nevertheless, it is impossible for the world to go on without its successive saviours."*

Whatever theological interpretations some people might want to place upon such utterance, those who take a Unitarian Universalist position would not be willing to accept that the difference between such outstanding figures and ourselves is in any sense a difference of kind. It is a difference of degree, and every one of us is in some degree able to be a vehicle of this spirit in the world, to be to that extent Christ — to be able to say, as Angelus Silesius said:

> *"Should Christ be born a thousand times anew,*
> *Depair, O man, unless he's born in you."*

This is one of the most significant of all of the meanings of Christmas, and is one we are in danger of missing if we leave out the specifically Christian contribution to the festival, for the specifically Christian contribution is that of incarnation. Expressed and symbolized in picturesque legend, what it says is the same as the Stoic writer Epictetus was saying at the time when the legend was growing:

> *"You are a distinct portion of the essence of God, and*
> *contain a certain part of Him in yourself. Why then are you*
> *so ignorant of your noble birth?"*

In other words, there is that in each one of us through which we transcend the narrow bounds of individual selfhood and by the power of which we can raise our own lives and the lives of others to higher levels. Different persons realize this process in different degrees, and there are some persons who realize it in so high a degree that around them the myths and legends crystallize, and they come to be hailed as saviours.

We can best look at this process through the eyes of poets, for after all, only a poet can give satisfactory expression to it. That is why we find the poetry of Christmas so largely satisfying and the theology of Christmas so largely unsatisfying.

Christ is you and me — yet he is ourselves transposed, as it were into a higher key, to save us into deeper wisdom and larger love, and manifested supremely in those persons who have done most to lift the whole human race towards higher levels of life.

This universal truth is the innermost core of the meaning of Christmas, and it is one in which Unitarian Universalists can fully share. In fact, it was a great Unitarian, James Martineau, who said in memorable words a century ago: "The Incarnation is true not of Christ exclusively, but of Man universally." In celebration of this deep reality Unitarian Universalists join, and it gives meaning to all that is said at Christmas about peace and goodwill. For it is upon these potentialities within humanity that peace and goodwill in the last resort depend.

For One Season Only?

There are those who say that this is a spirit which, if it means anything at all, should be evident throughout the year, and not just at one season. Of course, the Quaker poet John Greenleaf Whittier had a valid point when he wrote:

> *"The outward symbols disappear*
> *From him whose inward sight is clear;*
> *And small must be the choice of days*
> *To him who fills them all with praise.*
> *Keep, while you need it, brothers mine*
> *With honest zeal your Christmas sign;*
> *But judge not him who every morn*
> *Feels in his heart the Lord Christ born."*

But how many people do in fact live at this level all the time? The great value of seasons and celebrations is that they come as continuing reminders of the need to raise ourselves out of the rut into which we can so easily slip and start once again to experience life more fully and deeply. W. H. Auden expressed the other side of the picture when he wrote in *For the Time Being:*

> *"Music and sudden light*
> *Have interrupted our routine tonight,*
> *And swept the filth of habit from our hearts.*
> *O here and now our endless journey starts."*

So Christmas can come for Unitarian Universalists no less than for others at a time when we can "sweep the filth of habit from our hearts" and enrich our lives from the many-sided brilliance of the season. Those who belong to denominations which impose a theological straitjacket upon their adherents will look at only one facet of Christmas, but even from that they can uncover deep insights. More fortunate are those who can, if they choose to do so, look at all the facets, and experience the flashes of fire from the jewel as it turns in their hands. They can join in the songs and gaiety and legendry and poetry of the season without any feeling that it all has to be taken literally and desiccated into the forms of any one theology. With Edwin Muir they can say:

> *"I am debtor to all, to all am I bounden.*
> *Fellow-man and beast, season and solstice,*
> *   darkness and light,*
> *And life and death . . . Forgotten prayers*
> *To gods forgotten bring blessings upon me . . .*
> *The dead in their silences keep me in memory,*
> *Have me in hold, To all I am bounden."*

Phillip Hewett

Symbols and Practices Associated with Christmas

The most universal element in the Christmas celebration is the religious service, whether it be the Catholic Mass or any of the various Protestant forms. Throughout the Christian world people go to church at midnight on Christmas Eve or in the morning or at midday on Christmas day. It has retained its religious character, and a Christian orientation, despite the degree to which it has been affected by old pagan rite or modern commercialization. Fun and frolic culminate in worship, and without this as its climax the festival would lose its essential character. It could be very easy for many American liberals to forget this.

Material representations of the nativity scene are practically universal. The commonest form is the creche. It is found in homes and churches, under Christmas trees, and in street processions. Perhaps its most elaborate use is in France. Here it is arranged by children in the living room and lighted for the religious service at which hymns are sung, incense burned, and bells rung. Tri-colored candles are used to light it in honor of the trinity. It is carried in street parades in Poland and Czechoslovakia. It, or the "Precipio," has elaborate use in Italy. In Sicily wandering players enact nativity scenes in churches. In Scandinavian countries the homes are decorated with straw on floors and ceilings, even under the tablecloths.

Some credit St. Francis of Assisi with initiating the dramatization of the stable scene. He is said to have brought live animals into the churches to dramatize the nativity scene. Out of this effort, it is believed, the creche came, for figurines and and miniature stable were much more accessible and convenient.

Christmas carols are sung almost everywhere. While other hymns and classical music are associated with the festival, the carol is the real Christmas song. Carols are joyous songs. Many are of the ballad variety, and some almost nonsensical in content. William Wallace Fyfe says, "We find that our own authors familiarly use the term carol to signify a song of joy and exultation."[1] Percy Dearmer writes:

> "Carols are songs with a religious impulse that are simple, hilarious, popular, and modern. . . . They are generally spontaneous, and their simplicity of form causes them at times to ramble like a ballad. . . . The typical carol gives voice to the common emotions of healthy people in language that can be understood and music that can be shared by all."[2]

15

"Though sometimes trivial and even nonsensical, their scenic and picturesque qualities, no less than their strong human appeal, have always endeared them to the common people."[3]

In England there is a record of great activity in carol singing prior to and following the Puritan regime. The carol was exceedingly popular in Germany. Martin Luther is supposed to have travelled about with carol singers in his student days. From these two sources come many of our most loved and most familiar carols.

Considerable has been written on the origin of the carol, especially in Christian practice. Some suppose it was first meant to be used with the dance, the background of which goes outside the Christian tradition. W. W. Fyfe, who is an authority on the carol, believes that there are positive backgrounds among the Greek, Latin, and Celtic and Germanic peoples.[4] St. Francis of Assisi is thought of as contributing to the use of the carol in the Christian church. He is said to have adapted the birth story from Luke to a play form and used it, with the Pope's permission, to teach the doctrine of the incarnation. As already noted, St. Francis used live animals and actors, and sang with his people as the play was enacted. These songs were simple narrative carols telling of the birth of Christ. Later, when the creche was used it was carried about by carol singers. The Wiegenlieder of Germany and the noels of France are related and similar.

The carol is closely associated with the drama in that some of its earlier forms were used in conjunction with the mystery plays of the middle ages. The English "Coventry Carol" and the German "Joseph, lieber Joseph mein"[5] were meant to be used with mystery plays. Duncan in his "Story of the Carol" quotes Sir John Stainer as follows:

"There can be no doubt whatever that the singing of carols grew out of the medieval mysteries, and the habit of the priests of placing a crib containing either a living bady or a bambino doll in the chancels of the churches, and in other ways trying to teach the rustics by means of pictorial representations."[6]

Carol singing in our day has lost some of its hold upon people. We are less spontaneous in their creation and use, and they are more confined to churches and homes and less evident in spontaneous community activities, although far from absent. The more formal community festivals make great use of them in plays and pageants, and they are favorites with special singing groups. There are many helpful collections.[7] We could gain much from the creation of carols with more contemporary significance.

Santa Claus has his counterpart in almost every corner of the world touched by Christian culture. Our name, Santa Claus, is, of course, a corruption of the Dutch name for St. Nicholas who was Bishop of Myra in Lycia during the fourth century. St. Nicholas became the patron saint of boys. He was tall and thin, tradition says, and rode a scrawny horse. Interested not only in children but in unmarried maidens, he often provided dowries for the impoverished among them. St. Nicholas was adopted by the Dutch, and in time Western culture transformed him into a jolly, round and red-cheeked spirit more in keeping with his nature. In France he became Pére Noel; in England, Father Christmas. In America he has shown a characteristic adaptability to the times. He comes down chimneys, appears in parades, goes to parties, and so on. He began travelling on foot and by horse. Probably due to Clement Moore's genius, he took to the Laplander's mode of travel, and to this day the reindeer have an edge on the airplane.

Santa is represented by Mother Star in Poland; by Kristkind in Bavaria; Jul-Nisse in Denmark; Kris Kringle in Germany, and by Grandpa Koleda in Bulgaria. His equivalent appears in Italy as the beneficent old witch Befana who rides about on her broom stick distributing gifts to children. Old Russians remember Babushka who went about in search of the Christ Child, leaving gifts for every child visited just in case he might be the one. In Syria even a camel serves and children set out food and water for him. One suspects that Santa in his many forms represents a benevolent spirit in primitive society that countered the work of the more threatening spirits. Despite the permissiveness of this Christmas spirit, here and there a spirit of a different sort is associated with him, probably for disciplinary purposes. Santa in early times was accompanied by a disagreeable companion who punished children by leaving a rod and ashes in their shoes and stockings. There is Karkantzari, the half human and half monster of the Greek legend, who wanders about during the twelve days of the Christmas season. He is a mischief maker and the priest is needed to make him go away for another year. Certain elements of the Christmas celebration in some parts of Europe are rooted in efforts to counter the work of evil agencies.

The Christmas tree, or "tennenbaum," is German in origin and was probably derived from primitive religious practices. Its use spread widely. The evergreen stayed green when other plants withered. It was accordingly considered to be related to the life-giving powers of the sun. The German word for tree is "baum," or "Father Sun." Thus we see its possible association with the idea of the sun's rebirth. Harold Bayley says:

"The name *fir* may evidently be equated with fire, an idea

17

which is corroborated by the fact that the Welch for fir-tree is *pyr* i.e. the Greek for fire. The Greek for *fir* is *peuke*, i.e. the Great Father, or *Pére*."[8]

The Christmas tree is supposed to have been brought to England by a German governess in the family of Queen Victoria. It is found in America in the 1870's. It represents the general interest in greens at the Christmas season, an interest possibly related to the Roman Saturnalia that made extensive use of greens. Holly and mistletoe, although less frequently used, are still popular with us, and each has its age-old history. Both were used in Druid worship. According to Pliny, "The druids esteem nothing more sacred than the mistletoe and the tree on which it grows, provided that tree is an oak."[9] The mistletoe lived in all seasons. It was considered to be the seat of life of the oak. Its twin leaves and twin sets of berries represented the celestial spirit of regeneration. It was thought that a potion from this plant would make a barren person fertile. So, too, the holly shrub in many ways had its significance, e.g. its thorns were supposed to trap evil spirits.

Candles, fire and fireworks have a conspicuous place in the Christmas celebration. The primitive worship of the sun and of fire itself, the darkness and cold of northern countries, and the natural cheer and warmth of fellowship which humans have experienced about the hearth are no doubt responsible for the popularity of fire at this season. Candles are universally used because they are so convenient and have been of such service to man. Fireworks are widely used in the Bavarian celebration. The hearth always lures people to it — stockings are hung by it, Santa comes down the chimney, the yule log is burned in it and bits of it saved to start the next year's fire, etc.

The yule log, like the mistletoe, was supposed to have magical powers.

> "It is remarkable how common the belief appears to have been that the remains of the yule log, kept throughout the year, had power to protect the house against fire, and especially against lightning. As the yule log was frequently of oak, it seems possible that this belief may be a relic of the old Aryan creed which associated the oak tree with the god of thunder."[10]

Special foods are conspicuous in the festival. Christmas cakes, such as the "Kranai" in Bulgaria, are found in Europe. They often contain coins or other good-luck pieces. In England the boar's head was traditional, and the plum pudding holds its place to this day. In Poland wafers blessed by the church are given to, and broken and shared by, members of the family. In France there is a feast known as "reveillon," a meal of oysters, sausages and special wine. There are fried cakes in Greece, and so on. In America the idea of a feast is more important than what is eaten so long as it be expensive and extravagant, although the turkey and special candy are most popular. Probably the feast is the commonest of elements in all celebrations.

Stockings and shoes as repositories of gifts that children receive are widely used. In Holland, Belgium, and Italy shoes are set out with food for St. Nick's horse and gifts are placed in them in return. There are similar practices in Scandinavia. In places the color of stockings are important. In America the gifts seem to more and more gather about the base of the Christmas tree — obviously the stocking or shoe wouldn't do for the number and kinds of gifts our children receive. Stockings are still used among us by people who do not like to let go of the customs of their childhood, and possibly to appease early-rising children until the presents about the tree are opened by the family together. Why, above all things, should foot wear have been used? Probably one guess is as good as another. They were at least convenient receptacles.

Even the Christmas card has a history. Nothing has been more exploited in America than the Christmas urge to remember friends and loved ones by messages and greetings. Nevertheless, the Christmas card remains important as an agent of good will. Sir Henry Cole of England is credited with starting the practice of sending cards. They were reminiscent of the bordered and decorated sheets of paper prepared for children on which to write their Christmas recitations. Christmas cards appeared in America about 1875, when Louis Prang of Boston produced some. They were highly decorated and very expensive.

There are some special customs that suggest possible enrichment of our own celebration. Conspicuous among these is the practice in Scandinavian countries of setting out food for birds and animals, the bringing in of all traps during the season, and otherwise extending the spirit of the festival to other forms of life.[11]

— Students at St. Lawrence Theological School

[1] William Wallace Fyfe, *Christmas, Its Customs and Carols,* (London: J. Blackwood, 1860).
[2] Percy Dearmer, *Oxford Book of Carols,* (New York: Oxford Univ. Press, 1928).
[3] F. J. Gillman, *Evolution of the English Hymn,* (New York: MacMillan, 1927).
[4] W. W. Fyfe, *Op. Cit.*
[5] William G. Polack, *Famous Christmas Carols.*
[6] Duncan, *Story of the Carol.*
[7] Satis N. Coleman and Elin K. Jörgensen, *Christmas Carols from Many Countries,* (G. Schirmer, Inc. Text and Music, 1934).
   Marx and Anne Oberndorfer, *Noels,* (Chicago: H. T. Fit/Simons Co., 1932).
   Herbert H. Wernecke, *Christmas Songs and Their Stories,* (Philadelphia: Westminster Press, 1957).
[8] Harold Bayley, *The Lost Language of Symbolism,* (New York: Barnes and Noble, 1952), p. 271.

[9]*Ibid.* p. 23.

[10]Sir James Frazer, *The Golden Bough,* (New York: MacMillan, 1935), Vol. X, p. 261.

[11]Many of the details of information in comments on Christmas practices have not been given pin-pointed references. The reader is referred to sources generally. The following have been foun especially useful:

Mary P. Pringle, *Yule-tide in Many Lands,* (Boston: Lothrop, Lee and Shepherd, 1916).

Christmas in Many Lands, Prepared by Informative Classroom Pictures Association, Grand Rapid, Michigan. A good source of condensed information and pictures published for school use.

Elva S. Smith and Alice I. Hazeltine, *The Christmas Book of Legends and Stories,* (New York: Lothrop, Lee and Shepherd, 1914).

SOME WINTER CELEBRATIONS

A great many holidays cluster in November, December, January. These are some of the most widely celebrated.

October 31
> Halloween

November 1
> All Saints Day

November 2
> All Souls Day

November 5
> Guy Fawkes Day — Feast Day of Blessed Martin de Parres (patron saint of interracial understanding)

November 11
> St. Martin's Day
> Teutonic New Year
> Veterans Day
> Remembrance Day

November 15
> Roman feast of Jupiter

November 17
> Feast of St. Hilda (patron saint of business and professional women)

November 19
> Feast of St. Elizabeth of Hungary (patron saint of charities for the poor and of bakers)

November 22
> St. Cecilia's Day (patron saint of musicians)

November 25
> St. Catherine's Day (patron saint of philosophers, jurists, maidens and women students)

November 26
> Sojourner Truth Day

November 30

St. Andrew's Day — Advent Sunday — the beginning of the Christian church year, starts on the Sunday nearest to St. Andrew's Day. The Advent season, a time of preparation for Christmas which includes 4 Sundays, continues until December 25.

December 6

Feast Day of St. Nicholas

December 7

Feast Day of St. Ambrose (father of church hymnology)

December 10

Nobel Prize Presentation Day
Human Rights Day

December 15

Bill of Rights Day

December 16

Posadas Day — nine day celebration begins recalling journey of Mary and Joseph and Bethlehem
Philippine Christmas begins (continues through January 6)

December 17

Roman Saturnalia began (lasting 7 days)

December 19

Festival of Opalia, wife of Saturn (lasting 2 days)

December 21

Winter Solstice begins
Landing of the Pilgrims, Plymouth, MA 1620
Birthday of Mithras, Apollo, Dionysius, Odin and the Phrygian god Attis

December 23

Birthday of Joseph Smith, Mormon leader 1805
Caribbean Christmas festival (lasts for 2 weeks — a unique feature is the jig-dance which dates back to the Elizabethans)

December 24

Christmas Eve

December 25

Christmas Day — At least 105 nations celebrate this as a holiday.
Clara Barton and Evangeline Booth were born on this day.

December 26

Boxing Day (so named because boxes of gifts were given to servants)
St. Stephen's Day (first Christian martyr)

December 27
> St. John's Day (in Scandinavia, a day to visit friends)

December 28
> Holy Innocent's Day (or Childermas, commemorates Herod's massacre of young children; western churches celebrate it as this day, eastern churches on the 29th)

December 31
> New Year's Eve
> Hogmany Day (in Scotland)
> Noche de Pedeminto (Wishing Day in Mexico)
> Omisoka Day (in Japan — time to pay debts)
> Watch Night
> First Night

January 1
> New Year's Day — At least 125 nations celebrate this day
> Circumcision Day (of Jesus)
> St. Basil Day (in Greece — eating Basil cakes)
> Tournament of Roses (in Pasadena, CA since 1886)
> Mummers Day (in Philadelphia, PA since 1876)
> Mobile Carnival (in Mobile, AL since 1831)
> Roman Feast of the Kalends of January

January 2
> Feast of Saint Macarius (famous for sugarplums)

January 5
> Twelfth Night (Shakespeare's play written for this event)
> Epiphany Eve
> Old Christmas Eve
> Glastonbury Thorn Day in England (the thorn blooms in Glastonbury and pilgrims go to see it)

January 6
> Twelfth Day — the twelfth day after Christmas
> Feast of The Epiphany (Epiphany means "manifestation" and refers to the star leading the Wise Men. The following Monday is kept as "Plough Monday" in England.)
> Old Christmas Day
> Three King's Day or Day of the Three Wise Men
> Greek Cross Day (Tarpon Springs, FL)
> Four Freedoms Day

January 7
> Christmas Day in Ethiopia
> Christmas Day on Julian calendar in Russian Orthodox churches

January 10
    Anniversary first session of the General Assembly of the United Nations, 1946

January 11
    Old New Year
    St. Knute's Day (Tyrendedagen-traditional day in Sweden to dismantle Christmas trees, in Norway to have "Christmas Races" in sleighs)

January 15
    Black Christ Festival in Guatemala
    Martin Luther King, Jr., birthday

January 17
    Old Twelfth Night

January 21
    St. Agnes' Day

January 22
    St. Vincent of Saragossa (patron saint of winegrowers)

January 25
    Feast of the conversion of St. Paul

January 27
    St. John Chrysostom (patron saint of preachers)

January 30
    Feast of the Three Hierarchs (St. Basil, St. Gregory, and St. John Chrysostrom)

January 31
    St. John Bosco (friend of boys, patron saint of editors)

February 2
    Candlemas Day
    Groundhog Day

MOVEABLE DAYS

October/November
    Deepavali, or Festival of Lights (Malaysia and Singapore) marks the slaying of mythological king by Lord Krishna

    Diwali, or Festival of Lights (India) five day celebration including New Year's Day, the triumphs of Vishnu and a day devoted to brothers and sisters

    Mooncake Festival (Singapore) downfall of the rule in ancient China

November/December

Chanukah or Hanukkah, Jewish Festival of Lights or Dedication, marks the Maccobean victories and relighting of Temple lamps (8 days)

December

Kris Kringle's Fair (Nuremberg, Germany) began in Middle Ages, runs from early in month to Christmas

Guru Tegh Bahadur's Martyrdom Day (sacred day for Sikhs)

December/January

Birth of Guru Govind Singh (remembered by the Sikhs)

January

Ume Matguri or Apricot Festival (Japan)

Magh Mela Fair (annual purification festival for Hindus with ritual bathing in the River Ganges)

Tsao Chun, Festival of the Kitchen God (preparation for Chinese New Year)

January/February

Hs'in Nien, Chinese New Year (between January 21 and February 19)

Shivarotra (Hindu fast in honor of Lord Shiva)

Tet Nsuyenden (New Year festival in Vietnam, celebrated the first week of the first month of the lunar calendar)

II. The dialogue
of Christmas

*The dialogue of Christmas
    is crosstalk
Between the rampant reason
    of my self
And fractured ghosts
    of ancient legendary.*
                    Leonard Mason

We have met together, this evening, to commemorate the event from which all these consequences have flowed, and are yet to follow. The occasion is indeed worthy of our observance. If Heaven itself saw fit to celebrate it, with pomp of angelic retinue, with songs and acclamation of praise, well may future generations, in all coming time, follow the example. And it will be celebrated. The longer the world stands, and the more fully the consequences of that event are disclosed, the higher will it rise in the estimation of humankind, until it shall be universally acknowledged that, with respect to its influence, whether on the civil, social, intellectual, or spiritual condition of our race, all other occasions sink into insignificance in the comparison.

But let us not forget that, if we would observe the occasion acceptably, or indeed to any valuable purpose whatsoever, we must do it ''in spirit and in truth.'' Without this, all rites, all ceremonies, will be in vain, — but empty, idle pageantry. It is true, we naturally seek some appropriate forms and symbols, by which to express our estimation of memorable events; and this is well, — it is becoming. But still they are only forms and symbols, which represent a deeper reality, or else they are but a mockery. It is in the heart alone that our Saviour can be honored, or the benefits of his mission acknowledged. Let that mind be in us all, which was in our Lord Jesus Christ. The proper offering, on this occasion, is a heart transformed into his likeness. While the garlands of evergreen, with which you have decorated this temple, shall pass away, faded and worthless, in a few weeks, the spirit of Christian meekness, of love to God, of devotion to truth, and of universal benevolence to humankind, will be an ornament precious in the sight of Heaven, and more lasting than yonder stars that are shining in the firmament.

— Hosea Ballou 2nd

(from a sermon, ''The Birth of Jesus Christ'' preached in 1839)

29

What meaning does Christmas have for us? Its deepest meaning for me lies in its being the annual rebirth of hope. Set at the darkest time of the year, the time when days are shortest, Christmas is an annual reminder that days will become longer, that warmth and growth can give us the metaphor for articulating the hope in the cycles of human life. Darkness, despair, death in our lives will give way to light, to life, and to rebirth.

Christmas permits us to bring forth the child in all of us; it is always a celebration of children. Through songs, bells, and bright colors we express our belief in the joy and unity of humankind.

— Betty Pingel

Christmas is the richest of all celebrations, having gathered to itself a great storehouse of treasures in its journey down the centuries and through many lands. Much of its stuff is woven of myth and fancy; it belongs to the realm of poetry and imagination. Many of the greatest values in life do belong in this realm, and we are best able to avail ourselves of their full worth when we take them for what they are without confusing them with sober fact.

— E. Burdette Backus

Perhaps the most characteristic element of Christmas, and the most valued thing about it is what we call "the Christmas spirit," its joy, its reassessment of life as good, the warmth of human relations that it engenders, often renewing human contacts, modifying class distinctions and old enmities in joyous fellowship of old and young, and in the giving of gifts and services. This persistent spirit is difficult to explain as a seasonal thing, but no one questions its genuineness.

— author unknown

As a religious humanist who no longer believes in the virgin birth, I have given many reasons why I still celebrate Christmas. I have pointed to the fact that this is the time of the winter solstice, that it has been a time of celebrating the return of light since prehistoric times. I have highlighted the customs of other cultures and other religions at this time of year. And I have even said that it "just happens" to be a good time of year to celebrate the birth of all children or the lives of all great people, or to intensify our constant campaign for "peace on earth."

But there's no getting around it. In our culture, Christmas *is* celebrating the birth of Jesus. And I am strongly attached emotionally to a host of things connected with Christmas in which I no longer believe. I no longer believe in the words of most of the Christmas carols, cantatas, and oratorios, and I find the theology on which they were based morally repulsive. But I not only like to hear them, I love to sing them.

Christmas puts me once again in direct contact with the ideal Jesus of my childhood faith:

— a Jesus who was perfect love and compassion;

— a Jesus who truly loved his enemies and gave his life in serving the poor and unfortunate;

— a Jesus who loved children and approached the world with a childlike faith in what people could become. Almighty God, Creator of the Universe, had come to earth, and He loved each human being with an infinite love and saw the wonder of our true potential in a way no one else ever had.

There is magic, there is power in this ideal and what it commands me to become. The sacred power of this portion of the Christmas myth is what I bow before at this season of the year.

— Donald J. Jacobsen

Christmas is a most illogical season, anyway. Like Santa's reindeer, it takes a leap up from the old earth, plagued as it is with human hates and fears, and drenches us with a shower of the most amazing dreams and hopes we could possibly imagine. It is not a matter of atomic bombs, guided missiles and weapons of death, and the stories of our inhumanity, but something totally different. The leaders of states and the politicians bow out, and a child takes over; a child symbolizing the continual rebirth of hope and life. The embers of old, forgotten dreams are blown into flame again, and we see then in the clear, white light that we are all companions on this amazing star-adventure.

— Alfred S. Cole

"Why do you celebrate Christmas? You do not believe in virgin births. You do not believe that Jesus was a deity. You probably do not believe in angels."

True, but we believe in songs which are born in the hearts and minds of people. We believe that some stories deserve to live forever because of what they tell us of ourselves. The angels singing an anthem of peace and goodwill deserve to be heard forever because they are the angels in human hearts. The humble shepherds, who had ears to hear and hearts to receive a message of joy, deserve to live to the end of time. The wise men, so faithfully seeking the way of a star, deserve to go in search again each year as long as years shall be, for they are the story of our quest for ourselves.

— Ernest H. Sommerfeld

Scholars tell the Biblical story of the birth of Jesus was subject to much rewriting before it was canonized in its present form. As an historical event not much of the story can be corroborated. But there is no doubt that each December the story gives birth to a spirit of goodwill and love. The centuries have questioned whether Jesus was a God child or Mary and Joseph's natural child. But there is no doubt when he came of age he was a spiritual giant who had a profound effect on western civilization.

The nativity story may be poetry and not fact, but then again, it may be something else. Perhaps it is not so much that the stories are untrue but that our own lives are untrue and the nativity reminds us of who we really are. There is so much in us that is untrue to the divinity which is our real nature. Our selfishness often exceeds our generosity. Our narrowness squeezes our goodness. Our present is short of our potential. The nations likewise fall short of the promise. Wars, violence, hostages, and assassinations are a paradox to the promise of peace and goodwill.

But each December the sacred hope is reborn. Beneath our surface flaws lies a loving nature, divine in essence, and the nativity story brings forth the best within us. Nations pause and wars have been known to stop on Christmas Day. Scrooges become cheerful. The wonder of Christmas is that it reveals who we really are: saints in tattered clothing, children of God who mask their divinity most of the year. It is Christmas that is real and we are untrue to it too much of the time.

— David H. Cole

Christmas is not so much a matter of explanation and interpretation as it is a mood and a feeling. It is a time in the cycle of the year set apart by hope and fellowship and generosity. Christmas is the season of the heart.

— Gordon B. McKeeman

The need for some measure of ritual seems to be deep within our bones. The need for a measure of stability among the flux and fluctuations of human life is real. The need for an annual calling to consciousness of some of the necessities of human life and of some of life's ideals is the secret of the Christmas season.

For many of us, even though we have left behind many of the literal meanings of Christmas, this season continues to be important and is cherished by us. There is too much emotional residue left in us, too many beautiful memories of Christmas past, to allow us to disregard the magic of this season. As a matter of fact, there are many dimensions of this season which should not be discarded.

It seems to me that the mark of liberal religious maturity is to draw upon those universal aspects of the season which have profound and enduring values while we leave behind those aspects which are no longer meaningful or credible.

There are universal dimensions of this season which were celebrated religiously long before Judaism and Christianity existed. Both built upon the deep abiding aspects of this seasonal celebration and added their own particular stories to this ancient festival of light and life.

This seasonal celebration is one of the touchstones of the human life story and if offers us an annual opportunity to relate to the human story in its abiding magnificence. This season is important in a "human" way and in a "humane" way. It is important humanly because it is a celebration of light without which there could be no life and it is a celebration of human birth. It is of importance from the humane perspective because it is a celebration during which we raise high life's ideals of human identity, peace, love, and good will among all persons.

Christmas is a many mood time. It occurs during dark December when the days become shorter and colder, and the nights longer and darker. It is the time during which we decorate and enliven our homes with festive colors. We bring green trees indoors to remind ourselves of spring and life. We send messages of care and love to far away friends and we reassure those near us of our love. We string our brightly colored lights to lighten the burden of darkness. We brighten up the dark December days with the ornamentation of Christmas, a human habit which is deep in our bones. It must not become merely a habit. We must each year rewrite its meaning.

The Christmas season should be more than frantic hurry. We should not allow the meaning of Christmas to slip through the net of our needs and desires. We should not forget to see the lights. When we forget to look for the meaning of Christmas, not only are we oppressed by the darkness of the long nights, we also become oppressed by the darkness of our own thoughts.

Each Christmas is new. Each Christmas directs our hopes into the future. Christmas is an island in the dark of the year. Amidst the immensities and uncertainties of our age, the ancient festival of Christmas is an island of stability and hope.

— Stanley R. Stefancic

In many ways this is the season of the great "blue funk." Color it midnight blue. Earthquakes and fires remind us of our mortality. Senseless crimes remind us of our bestiality. A fading economy reminds us of our thin veneer of abundance. Yet there are lights. The eight candles of Hanukkah remind us that freedom of conscience is still stronger than any historical tyranny. The candles of Christmas, shining out from millions of homes, remind us that goodness overcomes darkness and that hope is stronger than despair. The flame of the chalice reminds us that, in the midst of dark ages, people still long for truth and search for it. We are people of the light, and we are entering the season of lights. But take heed: no one can curse the darkness for you; if you must curse, curse boldly. Likewise, no one can kindle light for you. You must light your own. But if you light it and hold it and hold it beside others, you can change this season of "blue funk" into the gold of well-being.

— J. Bradbury Mitchell

It is as though in the depth of winter darkness, at the farthest end of our pendulum swing into the void and darkness of space, we sense something of our true situation in relation to unfathomed reaches of space and existence, our actual condition close to the edge of cold nothingness and death, and we grasp for recognition and expression of what in our life might save us, or at least afford comfort and warmth and hope. That human grasping, recognition, expression . . . is Christmas.

The festival of Christmas has survived through the centuries as a deep and meaningful human response to life and existence. It is far, far older than the Christian church. Yes, the festival includes certain surface elements of cheapness and tension and shallowness, but underneath there is a basic human appeal having deep meaning and benefit.

No theology or cherished church doctrine has a monopoly on kindness and friendship and hope, on joy and the opening of the human heart. No theology or cherished church doctrine has a monopoly on human response to the marvelous existence in which we live and to the people with whom we live on this whirling planet. No theology or cherished church doctrine has a monopoly on ideals and aspirations. Those are what would shine through at the time of Christmas. Christmas — which utilizes extensively the motif of light — itself is a light that would shine in darkness, in the darkness of the remainder of the year and in human minds and hearts, a light to show us the better that is within us and can be made evident.

Christmas is for everyone, for everyone who can affirm unashamedly and joyously the meanings to be found in abundance; the wonder and promise of birth; the magnetic, ancient dream of peace among us; the discovery that wonderful things do happen, that the better in people *is* there, *can* come to the surface; the joy of sharing, of giving and receiving, of expressing love and friendship; the power in the life of one person, such as Jesus; the tug of warmth and hope in human hearts; the dedication of highest ideals; response to the cycle of human existence — all those meanings and others are in Christmas, the season of light. May it so shine in our lives and the lives of others that promise becomes fulfillment, that hope becomes reality, that tears of the past become a sparkle of brightness to be.

— Robert Nelson West

Christmas is not an easy time for many religious liberals either theologically or existentially. What, we ask, are we to celebrate — Christmas or Hanukkah? Are we to build creches or light menorahs? Or should we, instead, with pagan abandon, sacrifice our passion to the golden fire of the mistletoe, or, with consumerish complacency, render our gold in tribute to the profit-gods of the department store? We have trouble deciding just what has most claim on us, although by default mistletoe and commerce often win out. Existentially, the winter season has contrasts that cut past our bones and into our souls. As we approach the end of the year, we know the hard continuing freeze is on its way. We feel the diminishment of day before encroaching night. We are confused because the world is going one way and we would go another. Suddenly, we want warmth and light, companionship that reassures and acts that speak of a brighter, gayer world. But, none of this is cause for not pursuing the winter celebration. It, rather, is the reason for it. If you cannot choose between creches, menorahs, mistletoe kisses, or gifts, use them all. They are there for you, not you for them. If the cold and gloom threaten, don't let them. Look on them as but another of nature's backgrounds against which the brightness of human imagination and the warmth of human sharing stand out. We have reason to celebrate and many tools with which to do it. May this be a year in which all these come together for you.

— Don W. Vaughn

The *Other* Christmas Stories

The Christmas story is not just the story of the birth of a child, magnificent though that occasion be. Sometimes we are so enthralled with the inn and the manger, the shepherds and the angels, that we fail to notice the other great themes which weave in and out of the tale.

The Christmas story is, for instance, a story of sisterhood. After she has conceived by the Holy Spirit, Mary spends three months in the company of the elderly Elizabeth whose own womb also has been mysteriously filled. The two women greet each other with rejoicing and sustain each other in the wonder of their circumstances. The Christmas story is a story of sisterhood.

And it is a story of glory come to the poor. Whatever the exact nature of their material state, Mary and Joseph are hardly people of power or wealth. That God should choose them to be the agents of this holy moment is intimation that Jesus' mission will be a revolutionary one. The Christmas story is a story of promise come to the poor.

And it is a story of the wisdom of women. When the shepherds come upon the stable and report the prophecy of the angel (that a deliverer has been born), all who hear them are astonished. Except Mary; Mary knows. "But Mary," says Luke, "kept all these things and pondered them in her heart." The Christmas story is the story of a woman's revelation.

And it is a story of civil disobedience. For Herod instructs the wise men to find the child's location and report it to him but the wise men, warned in a dream that they should not return to the King, present their gifts and depart "into their own country another way." The Christmas story is a story of defiance and courage.

And it is the beginning of a story of exile and of triumph. For when they learn of Herod's intention to destroy their child, Mary and Joseph flee with the babe into Egypt and then, with Herod's death, return to dwell in Nazareth. The Christmas story begins a story which has changed the world.

It is important not to read this story narrowly but rather to feel its texture and discern its breadth. It is indeed the bearer of many messages. May more and more of them be disclosed to us, for the more of them we recognize, the more we may ponder the meaning of this season in our hearts.

— William F. Schulz

III. Joy shall be yours
in the morning

JL

Villagers all, this frosty tide,
Let your doors swing open wide,
Though wind may follow, and snow beside,
Yet draw us in by your fire to bide;
  Joy shall be yours in the morning!
    Kenneth Grahame
    (sung by the field-mice in Wind In the Willows*)*

Open the doors of the sanctuary for the people to come and rejoice. Enter into the fellowship of those who celebrate life with its warmth and its beauty, its pain and its healing. Come to the temple of delight for a season of simple pleasure. Come in imagery to behold the bright mystical star; to hear echoes of voices ethereal far away. Take counsel here of legendary lore, the wisdom of poetry and myth. Join together one and all in the spirit to Christmastide to stir into hope the vision of trust and justice o'er all the world; that peace and goodwill may bless and keep us in every generation.

— John K. Hammon

Now is the time of the winter solstice come upon us, when the sun in its outward course appears to pause, and resting, then, begins to turn again to drive the darkness from the north. Soon shall the frozen earth gain promise of new warmth and burrowed seed draw of springtime birth. So do we also meet these days with welcome and with cheer. Drive gloom and melancholy from our hearts, proclaim the birth of new found hope and joy to usher Christmas in.

— John K. Hammon

Welcome, rich season of bounty and good cheer! Wreathe every life with garlands of innocent mirth. Crown with green wreaths of joy the brows of those we love; weave in red berries of health, and the bright star of hope. Welcome blest season of peace, that bringest a truce to strife! And may thy white wings of peace spread over the waiting earth. Link all peoples and nations in the sure bonds of community, shed peace and good will, good will and peace, on all humanity.

— Percival Chubb

To you who gather in this hall
We greeting give, and welcome you
To glad mid-winter Festival
As ancient custom bids us do.

With Yule log, candle, mistletoe,
With holly, gifts, and singing
And stories of the long ago
Let hearts with joy be ringing.

— author unknown

Let this day begin the time for celebration.
Let us turn ourselves toward the season of the year,
when the trees are bare
and the grass is covered with snow,
and the sun begins to return once more
to warm our homes and our bodies and our hearts.
Let this day begin the holy celebration of Christmas.

— author unknown

It is the winter season of the year.
Dark and chilly.
Perhaps it is a winter season in your life.
Dark and chilly there, too.
Come in to Christmas here.
Let the light and warmth of Christmas brighten our
 lives and world.
Let us find in the dark corners of our souls the
 light of hope,
A vision of the extraordinary in the ordinary.
Let us find rest in the quiet of a holy moment to
 find promise and renewal.
Let us find the child in each of us, the new hope,
 the new light, born in us.
Then will Christmas come.
Then will magic return to the world.

— Ellen Fay

Another Christmas comes to us, and as always, it comes when we need it most. Just when clear nights are sending the mercury down as if it too were trying to escape the cold and curl up in the bulb of the thermometer, and when cloudy days bring the snow shawling out of the sky. Then Christmas comes: when the nights are longest, the paths the narrowest, the snowbanks highest, the walks the slipperiest, and the long, worn year just about worn out. Then Christmas comes — as old as memory, as fragile as an ornament, as familiar as the words of its carols and stories, and yet, somehow, new, untried, and shining.

— Max Coots

Into the bright circle of life and light, which is the Christmas season, we have come. Out of the routine ways of living, and the drab little ruts of habit, we have come to warm our hearts and minds at the cradle of the child. May something of the beauty, mystery, and promise of this lovely old story fall like silver rain upon the broken dreams, the hates and fears of all. Once again may we pause, look up, and in the far-off distances hear that old, old, music, the music of hope, brotherhood, sisterhood, and blessed peace!

— Alfred S. Cole

An ancient legend about making all things new reminds us of enduring possibilities of peace, of hope, of love and joy. We rejoice in the old and for the new.

— Gene Reeves

Dark, dark, dark the days, dark the month: see where dark earth's shadow lengthens, lengthens, dark, toward solstice day. Well, come then, let us make our lights, here in the dark, in the shadow, our lights, little lights, now until the great bright dawning come, the great awakening, every year, of Christmas day in the morning!

— John H. Morgan

We are the ones who keep Christmas. Christmas is what we want it to be. Christmas is loveliness, happiness, singing, laughter, giving, and sharing, if we will make it so.

May this season be a time of rebirth and renewal, a time of happiness and joy. Let there be light and warmth, and let us be their bearers.

— Holly Bell

May peace come to your house and your home. May peace come to you and to those who love you. May Christmas bring you peace! peace deep down in the heart of you; peace in the midst of you as you gather around the table.

— author unknown

Let the spirit of Christmas sing in our hearts as we leave this place of beauty and of love; let the vision of peace and goodwill to all people that we have gained together here today, inspire us all, that each new day may become a fresh birth of hope and joy, now and forevermore.

— John K. Hammon

Go into the world and bid others to follow the star:
Tell them the star means wisdom
Tell them the star means kindness
Tell them the star means understanding
Tell them the star means tolerance
Tell them the star means sacrifice
Tell them the star leads to a vision of a fairer
   world,
Tell them the star shines in the heavens and in their
   own hearts and if they will follow the light —
   their own light — they will bring peace and joy
   to others and find it themselves.

                    — author unknown

I wish for the dull a little understanding, and for the understanding a little poetry. I wish a heart for the rich and a little bread for the poor. I wish some love for the lonely and some comfort for the grieved. I wish companionship for those who must spend their evenings alone. I wish contentment for the aged, who see the days slipping by too quickly, and I wish dreams for the young. I wish strength for the weak and courage for those who have lost their faith. And I wish we might all be a little kinder to each other.

                    — Frank Schulman

May the candles we light this holiday season remind us of the glowing love within the heart. May the carols we sing uplift our spirits and renew our hope and vision. May the special moments we spend with family and friends strengthen the bonds of caring between us this time and throughout the coming year.

                    — Patrick G. Green

As the earth's tilt slants the rays of the sun, memories tug at other Christmas times. And so, ancient peoples formed circles of recall and celebration to create a sacred place. Let our circle of Christmas be of time and space with each one of us inside of it, with the memories we share.

                    — Robert Zoerheide

May the love of this season be with you through all the days of the year and give you strength and courage and faith. May the peace of this season be ever in you and bring you comfort and hope. May the light of this season shine in your heart and bring you happiness and laughter. May the joy that is in you be shared with others.

— Kenneth Phifer

May we now go into the world of the unknown, confident that we carry within us the renewed light of love, peace and joy, our own creativity and growth. As we move through life to the rhythms of the earth and sky, may we find comfort in the knowledge that, indeed, the spirit of our own divine child is born in us today. So Be It.

— Sydney Wilde-Nugent

May each of us find the epiphanies we seek, whether early or late, in life or in death, in Christ, in space, in stars, in the human embrace, in dark-night, day-light, in close encounters of every kind, in the peace of silence and the music of the spheres, in pain and in joy, in laughter and in tears, in moments and months, in days beyond years.

— Richard M. Fewkes

I wish for you at Christmas a joy that overflows and overcomes; that vanquishes all mean disabilities and maladies of the spirit. May you drink deep of the liquor of life, and intoxicate yourselves with its beautiful persistence. May all your Christmas presents retain their magic power to satisfy and fascinate, as once did the dolls and sleds and erector sets of childhood. May the darkness flee away forever, and the dawn break, endlessly.

— author unknown

I wish for you, all around you,
People who love easily and forgive quickly;
Whose eyes are stars when you are night;
Whose voices are trumpets when you are silence.
I wish for you
People about you who are gifts in themselves,
And whose presence in your life
Is an all-year-round present.

— James Curtis

Stars still shine in the skies above,
The people of the world yearn for peace,
Families come together in joy,
Children look to their parents for security and
    comfort,
All of us need love and tenderness from one another.
The Holy Days of Chanukkah and Christmas are here.
May you give and receive the most precious gifts:
Humanness at its very best. Shalom!

— Vester L. Vanstrom

As the chill hand of winter tightens its grip upon us, and sets a
death-watch over a tired, old year, let us kindle within our hearts the
gladdening flame of the yuletide season, that we may fling against the
blackness of the long, cold nights, and against the depths of human
misery and despair, lives newborn in love, good will and mercy
toward people everywhere.

— William D. Hammond

All the earth rejoices in the gladness of goodwill, and everywhere our hungry hearts await the word of peace. May we be messengers of Christmas Joy — bearers of its glad tidings, servants of its gracious spirit, and toilers for a world of kindness and good will.

— author unknown

Christmas is a risk for us to take. Shall we allow ourselves to be touched by sentiment? Awakened by song and story? Drawn into festivities, when our joy depends upon the goodwill of others? Dare we risk the disappointment of hopes raised high and excited expectations? May we have the courage to celebrate the season fully.

— Rexford J. Styzens

May all of you have the gladness of Christmas, which is Hope, the spirit of Christmas, which is Peace, and the heart of Christmas, which is Love.

— author unknown

Let us open our hearts to Christmas. Open them to all the hope that stands against a world that wastes with evil things; open them wide enough for gentleness in a world that is bitter and harsh; for loveliness in a world that is desolate; for faith and its joy and the song of its joy, that sings in the presence of God.

— A. Powell Davies

Holy is the true light and passing wonderful, which is the radiance within of reverent love. May it shine forth in our darkness ever stronger and brighter, and lead us and all people into the way of peace.

— author unknown

And now may benedictions come, like green garlands in winter, to each one in each day of life; to all, in our need to be and become, to serve and be served, to give and to receive, to love and be loved, unafraid at Christmas.

— Charles Grady

48

We celebrate Christmas once again. God bless it! Let us by one consent open our shut-up hearts and think of people as if they were fellow-passengers to the grave.

      LET CHRISTMAS BE ONCE MORE A KIND, FOR-
      GIVING, CHARITABLE, PLEASANT TIME. MAY
      WE KEEP OUR CHRISTMAS HUMOR TO THE LAST.

It is required of everyone that the spirit within us should walk abroad among our human neighbors and travel far and wide.

      THIS IS REQUIRED BY OUR JOYFUL ALLEGIANCE
      TO THE SPIRIT OF JESUS, A SPIRIT SUSTAINED BY
      THE BEST IN HUMANITY EVER SINCE HIS DAY.

The common welfare is our business; charity, mercy, forbearance are all our business.

      LET US GO FORTH WHILE IT IS DAY, AND TURN
      HUMAN MISERY INTO JOY.

Let us not be haunted at this season by the shadows of things that might have been.

      IF OUR PAST IS DARKENED BY ILL-WILL, LET
      NOT THE MIRRORS OF OUR OWN YESTERDAYS
      SHOW US WHAT WE SHALL BE IN YEARS TO
      COME.

Human courses foreshadow certain ends to which, if persevered in, they must lead. But if the courses be departed from, the ends must change.

      THE YEAR IS WANING FAST, AND IT IS PRECIOUS
      TIME TO US. WE HAVE THE POWER TO RENDER
      OTHERS HAPPY OR UNHAPPY.

We have the power to make their days light or burdensome, and their work a pleasure or a toil.

      OUR POWER LIES IN WORDS OR LOOKS, IN
      THINGS SO SMALL THAT IT IS IMPOSSIBLE TO
      ADD AND COUNT THEM UP.

The happiness we give is no small matter. A good word is worth a fortune. Let no idol displace Love, even a golden one.

      LET US CARRY THE TORCH OF GOODWILL, THAT
      THE LIGHT MAY BANISH HATE.

Let us honor Christmas in our hearts and keep it all the year.

      A MERRY CHRISTMAS TO EVERYONE!

      A HAPPY NEW YEAR TO ALL THE WORLD!

All: God Bless Us, Every One!

                        — Charles Dickens
                         (adapted)

We have a promise to keep which we made long ago in the silvery light of a star at the manger of a child.

> EARTH HAS RESOUNDED WITH THE HARSH CRIES OF HATE AND OUR HAND HAS BEEN RAISED AGAINST OUR NEIGHBORS.

We have a promise to keep, for that song of peace and goodwill from the midnight skies is faint and far away.

> WE STILL SEEK OUR NEIGHBOR ACROSS THE FROWNING WALLS OF FEAR, FOR DEEP IN OUR HEART IS THE HUNGER FOR PEACE.

Once again across the long years sounds that sweet old song, and from out our haunted sleep we awake to listen and bow down.

> HOW LONG, O MESSENGER OF PEACE, SHALL WE KEEP YOU WAITING OUTSIDE THE CLOSED DOORS WHERE PEOPLE TRADE THEIR SOULS FOR POWER AND GOLD?

Your dream, O Messenger of Peace, shines in our hearts today. The light from your star streams into our souls and hope is born anew.

> DAY BY DAY THE LIGHT SHALL GROW, AND YEAR BY YEAR THE SHADOWS SHALL FADE AWAY.

Voices of peace and goodwill, long stifled by the bitter cries of hate, sound again.

> THAT MIDNIGHT SONG OF LONG AGO SHALL FALL UPON THE EARTH LIKE THE GENTLE MANTLE OF THE SNOW.

— Alfred S. Cole

This is the season of all the seasons in the year

> WHEN A SPECIAL MAGIC OVERTAKES US.

It is the season of all the seasons in the year

> WHEN WE JOINTLY REMEMBER A BIRTH.

It is the season of all the seasons in the year

> WHEN WE REMEMBER THE PROMISE THAT ACCOMPANIES EVERY HUMAN BIRTH.

It is the season of all the seasons in the year

> WHEN WE REMEMBER THE PROMISE WITH WHICH THE STORIES OF JESUS ARE FILLED.

It is a season of the year

> WHEN WE CONSIDER HOW WE MIGHT FULFILL THAT PROMISE.

— Judy Deutsch

50

They told me that when Jesus was born a star appeared in the heavens above the place where the young child lay.

AND SINCE I WAS VERY YOUNG AND HAD NO TROUBLE BELIEVING WONDROUS THINGS I BELIEVED IN THE STAR.

It was a wonderful miracle, part of a long-ago story, foretelling an uncommon life.

THEY TOLD ME A SUPERNOVA APPEARED IN THE HEAVENS IN ITS DYING BURST OF FIRE ABOUT THE TIME THE BABE WAS PROBABLY BORN, ITS APPEARANCE RECORDED IN THE HISTORIES OF TIME.

And since I was older and believed in science and reason above all else, I believed the story of the star explained.

IT WAS A SCIENTIFIC FACT, FORETELLING NOTHING, MERELY THE SOURCE OF A LOVELY LEGEND.

But I found I was unwilling to give up the star. It seemed a fitting symbol for the birth of one whose uncommon life has been remembered long.

THE STAR EXPLAINED BECAME THE STAR UNDERSTOOD, FOR JESUS, FOR BUDDHA, FOR ZARATHUSTRA.

Why not a star? Some bright star shines somewhere in the heavens each time a child is born.

AND WHO KNOWS WHAT IT MAY FORETELL? FOR WHO KNOWS WHAT UNCOMMON LIFE MAY YET UNFOLD, IF WE BUT GIVE IT A CHANCE?

— Margaret K. Gooding

O Thou Creative Spirit, quicken in us throughout this Christmas season an awareness of the fullness of life that may be ours. As we lift up our eyes to the splendor of the heavens, whence shineth the Christmas star.

> MAY THE WONDER OF CHRISTMAS DWELL IN OUR HEARTS.

As we breathe the fragrance of fresh-cut greens, and behold the beauty of the cheerful holly, the festive trees, and the candle's light

> MAY THE BEAUTY AND CHEER OF CHRISTMAS DWELL IN OUR HEARTS.

As we lift our voices in well-loved carols, and listen to music great with the majesty of Christmas

> MAY THE SPIRIT OF CHRISTMAS WARM OUR HEARTS.

As we feel the quick response in those we love and cherish most dearly

> MAY THE JOY OF MUTUAL HELPFULNESS AND THE JOY OF SHARING DWELL IN OUR HEARTS.

As we watch the light in children's eyes, the light of vision, of joy and love, of wonder and delight

> MAY THE SPIRIT OF CHRISTMAS DWELL IN OUR HEARTS, ENLARGE OUR VISION, AND ENRICH OUR DAILY LIVING.

— Agnes Hazel Fletcher

Blessed are they who find Christmas in the fragrant greens, the cheerful holly, and the soft flicker of cancles.

> TO THEM SHALL COME MEMORIES OF LOVE AND HAPPINESS.

Blessed are they who find Christmas in the Christmas star.

> THEIR LIVES MAY EVER REFLECT ITS LIGHT AND BEAUTY.

Blessed are they who find Christmas in the age-old story of a baby born in a stable and laid in a manger.

> TO THEM A LITTLE CHILD WILL ALWAYS MEAN HOPE AND PROMISE IN A TROUBLED WORLD.

Blessed are they who find Christmas in the joy of gifts sent lovingly to others.

> THEY SHALL SHARE THE GLADNESS AND JOY OF THE SHEPHERDS AND SAGES OF OLD.

Blessed are they who find Christmas in the message of Jesus of Nazareth.

> THEY SHALL EVER STRIVE TO HELP BRING PEACE ON EARTH, GOOD WILL TO ALL.

— Unitarian Fellowship
Burlington, Iowa

From the pressures and grumpiness of enforced Christmas duties,
>GOOD LORD, DELIVER US;

From the sense of guilt at our own good fortune,
>GOOD LORD, DELIVER US;

From the feat of inadequacy towards those we love, especially at Christmas,
>GOOD LORD, DELIVER US;

From great expectations disappointed, more poignant at Chrstmastide,
>GOOD LORD, DELIVER US;

From cynicism, boredom, and ancient family feuds,
>GOOD LORD, DELIVER US;

From loneliness and despair,
>GOOD LORD, DELIVER US;

To spontaneity, and some small sharing, and joy in silly things, and immoderate laughter, and nostalgic memory, and friend's embrace, and tinselly decoration with no intrinsic worth,
>GOOD LORD, WE BESEECH THEE, BRING US CLOSE!

>— Kenneth LaFleur

This is the season when the child in the heart of all of us awakens and the embers of long-forgotten dreams are blown into flame.

>THE TRAMP OF THE LEGIONS IS STILLED; THE CAESARS LIE IN DUST, BUT THE LIGHT FROM THAT HUMBLE STABLE SHINES WARM AND BRIGHT.

Something old and almost lost amid the clutter of the years is calling from the skies and across the fields of snow.

>THE NIGHT WINDS ARE STILLED AND IN THE DARKENED HEAVENS THE STARS FORETELL OF LENGTHENING DAYS AND THE BIRTH OF SPRING AFTER THE WINTER'S COLD.

This is the sign that the light of hope, which shines in the dimness of our broken dreams, will never fade or die.

>O STRETCH YOUR HANDS, PALSIED BY FEAR, AND WITH THE SIMPLE TRUST OF THE CHILD, GRASP ANOTHER'S HAND AND WALK THE WAY TOGETHER.

Though the darkness press in upon us and the promise of Christmas comes like an echo of music upon the wind, let our hearts remember that loveliness, that light.

>— Jacob Trapp

IV. Guiding our footsteps to the holiest

Candles and fire and star!
These are the symbols of this most blessed
of all seasons:
Candles for the banishing of darkness;
Fires to draw out hearts and spread a
golden glow to the innermost recesses
of our being;
Stars to beckon us onward,
guiding our footsteps to the holiest.
Herbert Hitchen

Bring the candles! Light the tree!
There's something Christmas does to me —
It weaves a charm, it casts a spell,
It sheds a warmth I cannot tell.
Thank God (whatever else may be)
For all that Christmas does to me!

— author unknown

Once again . . . Christmas . . .
Cold without and warmth within,
Glowing hearthstone fires,
Stars in the eyes of children,
Fragrant evergreen,
Candlelight and vested choirs,
Songs of Bethlehem . . .
And for me, let there be Bells,
Echoing from frosty spires.

— author unknown

What happened at Christmas?
The Wise Men saw a Star.
The Shepherds heard the angels sing.
The Father was rejected at a crowded inn.
The King was troubled.
The Mother felt a baby's need.

What will happen to you?
May you find yourself
Rejected at the inn of busyness,
Troubled by the birth of hope,
See a star of promise,
Hear the heavenly song,
Feel the human need for you,
And find God revealed in all.

— author unknown

Christmas has no right
To burst upon us
Suddenly
And loudly
From afar
Lighting up
Right where we are
With nylon trees
And a long-life
Plastic
Star . . .

It is a lonely
Road
To Bethlehem
That must be walked
Slowly
And untalked . . .
Where no bright
Light
Or angel song
Intrudes
Ahead of cue
To wrongly claim
Arrival of the dawn
Before the night
Is walked
By each of us
On through.

— Francis C. Anderson

December dedicates
Its gentle snow
To the hurried ways
Its people go . . .
And asks each day
A bit of silence
On the Christmas way . . .
    A star to follow
    Through the neon night . . .
    A touch of love to reaffirm
    The pricelessness of right . . .
    A mistletoe of merriment
    To deck the dawn . . .
And a stable . . . softly . . . in my heart
Where I may pause to be reborn.

— Francis C. Anderson

The road from Bethlehem
Dwindles in twisted tinsel
And starlight dims
With faded hymns
Scattered "In Excelsior" . . .
With bills unpaid
We wonder if we made
The trip in vain
Again . . .
Or if some wild extended
Gloria
Might grab us
In the tired aftermath . . .
  To proclaim
  Persistently
  The path
  Of peace.

        — Francis C. Anderson

Will I have time to walk a bit,
Alone,
Along a winding desert road?
Or shall I, bent beneath my
  Christmas load,
Never think of it?

Will I have time to turn
  toward a star,
Silently watching from afar,
Sending me (with no price tag)
Its rays of hope
Unendingly?

Will I find a moment, in the
  first faint flush
Of dawn,
To kneel outside a stable door,
And find myself.
Reborn?

        — Francis C. Anderson

When the white wolf of winter stalks through the snow with the dead
    year in its mouth;
When the days grow short as a dying soul's breath;
When earth is iron and water is stone, when cold kills and darkness
    overwhelms the spirit in us.

Then it is that the strange thing happens!

Out of the depths of despair, joy blossoms.
Out of December death, life bursts forth!

For Christmas comes! Christmas comes like a star in the east, like an
    angel singing, like a god assuming mortality — like all the
    impossible things that mystify the mind and secretly delight the
    heart.

Now the carols ring and the children shout; now the candles shine and
    the fire burns bright on the Christmas hearth.

And now the white wolf slinks away into the night, and crouching in
    the darkness watches hopelessly its prey, for even a beast can
    recognize defeat, and in some dumb, inchoate way know that
    life has conquered death.

               — Waldemar Argow

ASSURANCES

Now these be eternal things:
    Pine trees shining against white snow;
    Laughter and tears and the heart's assurances;
    Sea water rolling under the sky;
    Mercy, compassion, the spirit's strength;
    Mountains leaning against the dawn;
    Courage and hope and the lingering faith;
    Starlight spangling the glory of night —
    The Christmas story in the human heart.

               — Waldemar Argow

HOWEVER DARK

However dark the closing year,
Bright Christmas brings a breath of cheer;
And with the New Year new hopes wake
That through the clouds the light will break.
Let us work on, and do our best,
And to the Future leave the rest.

               — Alice Stone Blackwell

Blessed are the parents
Who know how big is Christmas — and how small.
Who lead the way to the fireside
Rather than the toy-counter.
      Their children will follow them.

Blessed are the parents
Who stop in the midst of the party-going
And the gift-buying and the card-addressing
To hear the simple song of love.
      Their children will also hear the music.

Blessed is the family that knows
How big is Christmas — and how small.
Their whole year will shine
With happy memories,
      And a zest for living.

                  — Elizabeth H. Baker

FOCUS

To compass beauty, fragile, in a crystal;
To grasp truth firmly in a phrase;
To focus light into a single candle's flame;
To capsulate love's warmth and strength
      within the lines etched in one face;
So to capture grandeur in the plain —
      vastness in minutia —
      infinity within a moment lived;
This is genius, this is art and power —
This is knowing, feeling, life in every particle.

To compass beauty, puzzled, in an infant's birth;
To grasp truth firmly in a mother's hopes;
To focus light in figures trav'ling from afar;
To capsulate love's warmth and strength
      within a father's weary mien;
So to capture promise in the common —
      greatness in humility —
      the longing cries of ages in a single babe;
This is precious vision, this the real within
      a world of sham and fear —
This is Christmas.

                  — Robert M. Bowman

Whatever Child . . .
Whenever time . . .
Wherever place . . .
Is born a child of love and grace
Who grows to lead us up the road to a firmer,
        stronger humanhood,
We hail its birth, though high or lowly,
We mourn its death, but count as holy
What was taught and shown us through living,
        loving, learning, serving, giving . . .
And seek for no celestial throne:
A child is holy of its own!

— Anne Bradley

THE ESSENCE

Discard the myths and legends for
        what they are:
Strip away the accretions of the
        centuries;
Abandon the traditional half-pagan
        observances,
The feasting and drinking,
The spurious goodwill,
The alcoholic bonhomie;
End the materialism,
The commercialism,
The whole whirl of meaningless
        activity.

And what will remain?

With unimagined clarity
There will be experienced
An intermission,
A quietness,
A stillness of the spirit.
A strange awareness
Of the infiltration of human life
By some divine essence.
Bringing with it
An indescribable peace
Which is at once the mystery
And the reality
That is called Christmas.

— G. M. Caple

A WISH

For you, I wish:
    Soft snow,
    A gift, both given and received, wrapped in love,
    A candle and a fire,
    A bowl of crisp red apples, tangerines, and oily oranges,
    A blizzard of cards that bring those others closer than they were
        before,
    A tree that somehow kept its green when autumn came and went,
    The joy of old stories that seem forever new and songs sung softly
        under the breath of "peace on earth."

                        — Max Coots

EACH NIGHT A CHILD IS BORN

For so the children come
and so they have been coming.
Always in the same way they came —
Born of the seed of man and woman.

No angels herald their beginnings.
No prophets predict their future courses.
No wise men see a star to show where to find
The babe that will save humankind.
Yet each night a child is born is a holy night.

Fathers and mothers —
Sitting beside their children's cribs —
Feel glory in the sight of a new life beginning.
They ask "Where and how will this new life end?
Or will it ever end?"

Each night a child is born is a holy night —
A time for singing —
A time for wondering —
A time for worshipping.

                        — Sophia Lyon Fahs

Stars are brightest, this midnight of the year,
Time of darkness, time of cold,
Of reminiscence and anticipation.
In memories of summers past,
All thoughts of springs to come,
We light our candles,
Fragments of stars and sun
To light our hopes and dreams,
Make way for peace and love,
Still a distant dream, like spring,
Hope, made flesh in each of us.
Not shadows nor reflections,
Incandescent spirit, alive in us,
When stars are brightest,
This midnight of the year,
And life burns sharp in us.

— Charles Flagg

SONNET FOR CHRISTMAS

Oh fill your heart with fantasy and song.
This is the time to dream and not inquire
If it be true, but let our deep desire
Enflame our vision, make it glad and strong
To soar beyond our wont. It's far from wrong
To seek release. The year's demands conspire
Against our natures 'til our souls require
The melodies and myths of ages long.
The moon is full, the wind sings in the trees.
Bright mountains call, and clouds and faeries dance,
Ideals unborn and dreams half caught await,
And we can choose what we shall make the keys
To life. Shall love and joy and peace enhance
The fantasy made true as we create?

— Isabel A. Gehr

Light a candle in the darkness,
And you pierce the gloom;
Light a candle in the shadows
And love fills a room;
Light a candle 'mid a sadness
And stars come to birth.
Light a candle Christmas Eve
And you mingle heaven and earth.

— Max Kapp

I would not have this season pass away
    Until I see a star in strange light;
    And a green tree on a hill.
    Until my candle burns in ecstasy
    Against the loneliness and dark,
    Until I hear a sobbing and a song
    Until I find an altar still and bare
    Where I may leave my offering —
    And my prayer.

— Max Kapp

A MOOD OF EXPECTANCY

The earth has turned once more in its accustomed way.
And again our footsteps quicken,
Our voices are raised in familiar chorus:
The sights and sounds of Christmas
Greet our eyes and ears.
Almost as if we had never seen or heard them before.

There is a mood of expectancy,
What we are to expect, we do not know.
The least surprises are hidden beneath bright paper
and graceful ribbon.
The great surprises are the magic that happens
Whether we will it or not.

There is a mood of expectancy.
And the beauty is we do not know what to expect.
Tomorrow is an open door.
An untraveled journey.
An untouched feast.

Christmas is like that — it is a mood of expectancy.
For out of the birth of the humblest babe
May come one of the great prophets of the human spirit
And out of each of us, proud or humble,
May yet come truth and beauty and goodness we
    cannot now imagine.
Christmas is a mood of expectancy.

— Richard Gilbert

LET THE NIGHT BE SILENT

We have done almost everything
With the Christmas story,
Even though inexhaustible
Remains its glory.

There seems but little more to do
In verse or canticle,
So let the Night really be Silent,
And ourselves be still.

Let our contentious tongues
Have rest awhile this season;
One thing only let us do,
And that is — listen;

Scarcely for the herald angels,
Only for the oracular,
Sheer though inaudible,
Pleading of his star . . .

— A. E. Johnson

'TIS THE SEASON

Green leaves outside my window
Could lull me with their lie of endless summer.
No blustering wind, no sudden sift of snow
Heralds the change. And yet I am not fooled.
The signs are there — subtle, perhaps, but present:
A slant of light, the mist-filled morning air,
A soft grey anger in the swells of ocean
Warns me the darker season is at hand.

The sun, an errant lover,
Has wandered off. Only if wooed by me
Will it return. The ancient incantations
I now recite. I tell the ancient stories
Of hope made manifest; deftly prepare the feast:
Pack love and tinsel into every gift.
Most magical of all, I light a candle —
My act of faith, to guide the sun's return.

— Eileen Karpeles

66

Once more the earth has moved about its sun.
Once more, as waning daylight brings us near
The birthday of another solar year,
We think upon high purposes undone.
How many times the cycle has begun
With dreams held high and glowing hopes seen clear,
Only to lock in strife with doubt and fear;
To fail or falter, ere the course is run.

Yet it is not the years that deal us so,
But we ourselves, who throw our little light
Against the world of dull, insensate stuff
And fail to keep it shining. This we know:
In us a spark remains; we fan it bright
Again and yet again. This is enough.

— John G. MacKinnon

FROM BETHLEHEM'S DUST

Not of Augustus, or Herod, the legions of Caesar,
Not of the city imperial, famed and renown,
Not of the lineage royal, the station exalted,
But of the harrassed and driven,
The spurned of the Crown.

Far from the palace and villa, no wealth of a nation,
Far from the city celestial, the home of the rich,
Here is an obscure outpost, known not by earth's might,
We climbed to the height of our vision, leaving forever
The shadow and pitch.

This is the promise of time, the hope rekindled,
From humble beginnings to mount to the height,
As humanity's heart found the hope to aspire,
And Bethlehem's stable, its manger ennobled,
The balance made right.

Bethlehem was little known, its manger not the Inn,
But here the people's upward journey shall forevermore begin.

— George N. Marshall

LEGENDS OF THE SKIES

God planted a garden eastward in Eden
    And there set the tree of life;
With roots soil-snaking and brown bank wrinkled
    As though it were born for strife.
But high on the breeze, where green leaf quivers
    Blue-bathed against the sky,
A man looks up from the dust and the demons
    As the Lord of Heaven rides by.

God planted a garden southward in Eden
    And there set the tree of shade;
In glowing sand shone a pool of water
    Where jackals once had played.
And under the tree a daughter of Rachel
    Filling her water jar.
Looks up through the palms in the cool of the evening
    To the spear of a Holy Star.

God planted a garden westward in Eden
    And there set the tree of birch;
Air through its branches and bark of its body
    Send young men afar on their search
For slack reaches of water ending the rapids
    And the swell of a western sea.
On jet-streams of heaven their paddles now pull them
    Back to the silver tree.

God planted a garden northward in Eden
    And there set the tree of pine;
It shot up straight like an arrow to heaven
    Where Dipper and Pole Star shine.
Slant-eyed children warmed by the fireflame
    Look up to the star-silvered heights,
And see of a sudden a marvel of reindeer
    Leap out from the Northern Lights.

                    — Leonard Mason

KEEP CHRISTMAS

I see a child
The child sees me;
I cherish that child
Under yonder tree.

A tree that's tall
a tree that's wide
Shining bright
At Christmas tide.

Cherish the child,
Life's ancient spell,
And together we'll
Keep Christmas well.

— John Hanley Morgan

MARVEL MAKING

They made a marvel,
All those olden people,
Dying young, ill, plundered,
In cave, in hut, in hovel,
In wretched tenement
They made a marvel.

With music, dance,
With picture, poetry,
With holly, yule log,
Mistletoe, and light,
All the lights, little lights
To make a marvel.
Solstice.
And now we call it Christmas.

And so again I wish you,
As they did, in their way
Long, long ago: again I wish you:

Merry Christmas!

— John Hanley Morgan

SOLSTICE

The gray clouds cluster,
Colder blows the wind:
Darkness comes early to the land:
It is December.
The snows of winter gleam,
Sleet's iron fist descends.

We move in darkness: solstice.
Therefore make ready with the Light!
Light of star, light of candle,
Firelight, lamplight, love light.

These little lights can guide us,
And bring a steady peace
As we move toward Christmas morn,
And joy again the sun's release!

— John Hanley Morgan

TOUCH HANDS

Ah friends, dear friends,
as years go on and heads get
gray, how fast the guests do go!

Touch hands, touch hands,
With those that stay.

Strong hands to weak,
old hands to young,
around the Christmas board,
touch hands.

The false forget, the foe
forgive, for every guest will
go and every fire burn low
and cabin empty stand.

Forget, forgive, for who may
say that Christmas day may never
come to host or guest again.
Touch hands!

— William Henry
Harrison Murray

A gentle kind of madness
Comes with the end of December
A winter solstice spell, perhaps,
When people forget to remember —

The drab realities of fact,
The cherished hurt of ancient wrongs,
The lonely comfort of being deaf
To human sighs and angels' songs.

Suddenly, they lose their minds
To heart's demands and beauty's grace;
And deeds extravagant with love
Give glory to the commonplace.

Armies halt their marching,
Hatreds pause in strange regard
For the sweet and gentle madness born
When a wintry sky was starred.

— Anthony F. Perrino

Drab is the life,
and sighfully long,
which never has heard
an angel's song.

Dark is the night
whose sky-full of space
is starless of fancy
and its promise of grace.

So, let the merry bells be run,
    let the carols' claims be sung;
    let the candles kindle dreams,
    let love's season work its schemes;
    let life's hope be born again,
    let the joy of Christmas reign.

— Anthony F. Perrino

One of the colors of Christmas
is the green of growing leaves:
boughs of fragile fragrance
a wreath'ed tenderness weaves.

But there upon the holly branch
a drop of piercing red reminds
that caring much means bearing hurt
— a destiny that loving finds.

— Anthony F. Perrino

71

Much of the magic of Christmas
lies in the laughter of
children's delight
echoing half-rememberd joys
of warmth rekindled
by sound and sight.

The carol's merry music, the bright be-ribboned gifts,
the ever-young-green tree
renew the faded, jaded dream
to cheer and charm the children
that live in you and me.

— Anthony F. Perrino

The bleak and barren winter
Of seasoned cynicism,

The cold and crisp December
Of forgotten loves and dreams,

succumb again — as ever —
to the color of Christmas' hope
and the warmth of Christmas joy.

— Anthony F. Perrino

TOO FULL OR FULFILLED?

How full was the inn at Bethlehem? Too full!
How full are our lives? Too full?

Too full of society and societies to have room for family?
Too full of activities to have room for accomplishments?
Too full of responsibilities to have room for simple joys?
Too full of business to have room for religion?
Too full of busy-ness to have room for thought and prayer?
Too full of self-interest to have room for common needs?
Too full of regrets to have room for hope?
Too full of fear to have room for faith?
Too full of suspicion to have room for love?
Too full of conflict to have room for peace and goodwill?
Too full of noise to have room for angel choirs?

Make room! Clear away the debris!
Open the doors to your heart!
The things that matter will not clutter and crowd your life.
The things that matter will enlarge the orbit of your being until you are
    large enough to contain all that is worthy of being welcomed.

— Albert Q. Perry

72

If only for the Season . . .
Let us banish cynicism
    and welcome wonder.

If only for the Season . . .
Let us downplay our differences
    and discover the bonds
    of common origin and continuing cause.

If only for the Season . . .
Let us set aside worry
    and smile and laugh and sing.

If only for the Season . . .
Let us deny apathy and indifference
    and truly live by loving.

If only for the Season . . .
Let us subvert covetousness and jealousy
    and be both good gift getters and givers.

If only for the Season . . .
    The brief season
        of light,
        life,
        love,
Let us be wise enough to be
    a little foolish
    about candlelight and children and
    matters of the heart . . .
If only for the Season!

— Edward Searl

> *And suddenly there was . . . a multitude of the heavenly*
> *host . . .*   Luke 2:13

After the stores have closed and the final presents
    have been wrapped, —
Beyond the ding, ding, ding
    of Salvation Army handbells;
Beyond the steady, efficient
    computer click of cash registers;
Beyond the sometimes gay, sometimes reverent
    drone of Christmas MUZAK, —
There will come the deep silence
    of Christmas Eve.

It is the thoughtful silence
    of watching and waiting
The silence of the Winter's longest night.
You will look into the star-pocked dome
    of infinity and shiver compulsively.
Yet your heartbeat will give
    such wonderful comfort
That a feeling of utter holiness
Becomes an unuttered prayer.

At that moment
You will know
Why
The shepherds —
Who kept watch through the night —
Heard the hosannas of a heavenly host.

                                 — Edward Searl

The candle,
The evergreen,
The Infant Child:
These are the symbols of the season.

For we affirm that
   a flame
      banishes the dreariest darkness.
For we affirm that
   the Tree of Life
      endures the harshest time.
For we affirm that
   the spirit of love
      is renewed with the birth of every child.

So it is Light and Life and Love
We see
      in the Christmas fire
      and in the Christmas tree
      and in the Christmas child.

And it is Light and Life and Love
We celebrate.

                  — Edward Searl

We'll touch the candle of our hearts
To the flame of the Advent Star
And set the light to burn a path
Where the darkened places are.
And some who never lift their eyes
To the stars that flood the night,
May find their way to a Bethlehem
By our candle's friendly light.

— Ernest Sommerfeld

Against the darkness nature brings
We bring our light,
Our tallest candles burn to guard
The longest night.

We greet the shortest day with song
And friends with cheer,
We light a wish for peace to serve
The coming year.

— Ernest Sommerfeld

SEASON'S SEASONING

I wish you . . .
>Pure air and clear skies for your loves;
>A flock of geese and a pair of doves.

I wish you . . .
>Trees and grass and crystal water,
>Rainbows, cumulus clouds, and laughter.

I wish you . . .
>Silent nights, white snow, cranberries,
>Evergreen and a bowl of cherries.

I wish you . . .
>Appetite, zest, and red apples,
>A hearth and wood from the maples.

I wish you . . .
>Poems, surcease from care,
>A Bach suite and an Ellington air.

I wish you . . .
>Thoughts, pleasant surprises,
>Study and lofty surmises.

I wish you . . .
>Places to go and not to have to;
>Places to stay because you want to.

I wish you . . .
>Daily bread and daily work,
>A bottle of wine and a bright red shirt.

I wish you . . .
>Courage to be and will to do
>What love and sense have urged you to.

I wish you . . .
>New carols and a spray for cliches,
>A dog and a ride in a very old sleigh.

— Ernest Sommerfeld

DARK QUESTIONINGS

Will a black Mary, room
Denied, be led to the gloom
Of an ox-warmed shed
And a heap of straw for a bed?

Will negro shepherds come
At dawn, still trembling from
Music that shook the night
With sudden wings of light?

Will a star, bending low
Over the lean-to, show
Three dusky wise men in
To God's next of kin?

In after years will he
Too, nailed upon a tree,
Be called upon when men
Sharpen their swords again?

Ah, when will Islam, Judah,
Krishna, Christ, and Buddha,
Together bless with peace,
That war and rage may cease?

How many avatars
Of gentler gods than Mars
Must come again to earth?
How many a holy birth?

Ere all earth's children may
Sleep safe, and love the day?

— Jacob Trapp

I who have knelt before no gods this year
Have sudden need to kneel me in the snow.
When round me like the rush of wings I hear
The midnight chimes and carollings, I know
I am not meant to live on cynic's dole,
To speak the mocking word, and wear disdain
As one who wears behind a mask a soul
As parched for beauty as a drouth for rain.
I, who have lived insensible of loss,
Now kneel in wonderment of light that fills
A waiting world — from Bethlehem the cross,
And gentleness that walked forgotten hills . . .
How long ago: Ah me! How dull we are,
How slow of heart, how blinded by a star!

— Jacob Trapp

The Christmas Spirit we should never lose
And if we wish to change it, we may know
That we ourselves should change, and quickly so,
Should seek a deeper faith and find good news
From ancient, slender, subtle, guiding clues;
A birth, a star out where the wild winds blow,
A gleam of light, or comfort whispered low:
For Christmas is a spirit we must choose.

Be thou not proud! And be not stern of heart,
Because of wounds or pain, turn not away
Play thou the gentle and forgiving part
And be assured thou hast a part to play:
Give gifts of love and peace, though at a cost
And know thou that such gifts are never lost.

— Roscoe E. Trueblood

CHRISTMAS IS A FAITH

Your faith must be a blend of common things,
The life you lead and deeds you do each day,
Mingled with sun-lit towers and Milky Way;
Faith walks on feet yet soars the sky on wings,
It knows of sadness — still it often sings;
Its language helps you work and helps you pray,
Faith knows of fear but still remains the stay
By which your heart defies all threatenings.

Now Christmas is a faith; the faith that gleams
Through lonely midnight like one guiding star,
From shepherds' hillside up where angels are,
From flight and terror up to silvered dreams;
From a world cold and harsh with voices wild
To warmth and peace; a mother and her child.

— Roscoe E. Trueblood

THE ETERNAL SONG

Who laid the corner stone of (the earth)
When the morning stars sang together and all
those of God shouted for joy?   Job 38:6-7

The stars of morning at Creation's gate
Rang out a song before we ever came
Which lives though sung or unsung, just the same:
This song we sing in peace-time, hearts elate
And hymn it plaintively in times of hate,
It sometimes wordless comes without a name
Like truth or vision; like a feeble flame —
A candle in the window of our fate.
And never rings this melody so clear
And never sings so true with notes so bright
As when at Christmas with unbounded cheer
We hear it sound though starless be the night,
As if to say that back of clouds, grief, pain,
The stars serene remain — to shine again.

— Roscoe Trueblood

CHRISTMAS SONNET

And now, the greatest miracle of all,
Recurrent, silent, glorious as the sun;
Once more the lovely mother in the stall
Sings to her babe, the helpless holy one,
Immortal, changeless and with light suffused.
The ancient story is our heritage
Of beauty in a noisy world, confused
With greed and cruelty and senseless rage.
The quiet message lives. Oh wondrous gift
That, punctual in darkness, brings the song
Of angels, and the shepherds eyes that lift
As do our hearts, in worship! We who long
For peace and goodwill for humankind
That Christmas Star will seek and find.

— Sara Walther (adapted)

PRAYER AT NEW YEAR

I send no wish to the Impossible
Or prayer to Maybe, Perhaps;
No promise birthing pretense, despair,
Or Longing that sighs like a wrack.

In a world mad with our choosing
The warfare this year will glare,
Mornings will turn to darkness
And most will be worse for the wear.

So I wish you simply endurance:
Luck among the mines and snares,
Respite for some shining at table,
Less pain than you're able to bear.

With this an occasional glance
Into each other's eyes that care,
A minimum of broken lances
And a heart still able to swear.

— Clarke Dewey Wells
from *Sunshine and
Rain At Once*

TO YOU BE JOY THIS DAY!

The mercury is snuggling down
Into the little red bulb
To keep warm
But in my heart
There's a warmth that is pressing outward
Against all cold.
It radiates out to all the world
And I hope you feel it.

I love the old songs
Even though my voice cracks when I sing them.
I enjoy all the colored lights:
Chanukah candles in some windows:
Christian lights in others,
And just plain pagan lights all over everywhere!

I can't quite "catch sight of Proteus rising from the sea,"
But this time of year I can just about
"Hear old Triton blow his wreathéd horn."
This time of year was always one of rejoicing:
The Yule Log in Scandinavia,
The fir tree in central Europe,
Each spoke joy and love of earth and home and children.
Maybe Persephone's mother danced a measure or two
And old Bacchus tilted the flowing bowl
In honor of the season.

Maybe old Dutch Klaus did come down a chimney
(Some chimneys were big enough then.)
But our gas and oil furnaces would furrow his brow.
Never mind; they wouldn't stop him
Even if south of the equator this time of year
He might have to come down the air-conditioner.

So here's a Merry Christmas and a Happy Hanukah to you:
Health and Happiness
And the joy of children in your hearts as well as in theirs.
Let's hope the spirit of the season
Lasts a little longer this year
And still more next year
And so on until it's true:
"War shall be learned no more!"

— Robert Terry Weston

THE SNOW DRIFTS DOWN

Across the hill and dell, valley and upland,
Smooth as a blanket across the world,
Softly falling, falling,
Quietly, gently as a mother's kiss
On the face of her sleeping child,
The snow drifts down, touches, settles,
Lies on tree and shrub, on field and woodland,
Like a soft mantle,
Making all things new.
So be my heart this day:
The pain of things done and injuries unmended,
The fears of things unseen and long dreaded,
The ache of failures and mistakes of times past,
The sudden angry passion and the bitter regret,
And strength ebbing away with the inexorable beat of time,
All forgotten, or restored to innocence,
Clothed in gentle purity,
The universal forgiveness which whispers me,
"Behold, I make all things new!"

— Robert Terry Weston

The Christ is found not in some humble stable
    On Bethlehem's plain,
But in all hearts that seek to heal
    The world's dark pain.
Not on some Holy Night of long ago
    To angel strain —
While shepherds watched their slumb'ring flocks —
    Alone, he came.
But when in calm of quieter hours,
    Our souls aspire
To make the paths of truth and peace
    The heart's desire;
And selfless love becomes a mighty urge
    That stirs the mind —
A sacrificial flame that burns the dross
    And joy we find
In simple things, in gentle laughter free
    From pride of self;
It's then, we sense a Presence, all serene,
    So strong, so still.

— Horace Westwood

BE GRACEFUL

Be graceful in the winsome winter
 Bow gently on the ice-strewn walk
Tumble with elegance, if taken unawares
 You stumble on a hidden stalk.

It's not the wind's fault
 That your face is numb, as blizzards blow
Nor does the sleet glint down with malice
 As branches creak beneath the impersonal snow.

The balking engine and the sliding tires
 Conspire only to fulfill an icy law
Of physics and grumbling should be saved
 For your own folly. That's what grumbling's for.

Bleak as the winter is and bitter
 And desperate as the dark nights are
The snow-shapes and the magic frost
 Contain their own precise and lovely star.

A loveliness that young hearts know
 In frolic on the whitened land
And if you cannot share these rituals
 Find joy in memories — and then you'll understand.

       — George C. Whitney
        (adapted)

WONDER OF WONDERS

Wonder of Wonders
Is the Holy Mystery
Enshrining the Birth of every Christ Child!

Brave Akhnaton, prophet of purified religion,
Zoroaster, heroic champion of righteousness,
Meek Moses, divine leader of revolt,
Compassionate Gautama,
Uncompromising Socrates,
Confucius, the wise and wonderful counselor,
Mystic Francis, gentle brother to all that walks or flies,
Imperious Mohammed, welder of wild hordes,
And lowly Jesus, Prince of Peace
And Herald of heaven on earth.

Whence came these Holy Saviors?
Whence these embodiments of Moral Genius?
What Mystic Spirit sired them?
What Cosmic Womb conceived them?
What Spiritual Omen presaged their advent?

Were they not spawn of Giant Meteors,
Progeny of the Milky Way,
Sparks from far-off Suns and Stars
Come to illumine Earth's Spiritual Night?

Who sent them here?
What brought them here?
We Wonder!
We will never cease to Wonder!

                                        — David Rhys Williams

christmas
is
a time of
giving yourself
to see the smile of
pleasure
in another's eye.

a time of
all-encompassing love
for all you have
a feeling for.

carols, choruses,
music to fill
the mind and spirit
to overflowing with
warmth.

and, christmas
is
a time to receive
the gift of love
from another.

— julie wortman

THE ROAD TO BETHLEHEM

If as Herod, we fill our lives with things and again things;

If we consider ourselves so important that we must fill every moment
of our lives with action;

When will we have the time to make the long slow journey across the
burning desert as did the Magi;

Or sit and watch the stars as did the shepherds; Or to brood over the
coming of the Child as did Mary?

For each one of us there is a desert to travel, a star to discover, and a
being within ourselves to bring to life.

— Edward Ericson

V. Here's to epiphanies great and small

JL

*Here's to epiphanies great and small
whenever they occur. A blessing on all
Wise Men and Women, East and West.
Here's to the stargazers and pilgrims
everywhere, who are still foolish enough
and brave enough to follow their stars,
who travel by night, who bestow their
uncommon gifts on us all.*
                              Patrick T. A. O'Neill

W. H. Auden wrote that to pray is to pay attention to something or someone other than oneself. In this season when it is so easy to dwell on the riches that we have, to think only of the gifts we will receive and the feasting that we will enjoy, the friends we will see again and the many joys that will fill our lives in this festive time, let us also pray in hope and in love

for those who still suffer under the ravages of war

for those who bear the burden of oppression and injustice

for those who are without friends and are lonely

for those who live with constant pain

for those who have known disappointment and despair as their constant companions

for those who despise themselves and for those who despise others

for those who know only failure

for those whose lives have been shattered by tragedy

for those who do not hear the song of the angels and

for those who do not see the brilliance of the Christmas Star.

As we rejoice and celebrate in these gladsome days, let us find new strength that we might live and work for the day when peace shall truly be on earth and good will among all people the whole wide world around.

— Kenneth W. Phifer

O Spirit of Advent and Christmas past,
Prepare in us an expectant heart.
Thaw the wintry coldness of our ways.
Help us not refuse those waiting birth.
And teach us that Bethlehem is not a town,
    past or present,
But a place in our hearts,
Where the cry of the newborn baby can be
    heard.

                   — Burton Carley

May the spirit of this season help us find our way through the noise and turmoil of the days ahead into the heart of Christmas itself, to its quieter joy and its peace.

May we learn that we cannot hear the songs until our own hearts learn to sing them.

May we, whose needs are so great, know how close we are to what we seek, and how often the things we want so desperately are ours already.

May we be strong enough for the joys and the pains of love; and may we, with quiet persistence in our hearts, learn to enjoy the small happenings of our days and hours and find in them the meaning that touches us most deeply, that moves us most profoundly.

May we find that life is good. amen

                   — Charles Stephen

Let me possess myself
Be calm in mind and quiet in my heart.

Let me take time to watch the candle's light
And know it is the same
Vast silence of the silver stars.

Let me be of time dispossessed;
Stand at the birth and humbly
Say the name.
Let me in quiet, by the candle's sight:
Be akin to the stars and
Lost in time —
Be a Disciple of Truth's Eternal Light.

— John Q. Parkhurst

Oh great God, spirit of history's long changes, we gather now to confess a longing. Even when most content we are restless with knowledge of our earth home's delicacy, of the fragile bonds of the human family. We ask in the many ways we can to be good citizens of our terrestrial civilization, to be better neighbors.

Wherever there are children, and aging good folk, wherever there are ordinary fellow human beings, there would our best wishes travel. Closer here at home, may our burdens of care make us feel less clumsy and rather more effective. May we break through the commercial wrapping and ribbon that hide our own gifts of intelligent, imaginative compassion. And let light shine in us, make the fanciful poetry of the old Christmas story sing a new real song. amen

— Charles A. Reinhardt

PRAYER (to be spoken joyfully and vigorously akin to the ancient custom of shouting the Lord's Prayer)

O Creative Spirit of Life, we give thanks for the wonders there are: the human quest for meaning, for the poetry and myth of human imagination, for the bright stars in the night, for the joyful sound of voices uplifted in song, for the good company of women and men in houses of fellowship such as ours.

We would be mindful of the pain within the world, the loneliness, the hunger, the poverty which remains.

We join in the faith that in the midst of all which besets us we are called to be faithful to Life and faithful to each other. The spirit of Christmas is a spirit of hope and faith in the amazing possibilities which are open to us. Let us nurture this hope and this faith and proclaim it to the world, amen

— Bruce A. Southworth

O Child of Bethlehem, my gifts are rude and few: I bring this self of mine as a stable to shelter your birth; this darkness of my heart, this emptiness of my mind for your manger; these angry passions, these unlovely deeds, the accumulated errors of my wandering years I bring as straw which I shall break and soften and mold as a cradle for your head; and I bring my longing, my hope and my prayer that a light shall mark the place of your birth within my life.

— Emerson S. Schwenk

O Thou who art the life force sustaining us all, with sound and fury do we rent our lives with so much business and activity that brings no peace. The week ahead, now fraught with many temptations to tarry amidst the secular realms that have no life, is one in which we might find sustenance if we but pause, from time to time —

- looking up, to see a star we never stopped to see
- looking out upon the fields of frozen snow and trees now capped with a mantle of winter's light
- looking within to find a strength we little knew was there

Calm on the listening ear, the peace and inner power comes. Like a tender baby's cry in the night, our spirits are awakened to the meaning of this season. We sense the thoughts of motherhood — undim'd by the clouds of violence and greed. We understand a father's pride — undaunted by the demands of a world that had no heart. We feel the wonder that was even in the lives of kings, brought lowly, humble, before the gentleness and the hope that was latent in a tiny babe.

And now another year to celebrate this wondrous timeless miracle of worldwide birth is with us . . . to make of it what we will . . .

O Father-Mother God, residing in us all potential, help us to grandly raise our vision to a higher meaning than the usual . . . and make this season one of true religious depth and joy. In the name of all that's holy in the heart of humanity, we pray. amen

— Jan V. Knost

It's Christmas again, Jesus, and we light our candles and lightbulbs and deck the blackness with a multi-colored multitude of flashing, flickering, blinking, blinding lights, to mark your coming in deep December.

Things have changed since you came to the world in some anonymous stable thick in hay and animal smells.

We have been clever and learned new ways. We have learned to build great cities around us to hide us from the cold, the heat, the hunger, the sickness, the pain. We have come beyond stables, Jesus, the animal smells, the hay smells.

But the human family is cruelly divided still, in a thousand ways, as it was when you came. War is with us, only that we have learned more terrible ways of waging it; hate among people is with us; fear among nations is with us; the weak live in terror of the strong; four billion human souls crouch in the shadow of an atom bomb, waiting.

You came human-naked to the world, and you walked the long paths gently singing: "Love one another, don't be afraid to love, love is stronger than swords." We who have been so clever at building cities and cannons, we have yet to learn your human song.

It's Christmas again, and we light our candles and lightbulbs in deep December. But Christmas, Jesus, your Christmas, is a human light, and a human song, like your birthday in the hay, that first night.

You, Jesus, who are the true and beautiful soul in all persons, come into the night with sun and singing forever on this planet among stars. amen

— Kenneth Jacobsen

O God, keep us from missing life by small neglects
   that blind the eyes of the spirit;
Keep us from being overly analytical when we need
   to be understanding;
From talking too much when the situation demands
   listening;
From being too orderly when we may need the disorder
   of insight;
From being so involved in the immediate that we miss
   the long view of the soul;
From making such great efforts in life when the truth
   that saves is so simple;
From plodding along when we could hear celestial
   music and begin a magnificent journey to the kingdom of heaven
   which lies close at hand;
Keep us trusting, lighting candles in the darkness, knowking that with
the eyes of the spirit and the ears of the mind we may perhaps catch an
angel this Christmas.

— Ralph N. Helverson

O Lord, we are looking for something this Christmas, but we are not sure just what it is. It's more than gifts, more than laughter, more than the few moments of happiness and good cheer this season bestows upon us. We are thankful for those moments, but we are looking for something more.

Maybe it is peace of mind we are looking for, or that sense of claim that comes with understanding, with revelation; the ability to cope with the complexities of life, or the strength to face the frustrations with greater assurance and less fear.

Maybe we are searching for a more acceptable way to live in this ever-changing world — or for something to lean on. We *do* need support — we *do* need to believe in something — we *do* need to be inspired. We need to find something — some ideal, some promise to believe in.

So let this Christmastide breathe upon us a special sense of love and friendship; let the values which are of the mind and heart of the grown-up Jesus be part of our thinking. Let the Christmas message shine through.

Maybe someday, Lord, we will know precisely what it is we are looking for, but in the meantime, supply us with generous amounts of fortitude and calmness and assurance to deal adequately with the everyday, until the time comes when we will know for sure what it is we are looking for.

— David Blanchard

Creative Spirit of love and goodwill within us, we would feel the presence of the stars this morning. We would hear the silence which is the song of songs. We would be aware of the places in which we have fallen short, and seek that renewal of spirit which comes to us in the secret places of our hearts.

As we enter into the spirit of this Christmas season, and feel the magic touch of goodwill which comes with a friendly greeting, or remembrance, we would renew our spirits, and find strength for the days ahead. As we accept the joy of friendship and the security of family and community, we would resolve that all might be as fortunate as we. In the spirit of love, symbolized at Christmas by mother and child, we would enter this holiday season, that we may grow richer in the meaning and beauty of life.

— Samuel A. Wright, Jr.

Comfort thou my distressed spirit this day, O Eternal. With this yearly remembrance of the birth of the Nazarene Spirit into the world, comfort thou me. Make that selfsame Spirit to live in me that I too may know without any doubt, neither any fear, that Peace and Good Will shall one day prevail on earth. Touch this now inarticulate tongue that it may begin to speak peace again. Lift up the now closed flood-gates of my spirit that I may again pour forth love into this seeming loveless world. Open these eyes now blinded with tears of despair, that I may see, in wonder see, all about me those hosts of happy, dauntless comrades; and seeing, go forth rejoicing to meet and join them in their steadfast way of Peace and Good Will. Then, losing itself in that Great Companionship, my spirit shall find itself no more lonely. For in that Company of Comrades is never any thought of despair, neither any feeling of fear, but only confidence and great joy forever.

— Frank Carleton Doan

To thy children, O God, to thy children bring the sweetness of surprise. In this bright and blessed season stir us with wonder at all the things we have not known, nor guessed. Reveal thy surprises to us: the love in another's heart that went unnoticed in the furious pressure of the day; the courage in another's breast which we had thought could not be there; the clam unfettered wisdom in another's mind which we passed all unseeing on our way; the divine spark waiting to become a flame within another of thy children, a child whom we had fancied o so far from divinity. In this season, O God, grant to us the humbling and ennobling gift of such surprise as this — thy Holy, sweet surprise.

— Robert M. Bowman

Let us pray that strength and courage abundant be given to all who work for a world of reason and understanding; that the good that lies in every one's heart may day by day be magnified; that we will come to see more clearly not that which divides us, but that which unites us; that each hour may bring us closer to a final victory, not of nation over nation, but of humans over their evils and weaknesses; that the true spirit of this Christmas Season — its joy, its beauty, its hope, and above all its abiding faith — may live among us; that the blessings of peace be ours — the peace to build and grow, to live in harmony and sympathy with others, and to plan for the future with confidence.

— author unknown

O God, in our practiced pessimism it is difficult to be less than cynical about Christmas. We too have followed stars but they never led us to Bethlehem. We have known many wise men whose wisdom faded when tested by our experience. Angel voices for us usually turn out to be singing commercials. Words of peace are used to defend acts of aggression. Herod and Caesar still reign. The world as created is not as we would have it. And yet, and yet . . .

Somewhere a child just drew its first breath and the parents share in the primal joy of Christmas. A son estranged from his parents has decided to call home and the sound of his voice will bring the hope of reconciliation. Someone has given a gift where there was no expectation of giving or receiving. An aged person, ill and unloved, has just found mercy in the mantle of death.

O God, it's not your world, it's ours. Give us the courage to accept it, the grace to embrace it, the will to love it. Enable us, we pray, to appreciate and expand the moments of joy in life, whenever they come. Let them be for us bearers of hope which will enable us to endure any hour of despair, to the end that we, while the gift of life is ours, may help push back the dark with the flame of our faith.

— Paul Carnes

O thou who has called us out of the darkness into the marvellous light of life and love, help us to find our way through the noise and turmoil of the days ahead to the true meaning of Christmas, to its quiet joys and to its peace.

> Teach us that we cannot hear the songs until our own hearts learn to sing them, and that the most important gifts which we can give to one another cannot be wrapped and put under the Christmas tree.

Show us, whose needs are so great, how close we are to what we seek, and how often the things we want most desperately are ours already, if we will only stretch out our hands.

> Help us to be brave enough for life and love, and guide us in our search through doubt and darkness until we find the faith which knows no place or season — until we learn at last that though the very stars may wander, there is that within us which need never lose its way.

— A. Powell Davies

99

O God, we thank Thee that at the darkest time of the year there comes to us the brightest festival. Let the the gladness of its faith and the joy of its promise be warm within us!

Let us believe its hope: that sometime there shall be a world in which inhumanity is ended; a world of goodwill from which all cruelty is gone; a world in which the prophecies have found fulfillment, in which nations are at peace and hatred and strife are known no more. A world in which children's faces are bright like the face of the Christ-child, and love and gentleness have everywhere prevailed.

Let the darkness of our skies be cloven! Let the angel of this hope appear! Let the song be sung by the heavenly host, and let earth join in the chorus!

May the spirit of God be born in our hearts this day, that truth may direct us and love possess us.

— A. Powell Davies

Let the gracious spirit of Jesus, the spirit of the little child, as it knocks today at human hearts, enter our lives and bless them; that duty may become touched with beauty, and justice be forgotten in love. At other times we ask that we may do our tasks with consecration and patience; today we ask for more: that obligation may be changed to opportunity, and duty done with joy. At other times we ask that we may walk uprightly: today we pray for grace to bow ourselves to others' needs. Let our ears hear the cry of the needy, and our hearts feel the love of the unlovely. Give our hands strength, not to do great things, but to do small things graciously. Let our gifts today be not a sacrifice but a privilege. Let us accept kindness with humility. Heal the wounds of misunderstanding, jealousy, or regret, that scar our hearts; and let the gentler air of the Christmas spirit touch our lives, as though the cold of winter were touched by the kindlier breath of spring. As the old year ends, and the new year begins, grant us peace with the world, and peace in our own hearts, that those we love, and those whom we may help, may have sweet joy and rest.

— Francis G. Peabody

Let us enter into this Christmas with the strength of imagination. Let us not stumble on words or be caught up by images that do not seem to represent us. Let us transcend them all with the strength of imagination so that the essence, the meaning, and the truth are ours to use. And then let us use them, with continual imagination, to discover fruitful ways to improve the life around us. Let us stand beneath that special starlight of Christmas, find our neighbors in its special glow, and then warm our hands against the brightness of winter-night air with the special warmth that is found between people who care. amen

— Conrad Dippel

As we hear the familiar Christmas story this morning, let us open our hearts to the images which speak to our lives.

Each of us could travel a long and weary journey, only to find that when night falls there is no room at the inn.

Each of us could be a shepherd, patiently caring for those who need us, who depend on us.

Each of us could be a king, in search of the holy, ready to offer our gifts.

Each of us might sometime hear angel voices, singing of a glory we have yet to know.

"And surely, for each of us, there is a desert to cross, a star to follow, and a new being within to bring to life."

— Ann Fields

We are grateful for the color and warmth of this Advent season and we enjoy the changes that it brings into our lives. We are stirred deeply within us, by the call to goodwill among people and by the vision of peace on earth. At this season we are especially mindful of our oneness with all the living throughout the world and our affection goes out still more to the very young.

Yet, even more deeply within us, we wonder whether this seasonal brightness and cheer, and also the seasonal renewal of spiritual awareness, be not a fleeting excuse for leaving things as they are, an escape from reality. Merriment causes no qualms in us and we feel no guilt in the presence of rejoicing; we thank Thee for these blessings, but we look for something more.

We ask that over and above the jolly idealism of Advent we become ever more real and serviceable persons throughout the year. We wish that through our personal dedication to certain moral standards and ethical understanding, our personal characters would take on a quality of goodness, insight, and helpfulness which would bless those around us, all the year through.

Our thoughts are turned this day to all, such as the parents of Jesus, who were able to build something true and lasting. Beneath all the changes and appearances of life, may we become such real people ourselves.

— Gaston M. Carrier

There is a spirit that comes to men and women at this season of the year — it is the spirit of the child, familiar to all children, to whose eyes the unseen is yet visible with all of the mystery and loveliness of the actual — a spirit of which life becomes a sad tale of its loss. And, in the grip of this spirit compassion becomes commonplace, kindness is not servile, and generosity reaches out from the heart.

We pray that this spirit not be harried in its expression from all the round of Christmas duties and expectations. For, our greatest need in the affluence of our lives, where usually to want is to buy, is the gift of this spirit. Without it our shopping is a burden, and we measure the length of the season by the height of our desperation, and nothing remains save getting and spending.

It may be that we will put the gift of this spirit away with the decorations from the tree, the lights and the tinsel. Yet, it may be that it shall endure to grace our lives in ways unknown throughout the year. Let such be our prayer. And, if our prayer proceeds from the honest longing of our hearts, it may there find an answer.

— Paul Carnes

102

Our winter begins today — the time of darkness which we know always arrives, and which, we know as surely will pass in time into seasons of light and warmth.

The seasons of the soul have their own rhythm, their own reasons: Who knows the delight of some of us, reuniting with folk so dear? Who knows the anguish of some among us as our celebrations bring only a reminder of loss? Who knows the pain of uncertainty within others, plagued with doubts and fears — will there be another winter for me? Who can tell what hope is budding in some heart even as our sun grows cold and white in a misting sky?

The seasons of the soul turning in their own time, in their own way (unlike seasons of earth) bring to each of us a different experience of these days of Christmastime and solstice.

We have, in this winter of earth — we have, in whatever season of the soul — the most precious gifts to give away and to keep: we have ears for hearing each other, for listening to one another's need. We have eyes for seeing the signs, for knowing the beauty of another person, for perusing the uniqueness; eyes for telling our own unspoken stories. We have hands for reaching to help, for reaching to give and to receive — hands which hold, and caress, and forgive.

Let us, then, remember the forgotten. Let us seek to heal the injured, to nourish the weak, to revive the withered. Let us be there to love the unloved and the dying. Let our minds and our hearts burn with solstice fires, to prove that the human spirit lives and thrives; that whatever the season of sun or of soul, there reigns a dauntless determination to outlast, together, every dark time.

Let us be filled with the light and merriment that our celebrations bring, that we look ahead in hope and in faith to the Earth's rebirth, and the Springtime of the soul.

— Agnes J. Zuniga

The white mist floats down in the morning air a powder from the sky to cover the earth. It gives a new grace to the torn and ugly places. It is a miracle of beauty.

Let there fall upon us the grace of peace to quiet the anger of our lives, the grace of truth to end the agony of error, the grace of love to halt the enmities of strife. May it sift into our minds as the soft falling snow upon the earth, silently and ceaselessly.

Here, we are in a place of many memories. Here is a sense of old traditions and here are the symbols of our inheritance. Many have been here before us seeking the gifts of the spirit. Some have gone away empty-handed and some have been filled with its treasure. We, too, are seekers and among us there will be those who find and those who do not. The gift is here, the finding of it for ourselves rests with us.

It lies within us, the gift to see, the gift to be given and the gift to receive. Our discovery of the gift is the Christmas of the human life. Not in mangers or under trees; not in stockings or in stores, but within the self and within the heart is the source of Christmas.

May you make your discovery now and here, or tomorrow and elsewhere, but may it come to you a light within your life, a star above your day, a grace of being.

— John W. Brigham

As we enter the season of goodwill, may we not be bitter and may we not indulge in the rushing card-for-a-card and gift-for-a-gift teeter-totter, that makes us bitter. May we rather give as we feel and can afford and let the milling crowd swarm past us and not sweep us off our feet. Neither do we wish to envy others their splash of generosity and their need to display their popularity through parading the number and the cost of their remembrances. We would save ourselves from overtaxed energies and social engagements outside the home, that we may better keep our best personality for our family. We also pause to reserve time for the deeper celebration of "peace on earth." First things first may mean for us a strong effort to balance the personal and the social efforts for peace on earth. Great issues are being decided in December as well as in other months. We would not escape from the hunger and ill will that abound, just because we have a chance to follow the glitter. Instead, we would plan to share with those who cannot give in return, and give our children a greater gift than any that can be bought — a better chance for a peaceful world.

— Victor V. Goff

Now, in the shortest days of the year, nature has banked her fires, takes her annual rest. We, too, seek to grow in serenity. Soon the sunlight, by which our natural bodies live, will gain strength. Our thoughts reach back and are enriched through dwelling with the man of Galilee. The light by which our spirits live grows stronger, too. At Christmas-tide it draws so near we blossom souls anew. O may its influence benign be felt in all our lives, in home and office, mill and mart, in games and school and play, that we may grow as grows the light and spread a gleam of courage, faith and calm to those who have not found the power, serene yet strong, which comes from fellowship with Christs of every age and creed. We would be gentle, quick to heal the broken limb and harried mind, firm-standing in the righteous cause, afraid no longer of the tyrant's power, and quick to march in any ranks, however thin, that promise help for humanity, to pioneer in any sphere that may bring light and knowledge of a finer life; eager to serve, e'en though the pay is scorn, ingratitude, and jeers, sturdy to bear and the loads that come in spite of careful plans. We vow to seek the Christlike life through all the days ahead. amen

— Felix Danforth Lion

Faith, hope, love, these three
I offer you this season.
Faith that living affirms,
Hope that caring illumines.
Love that more matters than anything.
Faith, hope, love, these three
Not as gifts I offer them
For they are not mine to give.
They are yours and mine to share,
Humbly, with one another.
Fumbling, we hold their promise in our hands,
Faintly, we speak the trembling words,
Faith, hope, love, these three
I offer you this season.

— Richard S. Gilbert

105

Bring us to Christmas where, for a season, we may escape the routine world of fact and find the poetry of life, surprises in the familiar, until, with a new vision, we may see what we failed to see before.

Bring us to Christmas where, in the fireside world of fancy, we may find the innocence of life, the gift of a childlike heart again and encompass by loving more than we understand by logic.

Bring us to Christmas where, at the altar of wonder, we take counsel of simplicity and become attuned to the mystery in our own hearts and of the universal mythic image in all of us.

Bring us to Christmas where, in the world of imagination and delight, we tell stories with song and legend and another realm of human wisdom.

Bring us to Christmas where, in moments of the spirit's triumph in the daily round, we may overcome loneliness, face separation, accept change, contain conflicts, be sustained through all times of hardship, and live valiantly.

Bring us to Christmas where, in moments of great contemplation, we become more aware of primary concerns — peace in the world, justice for the excluded, community built by goodwill.

Bring us to Christmas where, by bringing out our best selves, we may light candles in the darkness and make prayers to the music of the world.

Bring us to Christmas by eyes that see, ears that hear, and hearts that understand.

— Ralph N. Helverson

Inexpressible joy fills our hearts as we enter upon the festivities of this glad season.
A season of expectancy and wonder,
A season of giving and forgiving,
A season of thoughtfulness and tenderness,
A season for friendliness and fellowship.
Let it be with music that we sing of Christmas.
Let it be in harmony that we dwell at Christmas.
May love enter our hearts and rule our lives as we seek to serve one another and thus reveal our kinship to Thee.

— Malcolm Sutherland

Let us learn to play with life at least for a time, for now we seem to work too hard at it. Let us learn to sing when we have only spoken, for the melody casts our words on winds of hope. Let us learn to enjoy cadences of poetry instead of pages of prose for they may be closer to the rhythms of life. Let us make room for fancy while we give fact a rest.

Let us take more time to build a snowman than to shovel a walk. Let us lift our face to the heavens and let the snow caress our eyes and tantalize our tongues, while we forget its treacheries underfoot. Let us learn to smile when we are tired with the work we have to do. Let us learn to laugh when our tensions give rise to anger. Let us learn to be merciful when we want to be judgmental.

Let us play for a time in the fields of myth and legend: for news and facts to make it, will be there always. Let us sample the whimsical words of the poets more than the studied works of the scholars. Let our thoughts roam in realms of imagination rather than linger in quagmires of reality.

And so, may hope find its way into our hearts even when our minds tell us there is no hope; may charity speak to us even when we have nothing to give; may loving kindness be with us when our store of love is exhausted.

Let it be so, for a time, for a season. And perhaps that season will linger and linger and take hold of us, never to let us go.

— Richard S. Gilbert

In the deep searching of the heart for that substance of the spirit that may grant us great inward joy; we grasp for a serenity to quiet the common irritations of the day.

In the deep searching of the heart we press for the dispelling of our every fear and the removal of anxiety — all false apprehensions, all delusions, all fancied hurts and angers. We aspire for truth and confidence, for sanity and for comfort.

Then let us welcome with great zeal the blessed season of Christmas, to deliver us from the frenzy of our disturbances and troubled cares. Let mind and heart be one to clear the way for the flooding in of beauty and color, for song to displace the rigid prose of yesteryear, for brightness to disperse all darkness and all gloom.

We would, in this time set aside, become open to the ecstasy of enthrallment, to the utter selflessness of giving, and to the sweet grace of glad acceptance.

Yet in the midst of our rejoicing we would be aware of that loneliness which comes to many isolated or kinless, and seek within our powers to transform melancholy into the cheer of care and friendship, which is the genius of this celebration.

May Christmas deliver us from cynicism and from mistrust, from dismal argument and false piety.

May we feel within ourselves the excitement of our festival with its deep, profound, and sacred tidings, its message of hope to herald in a great rebirth of consecration toward righteousness and peace and love.

> In silence now, let us dwell for a moment on the things which for each one of us have meaning and significance.
> — John K. Hammon

Holy and joyful is the Christmas season, wherein we call to mind Jesus of Nazareth, to rejoice in his birth and give thanks for his goodness. May this season the world over bring happiness to many, tranquility to all, and danger and terror to none. May international rancor and suspicion and inherited hatreds that mar our life, be washed away in the rising tide of human understanding, cooperation and mutual interest. We dare hope that in some not too distant day we will build in peace, and love will reign through all the earth. To hasten the coming of that date may we consecreate ourselves to "Peace on Earth."

— Tracy Pullman

We stand with eyes toward the east,
Awaiting the rising of the star,
And pray that love shall become flesh
   and dwell among us;
And that compassion shall be born
   in human hearts.

We celebrate the discovery of fact
   in the garment of legend.

Let every cradle be visited by the three
   good kings of Faith, Hope and Love.

Then Christmas is with us always,
   and every birth is the birth of God among us,
And every child is the Christ Child,
And every song is the song of angels.

To celebrate Christmas is to attest
   the power of love to remake humankind.
May we be renewed in the love which can save the world.

— Edward Ericson

VI. Through the
solstice crack

Time pushes the sullen door of winter;
   Hinges creak and criticize.
Through the solstice crack of winter
   Flood the earth's nativities.
         Leonard Mason

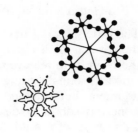

The Nicest Gifts I Ever Got

During this season of gift giving, a good exercise is to make a list of the best gifts we ever got. That will tell us what is important, for ourselves and for people we want to give gifts to.

While I remember a Daniel Boone hat and a magician set with special affection, the nicest gifts I ever got are in quite another category: the carillonneur at Rockefeller Chapel who let me strike one of the largest tuned bells in the world during his playing of *Ein Feste Burg;* my mother giving me a complete Shakespeare for my 14th birthday; coach Al Terry saying "Little Wells, grab your bonnet," and permitting me to enter as a freshman into my first varsity football game; a beautiful lady on a ship when I was still an acned teenager who kissed my face all over and told me she thought I was handsome; Dr. Henry Nelson Wieman telling me he had thought for several hours about a question I had raised and responding with a written answer the next day in front of the whole class; night after night my father playing catch with me in the back yard until it got so dark we couldn't see the ball; a Unitarian minister in Kalamazoo who put his arm around me after my father died and kept it there for a long time; a friend who flew several hundred miles to visit me when I was sick; a buddy who went to see three movies with me on the same day.

The nicest gifts people have given me have been enabling, confirming gifts, bestowing understanding and self-esteem, help in time of trouble and delight for ordinary days.

May I suggest that you, too, draw up your list of the nicest gifts you ever received. I think it will give some perspective to the kind of gifts we really want to give to others, this Christmas or anytime.

— Clarke Dewey Wells
from *Sunshine and
Rain At Once*

"I'm Gettin' Nuttin' for Christmas"

The little song, "I'm Gettin' Nuttin' for Christmas" presents itself as the lament of a child who has been extremely naughty and who therefore is to receive no Christmas presents. But when our children sing this song they sing it with great relish and enthusiasm. It is not as a lament, but as a kind of protest that they sing, a protest against the none-too subtle manipulation of their behavior through the Santa Claus myth of rewards for good children and punishments for bad. We should take heed of this protest for while rewards and punishments may bring people of any age to conform to the demands of an authority figure it is also true that a great deal of resentment may be generated in the process. The child sings, "I'm Gettin' Nuttin' for Christmas," with a pride that says, "I didn't knuckle under to your attempt to control me and take away my freedom of action through bribes!"

Contrast the approach of gift giving as a reward for good behavior with the philosophy of giving set forth in the Gospel according to John, Chapter 3: "For God so loved the world that he gave his only son, that whoever believes in him should not perish but have eternal life. For God sent the Son into the world, not to condemn the world, but that the world might be saved through him." Here we have a gift given, not on the basis of good behavior, indeed, if we follow the Biblical account God saw the world as sinful, but given rather as an unconditional act of love.

Should this not be our philosophy of giving at Christmastime? A gift given according to this model is given with no strings attached, no attempt to force another person to conform to our standards of good and bad behavior, but as an act of love. It is a gift which brings not condemnation, not feelings of guilt to the one who receives it, but the saving message that the recipient is valued and loved.

— Edward T. Atkinson

A Gift's True Value

When looking around in a gift shop the other day I noticed an item which I thought might interest or amuse my family in this season. It was a box of frankincense and myrrh. I paid a half dollar for it and went my way.

Once, these aromatic resins were very rare and fabulously expensive: suitable means by which kings might display their wealth. By tradition, frankincense and myrrh were two of the gifts by means of which the Magi expressed their awe and affection for the infant Jesus.

Now these items are common and cheap. After burning one of them, I would have to conclude also that they are considerably inferior to more modern products as a source of an exotic aroma.

All of which prompts me to suggest that it is always necessary to keep up-to-date in seeking for items with which to express one's faith and affection. Gifts of myrrh and frankincense will identify no one as 'wise' in our day. That which was once an expression of sanctity has become but an object of curiosity.

More basic, perhaps, would be the realization that frankincense and myrrh never possessed any real value of their own. They were never more than resins exuded by an injured tree. People gave them value and used them to express feelings of sanctity. With any gift, it is these feelings which are important. No gift has value in and of it itself, however expensive it may be. Anything can be precious, if it expresses love and trust.

— Albert Q. Perry

The Emperor's Tea

It was so cold the snow squeaked as Professor Stone walked up the hill from the university to his home. He was late for supper, having spent longer in the library than he expected. Turning the corner to his home, he noticed lights and many cars parked around the house. *Then,* he remembered! His wife was having a Christmas party. He should have been home hours ago.

Professor Stone entered the basement door, kicked off his rubbers, hung his overcoat on a nail, slipped up the stairs into the kitchen, and tried to appear as if he had been at the party all along. Almost immediately someone cried, "Here he is!" Open it! Open it!" And others tugged and pulled the professor into the dining room — into the dining room and up to the table, on which sat a rather large and somewhat odd-looking package.

The dean said, "Careful, Stone. I want those Japanese stamps."

The professor looked at the package. In the corner were many beautiful stamps — Japanese stamps. Cutting them out with his pen knife, he handed them to the dean. "You know," said the professor, "I think this is from that Japanese student we had last year. I seem to remember he was going to send me something."

"Open it, open it!" the guests cried.

Inside the heavy brown paper was a white package, tied with a broad white ribbon. "What a beautiful silk ribbon!" someone said, "May I have it?"

And the professor's wife said, "Be careful unwrapping that, dear, I want the rice paper."

As the professor handed the ribbon to the person who wanted it, he said, "That Japanese student said his father worked for the Emperor and could send me . . ." The sentence went unfinished for under the rice paper there was a beautiful lacquered box painted with many gay scenes.

"What a splendid example of Japanese art!" someone said. "Perhaps you will lend it to the museum?" And the professor said, "Sure. It wasn't a box the student was going to send. I think it was . . ."

"Open it! Open it!" they cried.

Opening the lacquered box, the professor drew out a large roll of beautifully patterned silk. "Oh, my," his wife said, "how lovely. There's enough here for draperies!"

"It wasn't silk," the professor said. "It was something of the Emperor's. It was . . ."

"Careful how you unroll that," someone said. "There's a box in it."

So there was! A carved ebony box. The professor stood up on a chair. Holding the box high in the air, he announced, "I am going to keep this box, for, though it isn't the gift, I know what's in it. It's tea! Our Japanese student said his father, who works for the Emperor of Japan, would sent me some of the Emperor's own tea." Opening the box, the professor showed his guests the inside — which seemed full of tea.

"It's just time for tea!" said the professor's wife. "I'll make you some Emperor's tea." She did this, and when each guest had a cup, they all tasted together. It was — awful! Each, to be polite, drank; and each, to be polite, asked for more.

The professor's wife dipped into the ebony box. But what was this? There was something buried in the box — something hard. Digging in, she found a small, exquisite ivory box, and in the ivory box — tea! This tea smelled wonderful, and this tea tasted — well, no one had ever tasted such good tea.

Far off in Japan, when the student's father told him of the kind professor, the Emperor agreed that a gift should be sent, and he ordered his chamberlain to deliver tea to the student's father.

The chamberlain thought, "What an exquisite gift. I must put it in an appropriate box." So he took a beautiful ivory box from his own home and in it put the tea.

The student's father took the ivory box and, saying to himself, "Such a gift must be protected with great care," he placed the ivory box in his favorite ebony box and filled up all the empty space with dried mulberry leaves.

The student's wife wrapped the ebony box in yards and yards of patterned silk, thinking, "Even this is not good enough for a gift of the Emperor's tea!"

And the student put the bundle of silk in his finest lacquered box. Handing it to his servant he said, "This is a package of the Emperor's tea. Sent it with great care to Professor Stone."

Knowing how precious the gift was, the servant wrapped the lacquered box in rice paper and tied it with his own white silk ribbon.

At the post office he said to the postman, "Think of it! This is a gift of the Emperor's tea for a professor in America!"

The postman picked the most beautiful stamps for the package — a valuable package, full of many charming things.

But the essence of the gift was the Emperor's tea.

And so it is with the gay, lovely wrappings that the minds of people have put around the precious gem of Christmas. Each of us must unwrap the gift for ourself, careful not to mistake the one for the other.

— Harold S. Stewart

A 'White' Christmas

Why is it that Christmas is ever associated with winter scenes of snow, sleighs, and being bundled against the cold? Santa Claus lives at the North Pole. We dream of a "White Christmas." There is even a song about "Frosty, the Snowman." It strikes me as strange, for Bethlehem is hardly a place of arctic clime. Rome, where Christianity came to power, hardly evokes wintry images of ice skaters. But somehow the nordics captured Christmas at least for Americans.

This cultural brainwashing is so strong that I find it hard to believe that people in Miami or San Diego can really and truly celebrate Christmas. How can there be Christmas with orange blossoms and blazing, hot sun? My tolerance for a proper Christmas barely includes Seattle within its ken. People scurry about this city blathering about their hopes for a white Christmas and I suppose that once a century it actually snows in Seattle on Christmas Day, but I doubt it! Given the choice, I suspect, we must opt for a rain forest over palm-lined beaches for a Christmas setting, but the margin is narrow. One cannot offer holiday greetings lying in a sunbeam and huddling under a raindrop does not offer a bounteous alternative. My pre-verbal conditioning tells me that a snow flake is the only proper backdrop for a Merry Christmas wish.

I once tried to calculate the percentage of the world that might have even a remote expectation of a white Christmas. I even tried to make the possibility fairer by confining my figuring to what is loosely called the Christian world. Even where Christmas is celebrated I suspect there is no more than an overall 10% chance that Christmas could be a real wintry day.

The only choice is . . . to readjust our thinking. White Christmas is a shuck and delusion. So Californians abandon your Bing Crosby and sing instead of "Sunshine." And for those in Seattle, let our holiday song be "Raindrops Keep Falling." So, I keep dreaming of a watery Christmas, just like the ones I used to know.

— Peter S. Raible

"I want the Sun God, Mithras, put back into Christmas," growled a hidebound traditionalist. "For more than a thousand years December 25 had been celebrated as His birthday," he continued, "until about 350 A.D., when the Church Fathers took over that date and its festivities to observe the birth of Christ."

"Diehard reactionary," I countered bluntly, "you may be right on your history, but Christmas wouldn't be Christmas without the Wise Men and the Shepherds and the Manger. Besides," I went on, "it wouldn't be Christmas either without a hundred other additions: among them, Christmas trees, Santa Claus, Dicken's animated 'A Christmas Carol,' grandmothers basting turkeys, and mistletoe antics."

"Additions or no additions," my opponent persisted, "Christmas wouldn't be Christmas without the sun's annual rebirth at this chill and gloomy time of the year and the promise of longer days and more and ever more of warmth and light."

"Admitted," I responded. "So why not join all the rest of us, Mr. Grouch," I urged, "and make merry — in the glimmering light of better days to come."

— Lester Mondale

And Snow

Hast thou entered into the treasures of the snow?
— Job 38:22

Snow makes no noise. Our boots tread roughly on the frozen ground, but snow comes silently and softens our harsh tread.

Like myriads of whirling dervishes, it fills the air, throwing white mantles across the shoulders of the hills, hiding all earth's ugly scars and stains. People do their worst, and in a single night snow brings serenity upon the ruined world, the devastated cities, and the ravaged fields.

Wind is an artificer piling it in drifts and strange, fantastic forms. The glow of lanterns never is so warm as when it falls on snow.

Take it up in handfuls. How it yields to shaping fingers! Take it up in crystals, one by one. What gems of loveliness! Snow understands geometry.

There is promise in the snow. Beneath its quiet depths, what growing things are waiting in the patient earth!

— Raymond Baughan
from *Undiscovered Country*

The other night with the first cold of winter I went outdoors and stood in the stillness, looking up at the sky. The near fullness of the moon accentuated the blue, and the few clouds of a white stream silently moving to the east heightened the stillness. It felt so good to get out of the house and away from the books. I was observing a ritual. Although only a few steps from my door, in a few seconds I was at one with all time, with all the generations that have gone before me and will come after. Standing, looking up, as they have stood and will stand. A simple ritual to be sure, but from it I felt a quietness of spirit as if by looking up I had been lifted up.

To each of us is given for the time being — a season. It has become for most ''a mixed bag,'' a time for sorting. May this holiday season give you all a time — to stand just a few steps from your door and, in looking up, be lifted up.

— John Papandrew

December is the woodstove or fireplace active again with plenty of wood to burn and time to enjoy it. December is the kettle on all day, always ready for friends. It's cold, lengthy winter nights, but the solstice promise of more light fulfilled. December is snow again, boots, skis and snowshoes checked and sleds taken off the garage hook. December is the menorah watched and lit, the tree purchased and gaily decorated. It's singing and listening, rehearsing and performing. December is lots of colorful holiday cards with notes that are read twice. December is excitement and expectation sharing and giving; gladly and sometimes sadly remembering other holiday times. December is love springing up over and over in many different meanings, reminding us that our joy can always be more, our hope can always be more, our life can always be more.

— Timothy Hume Behrent

In Praise of Winter

Let us not wish away the winter. It is a season in itself, not simply the way to spring.

When trees rest, growing no leaves, gathering no light, they let in sky and trace themselves delicately against dawns and sunsets.

The clarity and brilliance of the winter sky delight. The loom of fog softens edges, lulls the eyes and ears of the quiet, awakens by risk the unquiet. A low dark sky can snow, emblem of individuality, liberality, and aggregate power. Snow invites to contemplation and to sport.

Winter is a table set with ice and starlight.

Winter dark tends to warm light, fire and candle; winter cold to hugs and huddles; winter want to gifts and sharing; winter danger to visions, plans, and common endeavoring — and the zest of narrow escapes; winter tedium to merrymaking.

Let us therefore praise winter, rich in beauty, challenge, and pregnant negativities.

— Greta W. Crosby

Hush for a moment . . . and listen! Over there, beyond the clanging of cash registers and the howling of the north wind. Do you hear it? Someone is unpacking decorations. Listen again . . . someone is reading: about a man named John shouting in the wilderness "prepare," and an angel named Gabriel whispering in a young girl's ear "behold." Listen . . . someone is crying, alone. The sounds commingle, and the angel is heard again: "do not be afraid." Then another sound . . . the rustle of silk and the giggle of children putting on costumes. And still another . . . a choir is practicing: "Break forth, O beauteous heavenly light."

You hear it, don't you? Yes, that's it! . . . off in the distance. Footsteps, two people, one heavy and slow, carrying the weight of two, carrying the weight of the world. Listen, they come closer . . .

Teach us, O Lord, to seek silence in which to listen, to steal away a moment from the shopping crowd, to stop talking, complaining, worrying, laughing, just long enough to hear your Word become flesh.

— Thomas D. Wintle

Across the frozen fields of a distant past, brought very close by faith, there plods a young woman, heavy with child, leaning for support upon a kind and loving husband. The couple are going toward Bethlehem, a town that is everyone's home town no matter the place of their birth. There is a lighted, warm inn and there is a dark stable in a cave. There are many people in that town, but in the cave which awaits the couple there is no human witness prepared to meet the holy night to come.

Poor ragged Joseph, poor man of a poor land; gentle Mary, frightened and exalted with an unknown promise; these two alone, unwanted, walking to Bethlehem once again; shall they be better received than at the first? Is there place for them in the gaily lighted windows of our shops, and will our children be blessed by a return to holy love Will the old happiness of other Christmases be here in this to come? Will old bitternesses and estrangements give way to peace and good will?

O God, help our hearts to answer. Prepare us to welcome the ancient couple, ever new, but most of all to recognize them when they come.
— Wallace Robbins

My favorite Christmas story concerns the rather snobbish ox who shared the stable with the family from Nazareth. With considerable amazement he witnessed the visits of shepherds and the strangers from the East; heard all the talk about stars and angelic choruses; and finally watched Mary and Joseph flee with their son.

For days the other animals could talk of nothing but their human guests while the ox silently chewed his cud over in a dark corner. Finally he reproved his companions with this reflection: "I don't understand all this excitement. I don't know, I really don't know why you are so interested in that vagabond family. If they had been anybody worth knowing, they would never have stayed in this broken-down shack. As for the baby, — it was very like any other baby that I ever saw. They were very ordinary people, I would say. Very ordinary people indeed!"

Oxen are long-lived creatures, and this one proved to be the Methuselah of his kind. He was still around thirty-odd years later to witness the dismal end of the stable-born child. He then remarked to his companions, — "I knew it all the time. That chap was of no account. He was the very ordinary son of some ordinary people."

Then it was that the donkey who had carried Jesus many interesting miles spoke up to say, "Perhaps you are right. This man may have had a humble birth and a humiliating death; an ordinary birth and an ordinary death for such people, but he certainly lived an extraordinary life.

Regardless of how we react to this story, it contains a hint as to how our Christmas may become significant. Most of us can confess to being even more "ordinary" than the family from Nazareth, but our Christmas season may be a time of extraordinary living. Unusual neighborliness, unusual generosity, unusual expressions of love, and unusual attention to things of the spirit are all fitting tribute to bring to the stable-born one, who became the spiritual guide to many. May the Christmas season thereby, bring extra-ordinary grandeur to our otherwise ordinary lives.

— Albert Q. Perry

123

The Christmas Pilgrimage

If we truly desire to see Jesus in Christmas, we must go to the manger with the simplicity of shepherds. We will never see Him in the glitter of a palace except waiting to be crucified. It would seem, however, that we persist in believing that sooner or later we will see Him born amidst turmoil and luxury and go there. But we never see Him born because we are at the "inn" and He is in the stable. Unlike the Magi, many of us do not risk enough, dream enough, hope enough, or are hungry enough to leave our comfortable environment and travel beyond its borders to that land of purity of heart, poverty of spirit, and simplicity of life in order to see Jesus and keep Him in Christmas.

— Roland Bouvier

This Christmas give us a decent Christ. Give us the Christ of the Gospels, not gooped up by cheap dime store art or the mysteries of PhD. theses. Give us neither the one who-walks-with-me-talks-with-me like a mechanized Barbie doll; nor the one who emerges out of the ethereal blue that engulfs the ivory towers of the "serious" theologians; nor the one who is manifested in plastic; nor the one who wandered off into the hills like some crazy prophet speaking gibberish in Galilee or Manhattan.

Give us a decent Christ this Christmas! Give us the one who is neither a stranger to his world or ours. The genuine one. Give us the Christ who is the child of divinity in us and all; through whom all history speaks, through whom all the present is made joyful, and through whom all the future is a promise. Give us the Christ Christ wanted us to know, the one who said that the kingdom of God is within us, and that we are all children of the most high. Give us a decent Christ this Christmas! Not the cheap imitation we deify, not the foggy myth we try to demythologize; but the real and simple flesh-and-blood Christ who was born, who lived, who suffered and sacrificed for the sake of love and peace and goodwill.

— Bruce Clary

The real miracle of Christmas is that an uneducated peasant in an obscure corner of the Roman Empire should have had the insight, the ability, and the character to formulate and proclaim the religion Jesus did. Here was a man who saw the significance of his cultural and religious heritage in his world and who had the courage to attack the vested interests of his day in order to teach what he saw to be the truth.

Here is the real miracle — the personality of the man — not floating stars, angel choirs, or virgin births.

The birth of a child, any child, is a new incarnation and carries the promise of the great miracle of humans becoming divine, or reaching out to the stars.

— Donald B. King

A magical joy steals into life at Christmas time. There are celebrations and festivities. We greet strangers more easily and are more warmly open to all.

At Christmas we decorate our homes and hearts with light and color and joy. We are freer about being kind and generous as we'd like to be all the rest of the year — more friendly and loving.

Families unite and enjoy one another. We write to hear from old friends. Happy memories surface. We become pleasantly wistful as we remember persons and years now departed.

Why does Christmas have this wonderful power? What makes it special? Because its gladness and delight make us comfortable about being open and giving. At all levels of experience it's the time to give what's good: greetings, love, presents, celebrations.

Christmas is the season of joy because it reminds us of the good that is the Reality of Life itself; the prospect that a baby, a special infant, or any new born, has the potential to bring us the saving power of love.

This season with its gladsome delights is upon us. May your hearts be thrilled with its promise and joy. May love fill your life in this season of light and giving.

— Edgar Peara

A Short Christmas Sermon

It would be difficult to imagine that there is anyone who does not feel delight in some way in the score of big and little pleasures with which Christmas adorns our common life during these days.

One of the real miracles of Christmas for us in the 20th Century is that the man Jesus has survived what centuries have done to his memory, and that the human spirit of the man is alive among us, undimmed by ages of distortion and denial.

His life and teachings were obscured as people told themselves that certain doctrines about the manner of his birth and the meaning of his death were of the essence of religion. A faith he never knew and a church he never envisioned were erected around his name, and enforced by the prestige of his memory, with a narrow dogmatism that was no part of his outlook on life.

The miracle we should salute at Christmas-time and all through the year is that twenty centuries of theology and violence and misguided zeal have not wholly obscured the compelling figure of the man Jesus and the place he occupies in the story of humanity's developing sense of life.

Not as a god who once visited the earth do we revere the young Jew who made so profound and lasting an impression upon the flowing centuries since his time. Not as a disembodied divinity do we value his memory, but as a man of his own place and time who was gifted beyond the usual run of people sensing the deepest realities of our life; as one who saw past the circumstances and limiting conditions that cramp the understanding of most people and followed the light of his own integrity even to the death that his world made inevitable for the real immortality to live as a creative memory in the hearts and imaginations of millions of people to whose condition and needs he spoke the few scattered words we have as his lasting monument.

This is the Jesus who legend says was born on Christmas Day — a child of the earth, born of the love and need of a man and a woman for each other, reared as a child among children . . . a man who believed in the Hebrew faith of his ancestors and his time, and whose sense of life led him to stress unforgettably the humane insights of that faith; yes, a man whose intense, generous humanity has survived the human creeds, crusades, violence, and insipid sentimentalities that have been created in his name.

This is the real Christmas we celebrate — the birth and triumph of a prophet. This is the human miracle that undergirds the customs we freely delight in.

— Peter H. Samsom

126

Could Heart Forget

This is the season when the child in the heart of every one awakens, and the embers of the long-forgotten dreams are blown into flame. The tramp of the legions is stilled; the Caesars lies in dust, but the light from that humble stable shines warm and bright.

Something old and almost lost amid the clutter of the years, is calling from the skies and across the fields of snow. The night winds are stilled and in the darkened heavens the stars fortell of the lengthening days and the birth of spring after the winter's cold.

This is the sign that the light of hope, which shines in the dimness of our broken dreams, will never fade nor die. Friends, stretch forth your hands, palsied by fear and with the simple trust of the child, grasp your companion's hand and walk the way together.

Though the darkness press in upon us and the promise of Christmas comes like an echo of music upon the wind, our hearts cannot forget that loveliness — that light.

— Alfred S. Cole

To Live A Life — Not Merely A Season

The wonderful thing about Christmas is that it fulfills all our dreams. It suspends our indifferences and selfishness and fears and hates, and makes us for an instant spiritually kin. No one must be hungry or homeless on this day, no child forlorn, no heart forsaken, no race despised, no nation outlawed.

Christmas is the demonstration that no hope is vain, that the highest vision may be made real. It is as tho a spell were cast upon us, to save us . . . from our cruelties and lusts and make us ministers of love. The spell is fleeting — it passes quickly! But this means not at all that it is an illusion but that, real for this one day, it may be caught by the spiritual conjuration of our hearts and made real forever.

This is our task — to seize and hold and perpetuate the Christmastide! To live a life, and not merely a single day or season, which is delivered of prejudice and pride, hostility and hate, and committed to understanding, compassion, and goodwill! Then will there be no more Christian and pagan, Jew and Gentile, black and white, native and alien, or any division — but only the human family, one as God is one, and heirs of that promise.

— John Haynes Holmes

Antoine De Saint-Exupery wrote in *The Little Prince:* "It is the time you have wasted on your rose that makes your rose so important." It is especially important at Christmas time to learn to waste time. As I watched shoppers at the Mall on Saturday, I did not see a single happy face. Harried and hurried, everyone seemed preoccupied, irritated, or bored. Christmas can only be joyful if we slow down and waste some time. It is the time you have wasted crafting a scarf, stuffing a toy, writing a note to a close friend, reading, meditating, or thinking that makes Christmas come alive. There was a wisdom in the Christian season of Advent. Each Sunday preceding Christmas for four weeks explored the great religious themes of Christmas. Advent has been replaced by an orgy of shopping, commercials, canned music, and party-hopping. The glory of the incarnation is lost in the artificial glare of a secular orgy.

Walk, do not run, to the nearest Christmas! Wait and learn patience. Kick at pebbles, watch stars, notice all the quiet unimportant yet essential things that happen around you. These can be your ritual of waiting for Christmas. Christmas can be a renewal of a hope, a miracle of joy, but only if we waste some time making it a spiritually beautiful event.

— David H. Cole

Whatever faith we have, Christmas confirms it. Whatever hope is in us, Christmas exalts it. Whatever love abides with us, Christmas makes it more tender and more deep.

Christmas ages not with time for it utters the profound persuasions of the human heart; and these, being forever renewed by mysterious contact with eternal ideals, never grow old and cannot die. In Christmas and in the humble child of Christmas we find assurance that the invincible hunger of our souls is not a mere torment never to be assuaged, but an anticipation destined to victorious satisfaction. This hunger is that the broken shall be made whole; that light shall be shed upon every place of shadows; and that upon every uplifted face shall shine the radiance of divine peace.

— William Sullivan

For You

I wish for you at Christmas . . . (I don't really believe in wishing, but . . .)

That the holiday balloons you out of the basement of your burdens and that (since I'm told a holiday is a dancing day) you'll clomp away the cobwebs in your attic of anticipations and that (since someone told me holidays should be FUN) you'll not grow hectic-hearted over un-written cards, last-minute gifts, unbaked cookies and untrimmed trees, and that you'll ENJOY (not "suffer") the little children (hyper-active holidaysters, stockingeyed, presentprimed, always under-standing Christmas better than we do).

I wish for you at Christmas . . . (Remember, I disbelieve in wishing . . .) that you get everything you want, absolutely everything EXCEPT the things you don't really want, but only think you do (such as Love, Success, Respect, Fame, Perfection, Etc.) . . .

Instead, I wish for you acceptance of who you are, and a gift, rather baby-sized, of some inward star-beginning, something like a laughing lantern, a Christmas chuckle, steering and cheering you into the newest year (almost here) . . .

I wish for you a generous fragment, a piece of that promised Peace, and may your hands, heartfelt I hope, mold a portion of our common, daily Kingdom.

— James Curtis

Keeping The Season

The days have grown short, and the dusk comes early in the afternoon! From time immemorial, people have kindled these days with fire and fed them with beauty, hope, and joy. Let's resolve to keep them loving and leisurely this year, with plenty of friendly letters, with more giving of ourselves, and less giving of things. Let there be — peace, good cheer, and open hearts. Let there be — time for children, for strangers, for the elderly, and for the forgotten.

Above all, let there be a spirit of hope and expectancy, a readiness to believe the best of everything. Christmas is many things: it is carols and bells, it is a glowing hearth, kitchen smells, and frost upon the air. It is the mail carrier trudging through the snow, planes and trains bringing us home once more, and candles glowing softly in the night. Yes, Christmas is all these things, and more. But Christmas is nothing if not the rebirth of hope, and a new will to goodness in the human heart. You give but little to it, unless you give — yourself!

— John Cummins

I waited all month long for a simple thing:
>it lived in a flame that burned eight days,
>it lives in a sun that comes again,
>it was born with a child in a stable.
I waited all month long for a simple thing!

And in my waiting I received all this:
>presents that spoke to the giver's needs;
>appeals for money from unknown orphans;
>toys advertised 26 hours a day;
>simple trees sold for $5 a foot;
>plastic imitation mistletoe for drunken office parties;
>imprinted cards from persons I think I once knew;
>open-palmed welcomes from those who serve me all year;
>newspaper circulars to fill a truck;
>once-beautiful music masked into mockery;
>tinsel, glitter, skinny-Santas, midnight shopping;
>TV specials, boxed liquor, views of synthetic mangers;
>hustle, bustle, rustle, tussle.

And I still wait, for a simple thing —
>The rebirth of hope that springs from the human heart when
>reawakened by events of life that we sense as bigger than our
>own individual lives.

And, I rest assured that the wait, through all that comes, is well worth
it!

— Gayle Lehman-Becker

There are really two spirits of Christmas, each very different from the other, yet both deeply ingrained in our celebration of this season. And I suspect most of us have more of both within us than we ordinarily recognize.

The first, of course, is the one we usually talk about, the spirit of good will and peace. It is this spirit that bids us renew our hopes amid the gathering darkness, that kindles our generosity and our concern, that attunes our ears to the ever-renewed angelic chorus.

But the second, equally inseparable from the observances of this season, is the spirit of Scrooge's "Bah! Humbug!" We all know that hatred and distrust will not disappear from human relationships just because we say it ought to be so. We all know that peace on earth is a lot more complicated than it sounds in the Christmas hymns. We all know that if the world and the lamb, the leopard and the kid, the calf and the young lion all got along with one another as famously as Isaiah prophesied that they would, then some of these animals would die of starvation.

What it comes down to is that we give voice at Christmas to extravagant hopes that are beyond the range of any possible fulfillment. They are, as we say in our more sober moments, unrealistic.

But the real question is whether this is so bad. Perhaps the part of wisdom is to accept this reminder of the gap between the real and the ideal for what it is, a spur not only to our hopes but to our imagination and energies. It would be foolish to ignore the element of wishful thinking in our Christmas hopes. But how unspeakably more foolish it would be if we were to accept present reality as the last word and to stop dreaming altogether.

Our hopes are bound, of course, to be disappointed, at least in part. So long as time endures we shall remain creatures in the making, somewhere this side of perfection. Yet there is always hope for moving beyond the tragic failures of the past — if not all the way, at least a few steps farther. Our hopes are forever bound to fall to ashes; yet out of the ashes there can always emerge new hope — again and again and yet again.

— Max D. Gaebler

If I'd had my camera with me last Tuesday, in Boston, I'd have gone to some trouble to take a picture of the large handsome wreath on the entrance of UUA headquarters at 25 Beacon Street. Fashioned of lush greenery, tastefully trimmed with cones and a bow — the effect was somehow marred by a very heavy chain and padlock which secured it to the sturdy door. A necessary precaution for the symbol of goodwill, I was told, since valuable wreaths had been stolen on more than one occasion. It was a stark reminder and not to be ignored.

There is a certain fascination in noting contradictions in the customary blithe merriment of the Christmas season. Authors contrast bitter poverty with profligate spending. Psychologists have made it "OK" for those depressed by the holidays to air their feelings rather than repress them. Even the apalling statistics of divorce, teenage pregnancy, theft, violence, are brought out and commented upon in the glow from creche, candles, and electric stars.

Perhaps we are better able to consider harsh truths when we can fortify ourselves with bulwarks of carols, wassail, and "good will to all!" While we lean over to admire the sleeping child we dare to think of the fearful threat of global annihilation because somehow it has receded a bit beyond our circle of light and warmth. The temptation to become childlike now is dangerously seductive.

There *is* a legitimate comfort which Christmas offers to responsible adults. It is the reminder that while the earth endures we still have a chance to move toward a better time — a morning following the deep darkness of midnight. These very contradictions tell us that there is yet a little time.

The Simon and Garfunkel record on which the grim items on the "six o'clock news," don't quite drown out the voices of carollers, the greeting card design with news clippings of violence and hate which haven't completely covered the drawing of a simple manger, — even the wreath chained to the door, are all symbols of the indomitable hope which despite much to the contrary, still upholds and restores.

— Janet H. Bowering

Christmas is not the festival of blind faith but of defiant and resolute determination. "These things shall be," though the record of past effort is dark with shame, though the situation at the present moment is heartbreaking discouraging, though the citadels of evil give little sign of weakening. On Christmas Day, we say to ourselves and to one another, "Earth shall be fair!" not with the thoughtless exuberance of immature and childish fancy but with a very sober and very determined spirit of dedication, touched by a sort of shining glory that no darkness can destroy.

God grant that year by year, in part through our fidelity, the world may move steadily forward toward the ancient good of which the un-numbered generations have dreamed.

— Frederick May Eliot

Christmas is the time when the idealism of the human heart comes to the fore. It is the reassuring revelation of those qualities in human nature in which our chief hope lies. There is much, oh so much, that is wrong with the world, that mocks the sound of the Christmas bells; but as long as our hearts respond to the song of "Peace on earth, goodwill to all," as long as we have the grace to act on the injunction that it "is more blessed to give than to receive," as long as we sincerely feel that the great ends of life are served in causes that transcend their petty personal interests, there is hope that we shall yet redeem ourselves from our woe.

— E. Burdette Backus

December is the month of lights —
   lights crowning the heavens with glory through
   the lengthened night —
And in December, adding to the hosts of the heavens,
   are the lights of humankind, a multitude of lights
   made by us to brighten the ways we go.
And in the human spirit, December is a time of lights,
   rising over the depths of darkness are the lights
   of human ideals.
Hope shines brightest in December.
Courage sparkles in the face of calamity.
Fortitude is furbished by failure.
Over the wreck of reversal rises the strengthening
   light of resolution.
Because of darkness, the heavens shower their
   splendor.
Because of the gloom, lights of the face brighten
   the way we go.
Because of adversity, the human spirit finds lights
   of an inward strength.

                              — Carl J. Nelson

A Time of Darkness, A Time of Light

It is not just by chance that Christmas comes at the darkest time of the solar year. The ancients had their wisdom and knew the human heart as well or better than we, knew the rolling of time and the progression of the stars and the transit of the year closely and intimately.

As the year comes to darkness, so too there come times when darkness is in our lives — loss of one we love, illness and threat to our own sense of being and integrity, personal stress when we are overwhelmed and frightened by strange voices within ourselves, anxiety about the uncontrolled and unmanageable changes in the world around us, the break-up of our family by alienation or children growing up or changes in ourselves or those we loved pulling apart the fabric of hope, job security, crisis of one kind or another — the darkness falls.

> The darkness of the year comes upon us.
> And then Christmas.
> The festival of light.
> The celebration of a single birth,
> The celebration of a single star,
> The celebration of a single hope.
> And the light shineth in darkness . . .

There is a light for each of us that shines in the darkness. A single star, a hope. Sometimes we do not look. Often we need to be open to the guidance of others to see the light. Sometimes we have to let go of the darkness to see the light.

This Christmas may we turn our eyes to the star, the light, the hope, the love, that shines in the darkness.

> The light shines on in darkness,
> a darkness that did not overcome it.

May we all have a holy, happy, light-filled Christmas.

— Eugene R. Widrick

The Universal Humbug

Scrooge, of course, was right. Christmas is humbug. Light in the darkness is only light, and being in darkness is hardly a guarantee of light appearing — would it were so! So we are now nearing the longest night of the year — that is a geographical, latitudinal accident, and what does one do in Australia?

Of course Christmas is a humbug, not to mention the Saturnalia, or any of the northern hemisphere's midwinter celebrations, all with their unwitting, cunning admixtures of terror and hope, fear and faith. Fire in frosty cold is a healthy boost, and so also is the birth of a Superstar — we all can use them! It is, nevertheless, a cheering and pleasing humbug. I gladly participate in such seasonal self-deceptions for I don't think I need to deny my own desires to single out a season, a time, a ceremony, when I publically, communally, attest to my humanity.

Such is Christmas, such has been the late December event, for millions through the ages. For a handful of days, we willfully ignore the realities of worldwide distress, we indulge, we turn in upon ourselves, our families if available, we indulge appetites and greeds, we momentarily suspend our better judgments and routines, we behave irrationally.

I repeat: it certainly is all humbug. It is 'hum' — connoting a sort of turning-inward, meditation, like the Hindu 'Om' — and 'bug' — the bug is a primitive group of insects, successful, often fantastically-shaped, very individual —

So the 'Christmas Hum-bug' is a time when the individual hums private concerns, affirms whatever is to be affirmed, for himself or herself, gropes in darkness, perhaps lights a candle, or goes to church, temple, or somewhere, to proclaim a peculiar propensity for happiness over misery.

We have no final explanation for this quite illogical and most unrealistic ritual — but too many of us do it, for us to dismiss it.

So, we light a candle.

— James Curtis

The season of lights is upon us. Lights on Hanukkah candlelabra, on fir trees, on homes and office buildings. Lighted smiles on the faces of happy shoppers, shopkeepers, families anticipating reunions, children anticipating school vacations, and Christians rejoicing in the birth of Jesus. Cars are lighted at rush hour as the sun sinks earlier each day and fires are lighted in cool living rooms more to conserve than to observe these days. Lots of lights, everywhere.

A secondary characteristic of lights is that they cast shadows, often deep ones. Individuals, even whole families, can be lost in the darkness and perhaps ignored or forgotten by those possessing some seasonal warm glow. We must remember that in this time of the year to shine our lights in the corners and to reach out to friends or family or strangers who may feel abandoned in the dim cold of winter. Certainly that is an essential part of the meaning of Christmas.

— David More Maynard

'Tis the season already . . .
December always seems to sneak up on me. I no sooner begin to grasp the fact that November is here and Thanksgiving is coming up . . . is tomorrow! . . . was yesterday . . ., than I am seeing Christmas trees in store windows and that perennial Norelco television ad with Santa sledding down a hill on the three floating heads of the shaver. . . . How festive.

Another year is about to ring out. They seem to go by more rapidly the older one gets; time as a whole seems a bit speedier. There was so much I meant to do . . . meant to say . . . meant not to say or do. . . .

And then I get swept up in the spirit of the season. A round of Christmas carol records on the ole stereo . . . bringing out all the decorations for the house . . . feeling that there *is* something in the air this time of year that is enlivening, heartening, full of hope. Finally, the selection and setting up of the tree, the evergreen, the symbol of Life in the dead of winter.

. . . Then the celebration itself; the celebration of birth in the midst of cold and darkness and death. The celebration of the child within us all, the spirit which can come to us in the midst of pain or sadness or despair and keep the flame of our candle lit. The Light within that offers Hope shines on brightly. And around our winter fires we sit, looking toward that Hope and nurturing our flame — the flame which will later ignite into springtime. . . .

— Daniel Budd

"The light shines in the darkness, and the darkness has not overcome it."

There is something very powerful about the image of light. It has symbolized knowledge, hope, love. From ancient times it has been a sign of the divine, the Eternal Light, the Inner Light, the Light of the World.

Light is the theme of festivals celebrated at this time of year when days are shortest and nights are longest. By affirming that we live by the light of hope we banish the power of the darkness that surrounds us.

The eight candles of Hanukkah proclaim our faith that freedom will not die out as long as there are steadfast and courageous people willing to uphold it.

The lights of Christmas bear witness to the Light of the World in the form of a child. What better symbol is there for the light of hope than the child — new and fresh, open to the future, able to make choices that change the course of history.

We light our lights this season to remind us that the darkness, however powerful it may seem at times, does not overcome us, that there always remains within humankind a spark of hope that can be fanned into a light illuminating the path to a new order of freedom, peace, and love.

May the light proclaimed in this season be in your lives now and always.

— Frederick E. Gillis

The Festival of the Heart

Christmastime is the heart time of the year. It is the sublime hour when argument and speculation are intruders. Controversy seems out of place and theological vagaries have no response. We care not at Yuletide for the barren literalness of dogmatic religionists. They sound a discordant note in the gladsome music of the Christmas symphony.

The world does not ask on Christmas morn about miracles and astronomy. It is too occupied by the love light from the glowing eyes of a little child. It is seeing the miracle of love, and is singing its song of joy after a pilgrimage where it followed a star.

Wherever love has its habitation, there Christmas dwells. Every destructive, devitalizing, discordant agency of life may be ultimately and permanently dissipated by the spirit of love and unselfishness. Christmas proves that.

It is harder to hate at Christmas. Hearts are softened as the Day comes. Forgotten friends are remembered suddenly, and tears spring without shame when old memories are awakened. In the long, long year it is the one time when even the wisest and most inflexible admit the beauty of true sentiment, without fear of becoming merely sentimental.

A little more of that sentiment unobtrusively permitted to hover over life during the year would make Christmas last longer. It is certain that this old earth needs nothing quite so much as the technique of making Christmas last. Envisage such a world!

Love, unselfishness, devotion, gladness, music, starlit nights, angel voices, and shepherd hearts — all this is Christmas. The world gives all this an unhampered opportunity as the old year wanes. Its efficacy no one doubts. The power and glory of it spring from the beauty and incomparable splendor of one unselfish Life.

So at Christmastime, life and its little ironies assume new and proper proportions. We see the way more clearly, while the heroic quality of the person we honor gives us more courage to take that way. We hear the divine melody of an ancient song. Why and how the singers came disturbs us not. The song is the thing that matters.

The wide world is happier and would become progressively better if it forgot its sophistication and in childlike wonder, and with open mind and loving heart, let the Christmas song of "peace on earth, good will to all" become the motivation of all its days.

— Preston Bradley

Christmas, so it is said, is the green-shuttered colonial house in a field of snow, wood smoke spiraling from its massive chimneys, horse-pulled sleigh welcomed at the porch, inside the blazing Yule log. But what is Christmas if it is not also the kitchenette — small wreath on its corridor door, chicken-sized turkey in its electric oven — twenty stories up among the towers of a glass-and-stone megalopolis?

So what is Christmas, in its larger dimensions, but the season of doing that extra something that tells or tries to tell, others, wherever they may live, how much of value they have contributed to the days of one's years — how important they really are!

Christmas, accordingly, is the card that says, in the language of the heart: "You are no mere name in our address book but a living presence. This, more often than you can ever know, we welcome among the mind's most honored and appreciated guests."

— Lester Mondale

Reflections on the Meaning of Christmas

Christmas and Thanksgiving are two holiday celebrations that really do go together in many respects in spite of the indiscriminate mixing of the two in commercial enterprises. Both are a time of giving, of gift-giving and thanksgiving. To these two forms of giving I would add a third, namely, *forgiving*. The three together add up to the highest form of spiritual expression of which humans are capable, the reality of *love*. If Christmas has any deeper spiritual meaning left in our largely materialistic minded culture to me it is this — the reality of love given and received in human life. It is love's nature to want to give of itself to another for the sheer joy of giving itself. Love finds its complete fulfillment in the act of giving for the sake of the happiness and well-being of another. In so doing the self finds the deepest joy and fulfillment which is attainable in human life.

Love further gives of itself as an expression of gratitude and thanksgiving for the unsolicited gift of life-itself with its myriad possibilities and opportunities for goodness and joy into living actualities for all human lives within its sphere. Love is an expression of gratitude for the privilege and opportunity to make this dream become more and more a living reality for all.

It is also love's nature to give of itself on a third and deeper level of giving, the reality of forgiving. To forgive is to "let go," to let go of all the past hidden resentments, frustrations, animosities, and hatreds which poison the soul and rob us of our rightful selves. In forgiving, in "letting go" of all that would destroy us inwardly, love transforms and makes new all persons and events which are embraced within its spiritual radiance. Love truly "maketh all things new." Through its transforming power we ourselves are enabled, if only but for a moment, to become what we were meant to be, a human being who is whole and loving and free.

— Richard M. Fewkes

141

The Strange Arithmetic of Christmas
  by "Jeremiah Jenkins"

I deliberately requested your minister to allow me to write to you about Christmas. I was a teacher of arithmetic for fifteen years in a preparatory school, so I want to write about the inverted arithmetic of Christmas.

Christmas differs from figures and sums and dollars and crowds-at-a-football game. You can add all these together and get more. But with Christmas, you can add all the Santa Clauses on earth and there is still only one Santa Claus. Or all the trees and there is still only one Tree. Or perhaps all the births of children but there is still only one Bethlehem story. Or all the families, and there is still one family — yours!

It is when you start dividing Christmas that it begins to grow. It multiplies with division. It defies the rules. If you have six TV sets and give two or three away, you have less. But when it comes to the richness of love, the currency of gratitude or the document of faith, the more you give the more you possess. To teach is to learn. To encourage someone and give them your faith is to strengthen your own faith. To love is to know love.

Christmas is like a lot of things; it can be misused. I think it was never meant for raucous public displays. Its carols were not intended to be blared into the streets. Its colors probably were not meant to be emblazoned like advertising — or even associated with advertising. Christmas is the artistry of the world; it is the subtle touch, the gentle word, the endearing act, the loving gift. Share these qualities, divide them, and you will find miraculously that they have grown with division. This is the strange arithmetic of Christmas.

— Roscoe E. Trueblood

When Christmas Won't Come

All the outward show of the season is a vain attempt to create Christmas, to control it, to make it come. It will come, I have learned. But it comes in spite of, not because of, our efforts. It comes not in the outward show but rather in the inner darkness. The wise men could only see the star because of the darkness. It was a lonely cave beside the inn that was filled by the birth of love. The shepherds who waited on a lonely, dark hillside and trembled in fear where the first to hear the news.

Christmas is the promise that our emptiness will be filled, our hunger assuaged and a deep darkness be flooded with light. It is the promise that ''the God who has stretched us with loneliness will, someday when we have at last deserved it, fill us with his love.'' It is a promise that comes to people walking in darkness — the sad, the weary, the hopeless. It is there for those who feel in their soul's journey they are — like Mary and Joseph — wandering in a strange country, far from home. It is there for the pain-filled and the troubled and the lost.

Christmas will come, but we cannot make it come. And it may come most powerfully when we are most sure it will not come. The vain trappings of the season do disguise a great emptiness, but that emptiness waiting to be filled is the heart of Christmas and in that emptiness, that darkness, Christmas is waiting to be born.

— Earl K. Holt III

143

There is much in the Christmas season that speaks to deep human needs. The northern European countries needed the light-giving, warmth-giving aspects of the Yuletide. So the symbols of light have become an integral part of the season. Though much has been written deploring the commercialization of Christmas, the giving of gifts is still an offering of love. Evergreens, symbolizing the ongoingness of life, pervade the celebration.

Light, love, life — these are some of the universal needs symbolized in the Christmas season. But no less significant or universal are their opposites — darkness, death, hate. It is usually a mixture, if not a conflict, of these contrasting symbols that has come to characterize the season. It has given rise to the "Christmas Syndrome" of Christmas Depression — love/hate, elation/depression, togetherness/loneliness.

A way of not becoming entrapped in the "Christmas Syndrome" is to refuse to go along with whatever it is that works to spoil the season for you. What really counts at Christmastime are aspirations of hope and peace, feelings of goodwill and joy, and personal relaitonships — the sharing of warmth and love. These aspirations and feelings and relationships are not something that will happen just because it's Christmas.

This is especially so for those of us who are prone to loneliness. Faced with loneliness, we can meet it creatively — recognizing our deep need for relatedness — and strive to build relationships that are rich with understanding, empathy, and affection.

— Eugene Pickett

They begin as cogs, those protagonists in "A Christmas Carol." Bob Cratchit is not really a person, but a tool, a thing, a machine, hired to turn out as much work as possible. Scrooge is a stick-figure, fashioned of cupidity, loneliness, and self-hate. Both live in a social situation of organized moral anarchy. Dickens' answer, appropriate to the crisis, is that love can overcome such radical alienation, and weave bonds even between people who lack shared customs or beliefs.

We know that Dickens brought off the miracle of showing Scrooge the power of love. We face a task more difficult than Scrooge's or that of Dicken's himself, not only because ours is real life rather than story, but because the forces of estrangement and spiritual numbness are stronger now than in the London of Tiny Tim. In a way this can be turned to our advantage, for we have no choice really but to recognize and accept the implications of our extreme predicament.

The love which saved Scrooge is now a necessity, not an option, and it must be love in the tough and universal sense of community, quest, daring, and growth. A fragmented world needs people capable of such love to put it together. This putting together is not an abstraction, it is personal and immediate.

It has been said that the best we can do in this world is to increase the odds of something human happening. We of this church do that, for the most part, remarkably well. Thanks for increasing the odds!

There is power to create in our life circles, close and remote, precious bonds of tough and universal love.

May the blessing of such a Christmas be yours.

— Jack Mendelsohn

145

An old Buddhist said: "Tell me, what is this day you cherish so, that you call Christmas?"

And the Stranger from the West said: "Christmas is not a day, really. It is light, I think. It comes when days are shortest and darkest and hearts despair, and it reminds us that winter death is a temporary thing and that light and life are eternal.

"And it is hope. For it demonstrates how kind and generous and self-forgetting human beings can be. And we know that what people can be sometimes, they can, if they will, be most times.

"And, assuredly, it is love. Its symbol is a newborn babe, warm and safe in his mother's arms. To be sure, he was born a long, long time ago. Yet through the ages his influence as he became a man and the truths he taught and the love he incarnated have proved stronger and dearer in matters that matter most than all the kings and armies and governments of history. Oh, whatever else it may be, Christmas indeed is love."

"I think I understand," the old Buddhist said. "Christmas is like a lotus blossom. When it blooms, it holds, as in a chalice, the beauty of the world.

"Yes, you do understand," said the Stranger from the West. "When it comes, Christmas brings the light that redeems us from darkness, the hope that casts out fear and the love that overcomes the world. 'It is Christmas!' We rejoice. And, suddenly, the lotus blooms . . ."

— Waldemar Argow

The observance of Christmas represents a tradition and a continuity of values which give us a sense of poise and stability and tranquility. More than anything else, Christmas symbolizes home and family, the security which springs from one's awareness of having a place in the pattern of love and support and loyalty which is the family. Even when one is alone, the holiday brings this message poignantly home. The customs and traditions which cluster about Christmas all serve to gather up our half-conscious but deeply felt relatedness to those nearest to us.

This involves an element of pathos, too. For as we sense the very joy of the moment, we are reminded that it is but for a moment — that it can never be recaptured. We are inevitably reminded of our own childhood which has vanished, of those who once shared with us in the observance. The realization that what has been can never be again is a painful experience. And yet it is inevitable. Beauty and sorrow, pain and rejoicing so often go together.

Christmas brings us assurance of the power of love — a power calm and serene, yet so mighty in its calmness that it can heal all divisions among people, overcome all hatred, all suspicion, all distrust. May that power enter deeply into our own hearts and pervade our lives as the sunlight fills the day.

— Max D. Gaebler

Joy To The World

For the vision is yet for an appointed time, but at the end it shall speak, and not lie; though it tarry, wait for it; because it will surely come, it will not tarry.

— *Habukkuk 2:3*

Christmas with its shining sureness! The truth, the songs, the hope, the love, the insights, the purpose and the will — all here within! Mistake it not; the promise is no translation of the vision into fact. There are still dark and evil things to overcome. Yet it is here, hidden but indestructible, an inner light that glows with warmth and radiance as the journey lengthens. It is in the fiber of our beings. Its outreach is delayed yet for a time, but it will not tarry always. For it is deeper than hate, sturdier than evil, stronger than death. It will reassert itself in all simplicity and truth.

And the faith that wakes in all of us is this: that the earth is shaking to reveal the things that never can be shaken, that at the heart of life is neither chance not emptiness, but firm creative love. It sets the tasks we must fulfill. And in our toils, our conflicts, and our suffering, we learn of its unyielding power.

— Raymond Baughan
from *Undiscovered Country*

Let Christmas then bless us with its universal human gifts of love and rejoicing. Let it warm us in its gentle glow of affection toward one another, and humanity. Our stiff and frozen hearts can thaw in the gracious warmth of this holiday season when crowds of people in stores and streets are more patient and more cheerful toward one another because it is Christmas. We need Christmas desperately in our society today; we need its infant symbol to remind us of others, whom we scorn and whose dignity we debase; we needs its rich color and fantasy and magic to enrich our prosaic and bedeviled lives; we need its raucous materialism and commercialism to allow us to spend recklessly to express kindness to others, and to release impulse in a wholesome way. In these and a thousand ways we need Christmas. Away, then, with pious scolding! Away with care and the heavy heart, as we bask in deserved goodwill and generosity and honest joy! "God rest ye merry!"

— Russell R. Bletzer

There is a great paradox in Christmas. At a time of the year when all seems to be declining and decaying, when the sun is farthest from the earth and in the coldest part of the year, a great note of hope is announced. The paradox is just this — that the power of renewal becomes active where one would least expect it. This very season of ice and cold and emptiness contains within it the surprising seed of renewal. Following the lush fullness of the spring, we have the harvest. Then it seems that we are made to pay for the harvest by enduring the coldness of winter that follows it.

Yet amidst this, we celebrate new life. We celebrate the birth of a child. Is it not a paradox that this renewal, this birth, did not issue from rulers and governments and great powers but in the simplest of surroundings? The new beginnings were found in a pastoral country-side in the dark of night, in a stable, in a manger. In such unlikely places did new life begin.

Christmas is a time of many, many symbols, a poetic time. It is a time that is literally confused with symbols. There is a combination of religious and secular symbolism; there is a contrast of spiritual and material symbols. Yet all of it is Christmas. The modern Christmas is like a huge cultural basket holding the contributions of a long and full heritage of Christmas and midwinter celebrations. Therefore it is a mixed collection of symbols and meanings. The meaning of Christmas can be what you wish it, what you make of it. Thus, a sense of priority becomes the saving grace of the season.

— Alan G. Deale

Take Christmas.
Take the ancient, the medieval, and the modern.
Take what is sacred, secular, solemn, and silly.
Take Teutonic evergreen and Persian sun and Druid mistletoe.
Take Jewish flame and Greek feast and Roman present.
Take a Bethlehem babe in a stable surrounded by shepherds and kings
      with a brilliant star overhead.
Take a mid-eastern saint transformed through the centuries to a
      red-suited elf with a sackful of toys and a reindeer-drawn sleigh.
Take music from as many countries as the imagination can grasp.
Take Amahl and Scrooge and Rudolph.
Take lighted tree and punch bowl and greeting card.
Take mittened carolers and charitable gifts and candlelight services.
Take it all or take any part.
Take its light, its courage, its hope, its joy, its peace, its goodwill.
Take Christmas –– but to take it you must give it also.

                                   — Christopher Raible

A Christmas Creed:
    We believe that mistletoe is more significant than missiles.
    We believe that Bethlehem's star outshines our satellites;
    We believe that the gifts of the wise men have not suffered from inflation;
    We believe that the fear of the shepherds is more healthy than the fear of rockets;
    We believe that Joseph's dreams shall outwit Herod's hate;
    We believe that our journey to the manger is more important than a trip to the moon.

                                 — Frederick W. Ringe

Sing!

This is a good season for singing. I may not sing very well but everybody knows the Christmas carols and I can just sing and get away with it. Nobody notices unless I refuse altogether. So singing comes easy, now.

This is also a good reason for telling stories. The stories I like are both life-like and a little fantastic — believable, unbelievable, and somehow both at once. They let me imagine something other than hard facts that just say what is.

The idea of angels singing and animals talking for a holy babe born in a barn and laid in a manger allows me to love a little while in a world where everything is different. And get away with it.

A most amazing recognition this is: that I can get away with it. Life allows me; it lets me go again and again: for we are set at liberty.

This is a good season for believing that ''something happened'' and everything is different now. I don't have to be bigger, better, or beautifuler than anybody. I can love somebody and get away with it.

And what is ''it''? It is only that which I want in my heart of hearts — like loving, like being changed, like singing and having a story to tell. And once I have let myself go, there is something I can do no longer: pretend I am not allowed to be myself, in the community of giving and receiving. Such a life of freedom and love is itself the first and greatest gift.

— George K. Beach

151

Christmas In Spite Of Me

I hadn't felt as Christmasy as usual this year. I don't know why.
Maybe it was because the air stayed autumn-warm so late this year,
and the ground was bare, and even green long after it's usually white.
Maybe it was the lack of lights. Whatever the reason, I didn't get that
feeling that is half-child, half-adult. Maybe it was as much inner as
outer weather that kept Christmas arms-length from me; an inner
climate made up of something older, or tired, or busy, or bored. But
whatever the reason, the annual star, like a much-publicized comet,
didn't blaze so brightly as advertised over the ordinary fields where I
shepherd my concerns. But I need Christmas. I need it to remind me
that every year a child is born, every year an heir is given, every year
angels in disguises of all kinds sing glory and make promises in the
cold. I need it. We all do. The season is dark and cold.

But Christmas came. It fell out of the sky, white and cold, but not so
cold as the bare, empty days before. Christmas came, in the mailbox
with old friends' names folded up inside. It came hung in round, green
greetings let out of front doors to remind the street what time of year it
is. It came through my ears, in my eyes, in old echoes and fragile
memories. It came, as it always comes, like a light in my darkness.

— Max Coots

The Wonder of Christmas

The wonder of Christmas is that it means different things to us all at
different times, and so grows from the purely secular and selfish
symbol of presents to the spiritual and religious symbol of the life of
God in the soul of humans.

And that suggests that in all things, the great and influential experiences
of life are the things we grow up to appreciate. And that we should
ever be growing in appreciation, especially of the subtler, the finer,
the unassuming but enduring values around us.

And for this we have two sure anchors, not only at Christmas but all
through the year — the home and the church. For no matter how
things change from childhood to maturity, these two images remain
the same.

There is no need to tell you how strong is the thought of home today.
Nor how we suddenly realize at Christmas that what the heart is
hungriest for is not to be found in far distant places, or in big
excitements, but in small, intimate, homely things which matter so
much. Perhaps at other times we forget this, but at Christmas we
remember. For this is the day when people take time out to be happy,
and to be happy together.

152

As for the church at Christmas — well, it is practically impossible to think of the one without thinking of the other. Not the creeds of the churches, nor their disputations; not at Christmas. Rather the church as the meeting place of friendly people who speak the encouraging word, extend the helping hand, and think about each other between Sundays.

There it is, a quiet little flame burning on across the miles and across the years; the Church that has kept Christmas alive throughout the long centuries. How the very remembrance breaks through the shell of our worldliness and brings heaven close to earth again!

So whatever faith we have, Christmas confirms it and makes it stronger. Whatever love we bear toward others, Christmas makes it more tender and true.

And it is this divine faith and human love which shine through the never-fading Christmas story of the nativity of one whose whole life is summed up in five words from Acts — "He went about doing good."

So may we go about doing likewise, to the end that the story of our Christmases, a story of our growth in wisdom and stature become the story of many another who will follow us. Yes, and the story of humanity's slow, groping, spiritual growth to the fullness of the measure of the stature of Jesus.

— William Wallace Rose

Green, green, and green again, and greener still. This is our dream in winter. Not many today have wealth or space enough to deck out large banquet halls with gathered greens. But we still respond in some small measure of green to the season. Who is so poor in coin or spirit not to respond to all? Who does not dream?

The evergreens have been symbolic for a long, long time of life and hope in the midst of winter. Long before the birth of Christ, people in northern Europe celebrated the winter solstice with bonfires on hilltops and evergreen boughs and even whole trees in their tribal halls. If trees could maintain their green life through the long, cold nights of winter, surely the sun could turn in its course and climb the sky again and bring summer once more. The bonfires, the supplications had always worked in the past, and surely they would work now. They did. They still work.

This month the sun will turn back from the abyss and climb the sky toward summer. Green, green, and green again, and greener still.

— Thomas E. Ahlburn

Lo, How A Rose . . .

Christmas is not all happiness and joy. The Christmas rose has thorns as well as a beautiful flower. The imagery of Christmas includes both light and dark. So how do we cope with Christmas?

First, we understand and acknowledge that Christmas is both thorn and rose and recognize that Christmas sadness is not only for those few people who may find themselves left out for one reason or another. If you study the literature of Christmas you find that almost all of it is based upon an initial theme of sadness or loneliness. From the friendlessness of Rudolph, the Red-Nosed Reindeer to the selfishness of Ebenezer Scrooge to the cruelty of Herod the stories set a background of sorrow from which a theme of joy emerges. So also it may be with you.

Secondly, we must realize that Christmas, although a special day, cannot be separated from all the other days of the year. A rose bush grows within a larger environment, fertile soil, sun, and rain. Set apart from this larger environment the rose soon dies. So also Christmas grows out of a larger environment of love and generosity throughout the year. Again, remember when Scrooge made his great change in life, it was not just for Christmas Day, but for future days as well. To cope with Christmas we cannot believe that we can make the day itself special without dealing with all of the other days as well.

And, thirdly, Christmas cannot be overly planned. Joy and happiness rarely can be placed on a schedule any more than a rose can be forced to bloom at a certain moment of the day. In our approach to Christmas we must leave room for spontaneity and mistakes. If you think back upon it oftimes the warmest memories we have of the holidays are the times when a present failed to arrive on time or the Christmas tree fell down or the turkey was burned to a crisp. Of course a great deal of planning and preparation goes into getting ready for the holiday, but we will cope a lot better if we make allowances for human frailty and the unexpected.

On my desk in my study is a rose without thorns. It is made of plastic. It looks like a rose from a distance. But it doesn't smell like a rose and it is not delicate like a rose and it cannot reproduce itself like a rose nor does it give nectar to the bees like a rose. It is a rose without thorns and it is dead. "Lo, how a rose e're blooming . . ." What a wonderful image for Christmas; the Christmas festival, the festival of light and dark, of sadness and joy, the mystical union of opposites, the story of a king born in a humble stable, of Almighty God come to earth in the form of a helpless infant, the beautiful flower nestled among the forbidding thorns.

— Edward Atkinson

Christmas lives in those adults who in the midst of the annual stampede for goods remember that caring is the greatest gift, who through the tinsel and the trappings can still be patient enough to share the simple delights of the season, and who can teach the children to value one over the other.

Christmas lives in those who carry the burden of some great disappointment or some secret sorrow — and yet struggle to radiate a little cheer to those whose afflictions may be even greater.

Christmas lives in those who are bound by preoccupation and fear of involvement, who yet are working to learn how to share themselves.

Christmas lives in the persons of great learning who understand that knowledge is not all, and that, without involvement and action, there is little hope that learning will bring good to the family of humanity.

Christmas lives in those who, possessing all, sense that power and wealth mean little unless they are used to serve . . . for unto those to whom much is given, from them much will be expected.

Christmas lives in those, who living in a powerful and prosperous nation, remember that Jesus did not come to bless the complacency of the powerful or the selfishness of the prosperous — but to set people free.

Christmas lives in those in the slums and ghettos of the world, afflicted by poverty, who, in spite of their misery, dare to expect that the future for their children may somehow be better.

Christmas lives in those who in distant lands suffer daily under the affliction of wars which they do not understand, and devastation which threatens all humanity, and yet dare to believe that this senselessness will pass, and to hope that their children will *live,* simply stay alive, to grow up into a world of peace.

Christmas lives in those who, while others pray for peace and work for war, have the courage and patience to thirst after righteousness and to commit themselves to the great task of creating a world of peace and justice for the whole family of humanity. On a tablet in a small English church are inscribed words of praise for a man, "Whose singular praise it is to have done the best things in the worst of times and hoped them in the most calamitous." So it is that out of darkness we burst into light. So it is that despair is overcome by the radiance of joy. May Christmas come alive within you, within me, within us all each and every one.

— Richard A. Kellaway

The Sounds of Christmas

The sounds of Christmas — we all have heard them. They are the incessant playing of Christmas music in every department store. They are the familiar themes over the radio, and on TV, of Rudolph the Red-nosed Reindeer, Jingle Bells, White Christmas, Mamma Kissing Santa Claus Last Night, Frostie the Snowman and a continuing repetoire. They are the sounds of media commercials giving the latest countdown of shopping days until Christmas, of verbal advertisements suggesting gifts from the sublime to the ridiculous. They are the ringing of Salvation Army kettle bells, the voices of carol singers, Christmas sermons, and more.

There are sounds from the first Christmas. For many of us they are strange, far away, or forgotten. However, if we will listen, we can hear them in our time and place.

We can hear the deep stillness of the night speaking out of its silence, we can hear an angelic choir singing a song of Peace on Earth amongst those of good will. We can hear the muffled sounds of shepherds watching over their flocks, the sounds of sheep bleating, of cattle lowing, of a donkey braying, a baby crying, a mother crooning and a father whispering words of comfort and assurance. We can hear herders, simple folk and Wise Men sharing the wonder, strangeness, and beauty of the event.

We can hear all of these sounds and more if our twentieth century decibels do not drown them out at Christmas.

— Wilbur P. Parker

The carols we sing
Are echoes of the years of our lives,
Christmas visitors bringing with them
Memories of other scenes,
Of other times
Of other people
Of us, ourselves, in other guises.
We have sung these same songs
In the childhood which abides in us still,
We have sung them in young love
In the naive dream
Of an eternity of Christmases with the lover.
We have sung these songs to drown out hurt
And to amplify joy.
If, in this season,
We find that we are of many shifting moods
It can only be because we have lived
A life of many moods
Each recreated in the play of Christmas.
It is not a betrayal of the Christmas spirit,
To stare quietly into the snowflakes.
We cannot always sing,
And the spirit needs freedom to wander,
To re-visit old regrets
And to remember joy,
Returning, then, to remind us
From whence we came
All covered with snow and life,
Singing old songs in new places.
We sing together in the harmony
Of our humanness,
Remembering, at Christmas
Every tear, every hand,
Every singing of the song.

— Edward A. Frost

157

The Discovery of Christmas

Long ago, in the land of Israel, the shepherds pastured their flocks on many a hilltop, and looked down into the fertile fields in the valleys, and vineyards on the hillsides, the little villages and the winding roads and paths over which their neighbors travelled. Imagine a hilltop at night, with a silent watcher alert to guard the flock which was huddled together in sleep. The valleys fill with silvery mists, until the hilltop is like a little island in an unbounded sea. But the atmosphere is clear above, and the stars seem strangely near. Through the long hours of silent night the shepherd watches the majestic movements of the heavenly bodies.

The lonely watcher is rewarded, by discovering the universe. There are no stars except for those who sit in darkness. The light of day calls attention to the things of earth; but the night reveals the heavens. Many of the most majestic passages in our Bible come from those who, from the hilltops, watched the stars. Their meditations gave them spiritual insight, and they enriched our religion by their declaration of faith.

With the earth submerged in night, and the glory of the heavens revealed, people gained new faith in God. The strife and confusion, which beset ordinary life, fell away in such meditation; and peace and harmony were revealed in the heavens. Light and music and joy and hope stirred human hearts which for a few hours of meditation, turned thus from the temporary things to the eternal. Rich was their discovery.

It was to shepherds upon the hilltops that the Christmas message first came. The music, which was above the discords of the world, came to their ears. The light, which was above the mists of earth, came to their eyes. . . . Of old it was said, "They that sit in darkness have seen a great light." To them comes the revelation of the beauty and the order of the universe; for their ears is the message, "Glory to God in the highest: and on earth peace, goodwill to all." Christmas is a discovery — and it waits only for hearts that can respond to it.

— Henry H. Saunderson
(adapted)

The Star

To our ancestors in the far-off time, all nature was a mystery. Everywhere were spirits and demons and gods, beings to be feared and worshipped. But the greatest were the gods of the heavens, the sun, and the moon, and the stars. Their positions in the heavens at the time a child was born controlled its whole life, so people believed, and they turned to heavenly bodies to divine the will of God. For surely up there, in the starry firmament, surely there must God dwell, and there must prayers be sent. And when the very heavens change, and a new star is born, to burn bright in mastery — this surely is a sign, a sign to draw the shepherds, to draw the Wise Men, even from the East, to worship the newborn child.

Today the heavens are not so mysterious as they were then. We do not think we have to fear and worship the sun and the moon and the stars. Our magi, the astronomers, say that the Star of Bethlehem was really a dying star, whose bright death-fire was a gleam in our sky for a few weeks, and then went out.

But the Star has really remained, whatever our magi say. For its meaning to us will never pass away, and its light will never die out. Its message is the same tonight as it was twenty centuries ago:

"Peace on Earth, Good Will toward All." And we see it now as they saw it then, and still follow it.

— Robert Killam

159

There he sat, red suit, conical hat, fur-trimmed and all, on that chilly park bench, glancing skyward as though assessing the chance of snow.

I sat beside him. "How come you're not out there on the corner with your iron pot and bell?"

"I am not one of them," he replied, "I happen to be Santa Claus."

I smiled, pleasantly enough, but my doubt must have showed.

"I really am," he said, a trifle wistfully.

"But how can you tell if you are the real Santa Claus?"

"That is the question," said he, "How tell the true prophet from the false?"

"But do you really live at the North Pole?"

"Legend," he replied, "The fact is that I am everywhere."

"Are you also omniscient and omnipotent?"

"You mistake me for a friend of mine."

A little embarrassed, I yet persisted. "Perhaps you only think you are Santa Claus."

"That would be *my* problem, not yours. But I might point out that there are no children around."

"That is odd," I conceded.

"The reason," he said "is that I cannot be seen."

Like a chess player crying out "Check-mate" I said, "*I* see you!"

"And that is *your* problem, not mine."

We both looked up at the sky. "It might snow," he said, "It's better when it snows. But snow or not I must be going."

"Going where?"

"To distribute toys, of course."

"One last question. What is the spirit of Christmas?"

"Well, if you want to sound scholarly you might call it the ultimate potential. It's the moment when the best that is human surmounts all the stumbling blocks on the path to becoming. You care, so you help. You love, so you give. And you dream . . . you dream of the time when this brief season will be extended to the whole year."

"Don't you sometimes get discouraged?"

"Dear me, I've only been at this for a few centuries. Give me time."

Then he called out: "Blitzen, Blitzen! Where is that dratted deer?"

Suddenly there came a whole cloudful of snow, right upon us, and by the time I had wiped my eyes clear, I was alone on the bench. But there were hoofmarks in the snow and one dry spot on the bench, a very broad spot where he had sat.

— William L. Barnett

The responsibility of being Santa Claus must weigh heavily upon those who don the beard and red suit. There are few other opportunities a person has to be the personification of a myth. Indeed, I can think of no other. No other actor is believed in by his audience as is Santa. This is a very heavy burden for a Santa. I once played the part at a church Christmas party many years ago. (I was thin and beardless then.) I still recall the expression on one small face. She believed in me as few if any have believed in me in all my three-piece blue suits. Sally and I, being a thoroughly modern couple, did not push Santa, but no matter, our two children absorbed him into their lives; he is inescapable. Is Santa harmful? The question is nonsensical. Santa is! Santa lives! Like most myths he has a place in our culture that all the rational arguments of proper Unitarian Universalists will not shake. We deny him admittance to our church parties for fear he will overact. He comes anyway in some form. We believe, you see, that virtue is rewarded — sort of a Santa-ish idea, a myth of another sort but still a myth? Or is it?

— Carl H. Whittier

161

In Defense of Scrooge!

The Ghost of Christmas Past made Scrooge re-think and re-live his past life at Christmas time . . . How important it is at Christmas not to try to pretend that life is never filled with sorrow, or unhappiness. Of course it is. And, there are also memories of gratitude.

The Ghost of Christmas Present gave Scrooge a panoramic view of Christmas, the people shopping, some in affluence, some in want. Christmas being celebrated on the high seas, and in a lighthouse on a rocky coast. Everywhere, the season warmed the hearts of men and women. This universal aspect of the season is surely part of its grandeur. And Scrooge, I think, must have been impressed by the power of a season to warm so many hearts.

The Ghost of Christmas Yet To Be showed Scrooge his own death, lonely and unmourned. Thieves came and stole his very clothes and bed curtains on the day he died. His passing was noted with gladness or not at all. As in a dream Scrooge was not able to guess whose death and grave the spirit was showing him. The finger (of the spirit) pointed from the grave to him, and back again. "No, Spirit! . . . No!" The finger was still there. "Spirit!" he cried, tight clutching at its robe, "hear me! I am not the man I was . . . I will honor Christmas in my heart, and try to keep it all the year. I will live in the Past, the Present, and the Future. The spirits of all three shall strive within me. I will not shut out the lessons that they teach . . ."

And so Scrooge came out rather well. For him Christmas was a time of integration not of fragmentation. He remembered the past, the sorrow, the incompleteness, but also the gratitude. He was alive to the present, alive to the season — now —, and he also too thought to the future, to what kind of person he could yet be.

And so Scrooge is really the hero of "A Christmas Carol," a song of praise to Christmas, because it was Scrooge who allowed his cold heart to be melted and himself to be redeemed and cleansed by Christmas.

We should all try to do as well as Scrooge this Christmas.
— Paul H. Beattie

162

Magic Hour

No time of year has such magic as Christmas Eve. It is an eerie hour, so real that it seems unreal, a stanza of poetry and hours of dull prose. It has an unearthly grace, all its own.

Staid folk become suddenly stealthy, and there are odd silences and whispered conspiracies in the family. Old friends look at us askance, as if they were hiding some guilty secret.

Even sensible people, touched by some heavenly spirit, do things divinely foolish — learning, for one day, how silly we often are when we think we are wise, and how wise when we fancy we are foolish.

There is a strange winsomeness about Christmas Eve with its candles, its carols, its cookery, and its kindness, its fun and frolic touching us once more with the pull of playtime.

Age and childhood meet and mingle in its glee, memory blending with hope. For a brief time life moves with the lilt and lift of a lyric; we take a glad vacation from ourselves.

On Christmas Eve our gray wisdom does not seem wise, because it is hard and unhopeful. The clouds are off our souls, lifted by happy winds, and we taste the joy of being free of self, and know that life is boundless, as we wish our souls to be.

Aye, it takes us down from our towering pride, and teaches us, for one holy hour, that the humble of heart alone may hope to be happy. It makes us a child again, glad, trustful, unafraid.

Christmas Eve knows how to be merry, even in a dark, tragic world, and that is a secret worth finding out. It has learned a love that can heal the old hurt and heartache of our race.

God be thanked that, for one fleeting day, we can hear a music faint and far off, which will yet gather up our broken and discordant human voices into one triumphant harmony at last.

Merry Christmas! If it is not a fact, it is a high faith and a holy prophecy, our one winged and singing hope.

— Joseph Fort Newton

And stars, twinkling in the night air,
Became beacons leading to a babe in a manger, or a cave,
Or other humble place, in east or west,
A child in whom the human race was born anew.
And simple shepherds, so close to the earth,
Became heroes in a great miracle play,
Finding the new born babe before the great kings of the East.
And angels, those celestial non-creatures, made heavenly music,
To stir the heart for centuries.
(Oh, we know it didn't happen that way
But one must admit, it is very poetic.)
Only a myth, you say?
Of course, only a myth,
The stuff of which dreams are made,
The fictions of which hopes are made,
The fabrications of which joys are made.

Only a myth.
Yet those myths link us with those we never knew,
And will link us with those we will never know.
They will speak a poetry irresistible.
For we are sustained not by bread alone,
Or by reason,
Or by fact,
Or by the daily hum drum,
So much as we are by the poetry of human imagination,
Which paints pictures where before there were only colors,
Which forms songs where before there were only sounds,
Which writes stories where before there were only words.

Someone needs to be our story teller,
For human life is more than a bleak passage
Between the portals of life and death.
It is a story, a myth.
It is the myth of Jesus, or the Buddha or Confucius.
Heroes of the race.
Or it is the story of a life,
Yours or mine, a story with a beginning and an ending
And all that goes between of despair and hope.
— Richard S. Gilbert

164

In this season of growing darkness, as days shorten, as cold and encicling gloom deepen, let us turn to the inward light of the human community to be warmed by the world of legend and fancy.

Let us turn to the stories of miraculous births that remind us of the wonder and beauty of another human life.

Let us turn to the fanciful figures of jolly old elves dressed in red who remind us of the generosity and loving care nestled within the human heart.

Let us, most of all, turn to the tales of brave and courageous men and women who stood up for what they believed, and who tell us once again of the indomitable spirit residing within humanity.

In so doing,
May we, too, become bearers of light amidst the surrounding darkness. . . .
May we reach out to others with generosity and loving care, showing them the ''larger'' side of ourselves. . . .
May we reveal to those closest to us some of the wonder and beauty of our own existence. . . .
And may we find within ourselves, together, the courage and determination to be that which we believe, the freedom to become that which we would become.

— Rick Kelley

Do Your Christmas Thinking Early

Christmas is such a tremendous fact, not only in the calendar of the year, but in the history of the world, and indeed of all human life, that one day or one week is not enough to celebrate it.

It is a remarkable fact that all over the world history is dated from a birthday in an unimportant Roman province, the time of which no one really knows. This can only mean that the significance of Christmas far transcends the incident of the birth of a little Jewish boy, and so we do well to take time for that meaning to grow in our minds and hearts until we really understand it.

The Church has wisely recognized this need, and designated these few weeks before Christmas as a season of preparation, and called it Advent, just as before Easter we observe Lent.

The Advent season is a time for getting our hearts in tune, and that is no quick and easy matter. It is not like tuning in the radio with a simple twist of the wrist. The heart is a much more delicate instrument. We need time to think, to pray, and to look up at the stars. That is the only way to hear the angels' song.

Let us take time each day to think of the real meaning of Christmas, to prepare our minds and hearts for this great festival, for if the kindly loving spirit of the Christ is born in us, it will be Christmas always.

— Stanley Manning

Advent is the season of anticipation and preparation for the glorious festival of Christmas. It anticipates the star by which kings and shepherds alike are led to the heavenly voices within them, singing of the lovely eternities which have always sustained them — the lovely eternities which make kings shepherds and shepherds kings.

Advent is a season of hope and warmth, a time when it is well to look into hearts and not be surprised to find in them divine things in humble and human surroundings. It is a time to consider those forgotten things that give birth to joy, peace, and goodwill.

Advent is a time for loving again those who are lost and lonely, and to have sympathy for those who are never moved to tears of joy or sorrow, those who never hear angelic voices or who never see miracles in mangers, those who never follow the promise of a star.

Advent is a time to say to those who sit in the darkness that upon them the light will shine, that God is with them, and that the divine visits their lives not in golden splendor but in the rough-hewn simplicity of their needs and care.

— Bruce M. Clary

Oliver Cromwell once ordered the "heathen" celebration of Christmas ended in England; the New England Puritans objected to the celebration as well and in 1659 passed a law setting a fine on anyone "found observing any such day as Christmas . . . whether by forbearing labor, feasting, or any other way . . ."

But Christmas survives all efforts to subdue it. Cromwell and the New England Puritans were right, of course, about the "heathen," pre-Christian origins of Christmas. But they were wrong in trying to disavow it because of those origins. Its beginnings make it more universal, and those of us who have the touch of the heathen upon us can find good meanings in this season.

Scrooge, after all, was converted and promised, "I will honor Christmas in my heart and try to keep it all the year." So can we, whatever our theological beliefs, for Christmas is so much more than theology, so much more than the Bethlehem legends.

It is as ancient as the awareness of the winter solstice; and as contemporary as the inner need each of us has to hope and dedicate ourselves to peace upon the earth and within the hearts of men and women everywhere. It is as deeply rooted as human loving and sharing and giving, and it is as new as the birth of our children and the birth of wonder and the birth of new ideas and new love.

— Charles Stephen

167

Joy to the World

I suppose that the birth of Jesus, and the lovely legends that gather about it, have set more people to singing than any other event in human history. There's an enchantment about this season that all but the most churlish spirits must feel, and that brings out the best in this queer human nature of ours. Vanished, for a time at least, are our little meannesses, our artificial habits, our moods of complaint and resentment. Who wants to scold or squabble or be captious and carping? No, we are all members of one family, living together as in our parents house and eager to make it more snug and homelike.

Christmas is more than an official holiday. It's folks and family and friends. It's the mail carrier and the tailor and the one who leaves the paper on the front steps. Yes, it's tender memories of loved scenes in the days that are gone. It's listening for caroling voices that were hushed long ago. I like the saying that God has given us memories that we might have roses in December. Christmas is the time to open the doors of our minds and hearts, to forget our private concerns and worries and ambitions and share our good with others. It's a time when we can both hear and bear glad tidings, a time to give "beauty for ashes and the garment of praise for the spirit of heaviness."

— Samuel A. Eliot

Joy to the world!
But what is joy?
      Is it colorful? Is it expensive?
      Can it be gift-wrapped?
No, it is none of these.
      Is it happiness? Is it excitement?
      Is it blessedness?
Yes, it is these and more, much more.

Joy is for now.
It is completeness. It is consummation. It is holy.

Joy is that painting on that day at that time in that place.
Joy is that poem the umpteenth time through.
Joy is that smile exchanged that day.

And joy is the story of a babe and kings and angels and shepherds and
    stars.
It is not fact. It cannot be proved. But it is truth.

In that story is completeness and consummation.
    Because
In that life was completeness and consummation and holiness.

Joy to the world!
May this Christmas season bring you joy.

                   — Rexford J. Styzens

Christmas Wants

What do you want for Christmas? Of a truth, the answer to precious few questions serves so completely as a clue to the mystery of the human heart. At other times of the year we may dissemble and make-believe, but at Christmas our true nature reveals itself and we act from the hidden motives that dominate our lives.

Come with me this blessed Yuletide season and let the heart confess those wishes it has ever longed for, but never dared express. Aye, what is it we truly want?

I want a few faithful friends who understand my loneliness and who make it less, not by what they say but simply by what they are.

I want a growing capacity to appreciate and resond to the uncomplaining suffering of others, knowing that they fight as hard a battle against odds as ever I do.

I want a mind unafraid to travel, though the trail is not blazed, and a heart willing to trust, even when faith seems the most unreasonable of efforts.

I want a sense of duty tempered with compassion; a conception of work as a privilege; an instinct for justice tempered with mercy; and a feeling that responsibility is my debt for the opportunity of living in a day when great ends are at stake.

I want tasks to do that have abiding value, that make my life a lot better and the world a little brighter.

I want a sense of humor, including a sense to laugh much, often at myself; the grace to forgive and the humility to be forgiven; the willingness to praise and the capacity to respond to greatness and glory.

I want a glimpse of verdant hillsides, the never-resting sea, the horizon-seeking plains and the sound of a bird lifting my spirit higher than any bird can fly.

I want a few wistful moments of quiet amidst the raucous noises and feverish fret of the day, and when twilight descends like a benediction I want a sense of an abiding and eternal reality whose other name is God.

— W. Waldemar W. Argow

Why Celebrate Christmas?

To reflect upon the miraculousness of birth:
> For with the winter solstice, the sun has turned about to begin again the process of the rebirth of nature, and so we may once more marvel at the regeneration of plant and of animal and of human.

To celebrate the living of life:
> For in this life is our one and only opportunity to laugh and cry, to sense and appreciate, to feel and think, to accept and create, to do and give, to live, and love.

To recall the spirit of the great prophet, Jesus:
> For he preached no greater commandment than love of God and love of thy neighbor.

To join in the fellowship of giving:
> For this is a time for us to come together and give of our friendship and of our love and thus of ourselves.

— Robert Edward Green

The Christmas message is simply this: That what is highest and deepest in reality is not to be sought far off in other realms — in long agos, in far aways, in the heavens, or in distant ages to come. It is in this world, in this natural, historical, human realm that the sacred is and is to be discerned by us. That, as I understand it, is the doctrine of the incarnation.

If finding the sacred in this world is difficult for us, our difficulty is rooted not in disputes with fundamentalists about dates or dogmas or the historicity of certain biblically-recorded events. It is difficult because what is wrong in the natural, historical, human realm tends to preoccupy us. The sacred is hard for us to feel and hard to find.

The festival of Christmas itself can help to remedy this. If we can enter its stories, its customs, and its celebrations — enter in with energy and will and emotion — glimmerings at least of the sacred will make themselves manifest to us, first to our feelings; perhaps later to our minds.

— Roy D. Phillips

171

Christmas is the heaviest time of the year for a minister. Like the sales clerk, the garbage collector, and the mail carrier — the minister works overtime during the holiday season. With extra crises, increased counseling, and more worship services, 'the season to be jolly' often ends in stress and illness. Clergy tend to be human like other people. But I still adore the Christmas celebration. Not only the tree and the tinsel, the gifts and the candles, the great carols and the wide-eyed children; but the deeper meaning of a holiday which celebrates the birth of a Jew in ancient Israel. It touches a chord in the heart, far surpassing the mundane realities of the everyday world. I do 'rejoice!'

In theological language, through the event of Christmas I participate in the creative action of the ground of all being. For I learn that my separateness from others in space and time here on earth is but a secondary, deluding aspect of the truth: which is that in essence I am a part of one being, one ground; and I fully experience that greater truth — going out of myself, outside the limits of myself — in the rapture of Christmas.

In more simple terms, the joy of Christmas comes from the increased capacity to identify with all good things. I do not think of 'issues' and 'enemies.' The smile comes easier. I sing with more gusto. Everything appears to be different, not quite fantasy but bathed in a different light which shines in hidden crevices. 'All shall be well, and all manner of things shall be well' is the whisper I hear through the bells and the chimes.

So I wish the same joy, love, and rapture to all my congregation. If, in some ways, Christmas adds to our burden, it's well worth the penalty. Feel the music resounding in the soul. Taste the elixir of life and cheer. Hear the words of hope and trust. See the angels flying overhead. Touch old friends. Kiss your loved ones. It is real. It is glorious. It is Christmas.

— David O. Rankin

Practicing the Scales of Rejoicing

We had forgotten how to sing until angel voices from mythical realms
of glory split the night with their song;
We had forgotten how dark and deep the night until the pure light of a
birthing star opened our unseeing eyes.
We had forgotten the miracle of new life until some unknown poet
caught and sang the mystery.

How weary our step until the quickening holy day season.
How routine our stride before hearing a different song in the night;
How burdened with habit, now infused with time-honored freshness.

For the time being — eyes see a magical night of joy;
For the time being — ears hear melodies of the spirit over time's
tumults;
For the time being — hearts comprehend what minds but dully grasp.

For the time being is all we have, we who are mortal flesh;
Somewhere between the triumphant night of birth and the dark day of
death we stand;
Somewhere between silence of beginning and the eternal deathless
silence of ending, we pause. . . .
For the time being is all we have for practicing the scales of rejoicing,
For singing into the dark and unknown night,
For flinging faithful tunes against the cold silence,
For beating rhythms of the soul over the cosmic cacophony,
For making melodies of meaning in the midst of senseless space,
For drawing from constricted voices sounds of joy despite all sadness,
For the time being is all we have for practising the scales of rejoicing.
— Richard S. Gilbert

Christmas is more than a date in the calendar.
Christmas is a mood, a sentiment, a symbol.

It is the quickening of the presence of other persons into whose lives we have invested a part of our own lives.

It is a memory of other days when into one's path a special one appeared to turn an ordinary moment or a commonplace event into a hallowed experience.

Christmas is home and hearth, the full, free laughter of children, the remembrance of friends, and a moment of peace and the noisy conflicts within and without.

It is a gathering up of the transcendent dreams of the centuries, signalized in the birth of a child who became the Prince of Peace.

Christmas is a time when goodwill is re-born and again made real in the hopes and hearts of all.

- Clinton Lee Scott

The Christmas That I Celebrate

The Christmas that I celebrate begins and ends in an affirmation of life.

There is a human need for hope and if it be located seasonally with the shortening of night and the lenghthening of day, I shan't object.

There is a human need for joy and if it be portrayed in a manger scene and the birth of a child, I shall rejoice in the gift of life; I shall rejoice in knowing that as we grow in years the human family is always beginning again. Birth is the star that I shall see in the East.

There is a human need for belief, and if for many belief is faith, I shall try to make my beliefs as meaningful, and sustaining as their faith.

There is a human need for community, and if for many this means a gathering beneath the cross, I shall strive for a gathering of the human family around itself and from all the wellsprings where we have stopped to drink.

There is a human need for worship, and if for many this means a falling down and an adoring, I shall try to stand tall and let the strength of my belief show in the dignity of my labors.

There is a human need for love, and if for many this means a union with God, I shall seek to live lovingly. Let the legacy of those who come here be such that later it may be said, "It is clear that love walked here."

There is a human need for giving and receiving, and if for many it is done in the name of a child and in the hopes of receiving his blessing I shall give in the name of all children in the hope for their happiness. I shall endeavor to give of myself to the needs of the human family, and receive in return some measure of ennoblement.

There is a human need for an awareness of beauty, the beauty of life, and if for many this means living with God, I shall seek to sharpen every sensory perception, refine, and relate it to my whole life experience that my awareness be thus enriched.

There is a human need for peace, and if for many this is the most compelling voice of our time, we shall have it. We shall hear it as it has never been heard before and the whole world shall be filled with its music.

The Christmas I celebrate is thus a seasonal recognition of human needs and an attempt to satisfy these longings within the totality of my beliefs. The universality of Christmas lies in its seeking to meet human needs.

Christmas has suffered from excesses, abuses, and commercialism in the same manner that love has been profaned on the screen and the printed page. Just as I would not discard the concept of love because of its corrupters, I shall not grind Christmas beneath the heel of contempt because of its usurpers. Whenever you grow weary of this season, I ask that you look into the eyes of little children and you will see what is left to celebrate. In their eyes are joy, anticipation, hope, love, excitement, and wonder, qualities that are quite necessary to human happiness. This is the Christmas that I can celebrate, un-equivocally and without reservation. In the eyes of little children, in the indestructible immortality of idealism, there is the real meaning of Christmas. This is a Christmas that I can celebrate. This, I do believe about Christmas.

- Roger E. Greeley

Has there always been a Christmas?

When the first cave people sat in the first cave and warmed their hands at the first fire . . . was there a Christmas then?

Yes, in a way there has been a Christmas for as long as there have been people who needed one.

Christmas started with darkness and cold, with winter setting in, the days getting shorter and the nights colder, with people hoping for light and warmth and another spring and another year of life, coming closer together around the fire, comforting one another, helping one another to last out the winter.

Christmas started with people using all the magic they knew to help the sun stay bright in the sky.

There seemed to be magic in the flame which people could kindle and control . . . some of the magic brightness and warmth of the sun itself.

And magic in the growing things which kept their green throughout the cold, dark winter, which seemed to live forever when other plants withered and died . . . in an evergreen tree brought indoors to share its secret of eternal life.

Stranger than the evergreen was the mistletoe, which grew without a root, even oaks, turned brown by winter, were green and white with the leaves and berries of this magic plant.

The holly wreath was double magic, with live green branches curved into the sun's shape.

There seemed to be magic in music and dance, in singing and the ringing of bells, long used to call people together.

And a most profound magic in giving and receiving gifts, as precious grains of corn are given to the earth so that more will grow in its place.

The Jewish tradition has the story of the eternal temple flame, rekindled after conquerers had defiled the temple. According to legend, only one day's oil remained. Mysteriously, it lasted eight, until new oil was ready. From this tale has come Hannukah, the Festival of Lights, celebrated in December with the Menorah.

And then on a certain night in the little town of Bethlehem, a child was born to Mary and Joseph. He was named Jesus and grew to be a great preacher and teacher. He taught another kind of magic, the magic of peace, of kindness, of living so that all humankind could have eternal life.

People knew that this magic would work, but it was very hard to practise. They kept on with the candles and evergreens and song, and they added the star and the shepherds, the wise men, and the angels singing 'Peace on Earth.'

They celebrated the birth of Jesus along with the birth of the new sun.

Another part of Christmas started in the fourth century in Myra, where the bishop was a generous man named Nicholas. He tried to live by the teachings of Jesus, and he remembered the old magic of giving. People loved him, and he became the patron saint of children.

Fifteen hundred years later and halfway around the world, Clement Moore wrote "A Visit from St. Nicholas" and gave American children the picture of Santa Claus they love.

Over the years, Christmas has been celebrated by other writers from Dickens to Dr. Seuss, by painters and composers of music, by cooks of good things to eat, by every art and craft known to people everywhere.

We who have charted the course of the earth around the sun need no magic to keep our faith in the security of its path.

But more and more we come to know that the miracle of life on this earth depends upon peace and goodwill to all.

It is the light within the human spirit that we must tend.

It takes more than magic, and it is up to us.

Peace! Goodwill! Merry Christmas!

- Joan Goodwin

We are fast approaching the season during which we celebrate the birth of one who never had any money, nor owned any property except perhaps the robe that he wore. And it will be marked as usual with a great commercial orgy, given added impetus by the tycoons of advertising, who will extol the virtues of this or that product as an expression of the spirit of goodwill and peace. The children will be regaled with "tommy" guns and tanks as toy soldiers, admirable examples of the spirit of peace and goodwill and love. Over the heads of the harrassed shoppers will float the strains of "Hark, the Herald Angels Sing" scarcely heard above the honking of automobile horns, the hurrying feet of shoppers, and dim mutterings of "I don't know what I'll get for Cousin Lulu."

It does seem a little strange that this is the prelude for a season celebrating one so poor, and above all, so indifferent to the physical tokens, so much more interested in human minds and hearts. It seems that the commercialism of Christmas is like the tail that wags the dog, not realizing that it is only a part, and at that, a non-essential part of the whole.

Perhaps it would not be amiss to suggest that in celebrating Christmas, we spend some time in exhibiting the virtues which Christmas suggests, peace, goodwill, love, and friendliness. Your friends will think more of you for your friendly spirit and your goodwill, than if you wind up on Christmas Day a tired, drawn, crotchety victim of the battle of the bargain counter. It might not be remiss, either, to read the story of the nativity, to remember that you need not believe the story to believe what it is about, to feel the warmth and glow of Christmas.
- Gordon B. McKeeman

Let Christmas come. Let it come. I know, our problems continue, the world will be the same after Christmas as it was before, troubles will not go away. But let Christmas come, the season, the day, the special feeling of Christmas Eve, the good feeling of a good old day in which the child still living in us laughs in joy at many-colored lights sparkling on the snow, the crackle of bright-wrapped packages shedding their skins of paper and plastic, and the great music flowing along the streets, reminding us of the hope of peace, a world someday really new-born. So, let Christmas come. Come then, old season ever new: we welcome you in love once more to every hearth and home.
- John Hanley Morgan

I'm a traditionalist at Christmas. I'll try something new if it seems to promise a comfortable fit with the old pattern, but I'm wary of new decorating schemes or clever twists to the familiar pageant. And jazzed up carols are about as reassuring as an orange Christmas tree.

I can think of at least two reasons for my attitude. First, the Christmas celebration is for me, such a source of pleasure that I doubt it can be improved upon. Second, I like things to be simple — traditional but simple — and innovations tend to complicate matters. We make things difficult by crowding in many inconsequential activities. The ceaseless, "going places and doing things", characteristic of our culture is expressed in a whirl of seasonal events.

I think all this indicates a search for something that may be very close to us if we will pause to find it. This is not easy; it is uncharacteristic. Much of our pioneering progress and technical advance has come from our restless urge to find what's over the hill or around the bend.

But now is the time to wait — to let the caravan pass, a time to find your gift; the promise of hope, the open heart, friendship restored — whatever Christmas has to offer you.

Stand still a moment. Warm your hands at friendly hearthfires, listen to the choir invisible, watch the brilliant star.

- Janet H. Bowering

This winter began too soon, and much too cold. Up and down the street I met so few who said they had "Christmas Spirit". Instead they seemed to huddle inward from the cold, hurrying home like Dickens's Scrooge shivering his way from cold-blooded counting house to cold-hearted flat.

The trappings have appeared on schedule but canned carols and plastic garlands hang like humbugs in the air. And the news, as given by early morning thermometers and early evening TV screen hardly warms the heart. Obviously there is no "peace on earth — no good will to all." Obviously!

But the obvious is but the surface of the season. Beneath the evident is the fact that Christmas still commemorates the victory of the ideal over brutality, spiritual freedom over despotism, light over darkness. So it is that cold is warmed and despair rebuked. The fact remains that, as always, the light comes in the darkest season, warmth is rekindled in the coldest time, and to us a child is born in the very season of nature's death.

- Max Coots

Think of the magic and wonder surrounding the first Christmas you can remember. You were four or five or six when, of a morning in midwinter you came into the familiar living room and found it a fairyland of dolls, toys, sleds, stockings with sugar plums peeping out of the tops and tangerines in the toes, with all presided over by the Christmas Tree, shimering with tantalizing loveliness and light from its star-topped crown to its present-packed base. You took one look, gasped in disbelief, raced into the room to touch and make sure it would not vanish like a vision, and then sat down speechless on the floor, content merely to look and look and look.

Thereafter Christmas Eve and Night were times of unbearable suspense. You lay awake vainly trying to sleep, listening to every creak and rustle in the darkness-cloaked house for the sound of Old Santa coming down the chimney to fill those long, carefully chosen and hung-up stockings on the mantel. You waited, bursting with impatience, for the signal of seven from the grandfather's clock which released all the chidren from their beds to rush down to the now familiar but ever glad surprise of Christmas morning.

Then with the years, came doubt, then disbelief. Santa was not real, not alive, just fun, just make-believe. You felt a little hurt, perhaps let-down, but not really — for you began to sense that you too could play at Santa Claus; you could help him to be. So you became a co-conspirator in the Christmas mystery play that takes over our hearts and homes at this season of the year. You played the game, and did not spoil the fun for the little ones. As you grew up, Christmas became the expected, but it never became ordinary.

You had your own chidren. Santa was reborn! And how! You were surprised that you had forgotten and neglected him so long. Why, he even looked like you! You listened to your children's cries of delight. You saw the Christmas stars on the tree shining at you through the bright, gleaming eyes. You heard their soft, sweet voices singing, falteringly but bravely, "Away in a manger," and "Silent Night". Christmas was born anew.

Your chidren grew, and they too came to understand. Finally they went away, out into the world, and you found yourself asking each other, "My dear, do you think we should have a tree this year? It's such a bother, you know. Well, perhaps a little tree, on a table, for old time's sake."

And then there came the Christmas miracle once again, the old that is ever new and that renews all that is old. A new baby was born — that first grandchild! Who at Christmas could deny a babe, or deny a baby Christmas — who? Not you! Christmas was born again for you in all its splendor. The world is recreated and love reborn in every baby's smile. As long as there are babies, there will be Christmas.

- Donald Szantho Harrington

A Golden Christmas

She sat in front of the old black stove alone, except for the gray cat who slept curled up on the small braided rug. The room was quiet, too, except for the muffled cracking sounds of burning wood.

Eighty-five winters had come to her, and gone again, but they were with her still when memories came like a gust of wind to make the coals glow, then they would fade away like distant sounds at night.

The knitting needles in her hands moved in rhythmic patterns inter-twining yarns of black and gold like her years had knit themselves together in that New Hampshire house where generations descended slowly, like a floating flake of snow that hits a child's nose and melts away unnoticed in the midst of play.

The December sun was setting now, casting shadows in the room and she remembered scores of Christmases, silhouetted on her mind in permanent memories that wove themselves together like the golden yarn in the child's hat that she was knitting. She remembered special trees, cut from the grove beyond the hill and carried in the sleigh and then into the house, the tapers on those trees lit up the winter-darkened room and shone like stars in children's eyes, while voices joined and sang of Silent Nights.

She remembered the hush of calm and the quiet in the room when the song was done, and she felt again the heavenly peace that helped the tears to flow like the tears that she had watched, and wondered at, when her mother sat in this same chair so many years ago.

She heard the sounds again, from those special Christmas mornings past — the children's voices, one her own, squealing with delight when they saw the stockings stuffed and hanging and gaily colored presents waiting to be opened.

She held the scene and caught the sounds again in a precious moment that was cherished on that lonely winter day. The heavenly peace they sang about was hers to stay though the family was scattered from coast to coast and none but she remained from the people in her dreams. They lived in her, and in the nooks and crannies of that house, if houses can remember.

And this December day had brought them back again — the tree upon

181

the sleigh seemed just as real today as she shook it off to clean the snow and brought it in the house. She smelled the pine and savored it, and burned the candles in her mind. The knitting needles now were still and the chair had stopped its rocking. She saw the stockings hanging there by that same old fireplace, - she saw the presents wrapped with ribbons, and felt the same delight, and more.

She drank the wine of memory and smiled so softly to herself. The cat got up and stretched and yawned, the wood was crackling in the stove. The needles in her hands took up their work again as she rocked alone on Christmas Eve — a golden Christmas in her home.

- Frank Hall

A starry night! The tang of winter in the air! The delicate beauty of snow laden branches! The solemn dignity of a dying year! Under one roof, a happy family reunited! The cozy warmth of a fire crackling on the hearth! The merry eagerness of little children around a lighted tree! The contagious power of smiling faces! The hearty greetings of welcomed guests! The joyous surprise of hearing from friends far away! The wistful recollection of former days and festal occasions! The mystic presence of those whom ''we have loved long since and lost awhile!'' A holy impulse to share with the needy and befriend the lonely! And behind it all, the lyrical refrain of heavenly music ringing through the air, telling of shepherds filled with wonder, of wise men bringing gifts, and of voices celestial prophesying the final triumph of Peace on Earth through people of Good Will!

- David Rhys Williams

It is that season of the year again. That eminnently impossible yet joyously wonderful season of Christmas. "Christmas impossible?" you ask. The supreme truth and message of Christmas is indeed its seeming objective impossibility.

We live in a world gone mad. Each hour compiles new proof of strife and tension, of crime and misery, of wars seemingly inevitable, of hunger and cold, of hate and fear. The living reality of our days is not "peace on earth, goodwill to all". It is rather, strife around us and everywhere despair. Such is the world we know too well. Yet it is wise for us to remember that such also is the world our forebears knew before us. Into such a world Christmas comes as it has come for 2000 years, and into such a world the same spirit, by different names has come to those of other faiths.

We who view the Christmas story from a naturalistic perspective easily read the impossible into the attendant notice of miraculous events: chorus of angels, virgin birth, and the strange star. Yet is not the miracle only embroidered with these tales? The impossible event is that in times of deepest despair, visions and inspirations of hope, of peace, of love come to all.

The real Christmas message and miracle is that people still hope! It is that they still keep alive the poetry of love and peace and goodwill even when life seems to dim all prospect of such a vision. The impossibility of Christmas is that it comes. Its coming is more than an event ot the calendar. Its coming is a revitalization of the spirit — where people still hope, still see visions of peace, love, and fellowship. The impossible becomes plausible and life takes on a dimension richer than the obvious.

Come Christmas! Let us warm our spirits by its eternal light. Let us live again in the hope better than we know. Perhaps in living awhile by that faith, we can more fully be what we would, and can erase the darkness that seems to be.

- Richard Woodman

It was a tiny babe that lay there,
so frail and helpless in the warm, fragrant hay,
so completely at the mercy of people and things.
The noisy, cruel world outside
was filled with heartaches and oppression,
intrigue and treachery.
But within,
the loving gaze of peasant parents
gave promise of comfort and safety.
Friendly people came
to smile upon him and offer their gifts.
The child "grew in wisdom and stature,
and in favor with God and man,"
for his parents had trained him well
in religion as well as vocation.
He became a teacher-philosopher,
influencing the lives of paupers and kings.
Some people hated him,
Others called him "the hope of the world."

The Christmas story is ever re-enacted
in our midst.
A new-born child is laid in a cradle
to be nurtured and guided into adulthood.
What it sees, hears, feels,
it becomes.
Its environment molds it
into a noble, kindly, upright person
or an unhappy, perhaps tragic
caricature of a human being.

This message of Christmas
is always with us:
Every child
in every cradle
is potentially
the hope of the world.

-Hope Hilton

Christmas belongs to the newborn: babes in loving arms, swinging cradles, fur blankets; babes in crowded rooms, cold rooms,cheerful rooms; babes in huts, tents, split-level houses; babes in mangers.

Christmas belongs to the wonderful world of children, the world of impish smiles, innocent tears and unrestrained laughter; the world of effervescent hope, sudden heartache, spontaneous forgiveness; the world of easy make-believe, hard-won reality, dreams unnumbered; the world of questions that cannot wait and answers that do not help.

Christmas belongs to families together, separated; families giving, remembering, celebrating; families loving.

Christmas belongs to light's promise of delivery, winter's promise of spring, the morning star's promise of daybreak.

Christmas belongs to spirit seeking, becoming, uplifting; spirit in love radiant, wondering, at peace with the world.

- Jack D. Zoerheide

Christmas Revelations

Who of us can be so dull of imagination as not to be moved by the simple and exquisite beauty of the Christmas story — whether we can accept it historically or not? The thing for us all is that it is warmly human and that its center and core is a little child. And just because of that, because it is compounded of these elements that are universal, — motherhood, — fatherhood, — infancy, — hope for the future, — it touches our latent nature. For every true man and woman is at heart a child, just as every true man and woman feels the great, tender, shielding parental instinct when there are little ones in our midst. Children give us wonderful glimpses of what in truth there is in us, — their very presence reveals to us unrealized depths of tenderness and aspiration.

- Herbert Hitchen

This holiday season has always been closely associated with the words of Isaiah, *For unto us a child is born . . . and the government shall be upon his shoulder.*For many this means a very special emphasis on children, who seem to bring a fresh and hopeful spirit to awaken everyday adult lives. Church services, family celebrations, and commercial appeals all center on children. I enjoy and perpetuate this emphasis as much as anybody, but I worry about it too, because I think it partially misses the deeper meaning of the Isaiah passage.

There is a child in each of us - that part of us which is creative, imaginative, spirited, and loving. There is also an adult in each of us which is thoughtful, deliberating, protecting, as well as worying and sometimes controlling. The child is hopeful; the adult is cautious. Most of the time we live in the adult, but occasionally the child creaks through in moments of spontaneous laughter of hopefulness, fantasy or play. Then the layers of concern, born out of eleven months of problem solving, fall away. Then, it is true that for any one of us, at any age of life, "A child is born."

Take some time this holiday season to allow your child a rebirth. It's nice if you have little children around to play with, but it's not necessary. The child in each one of us, when freed for a time of adult caution, brings enough light, hopefulness, and spirit to brighten any home.

-John H. Nichols

Last night I brought the Christmas decorations out and started making my apartment reflect the season. Central is a creche, a family heirloom. As I was placing the figures of Mary and Joseph I began to reflect on the family. At this season, "family" takes on heightened importance, often creating as many sorrows as it does joys.

But, what is "family"? The religious conservatives are currently trying to have the U. S. Congress pass the Family Protection Act, which would, among other things, prohibit funding of educational programs which do not reflect "traditional male and female roles," meaning working husband, homemaker wife, and 2.3 children in the public schools.

I look on that nativity scene on my mantel: Mary, Joseph, and the empty manger awaiting the arival of Christmas day, when, by tradition, we would place the figure of the infant, Jesus. The infant Jesus. According to gospel tradition, that infant was a bastard son. What are our religious conservatives to say to that? As someone summing up Jewish law on the family stated, "Your mother is a biological fact. Your father is an act of faith." In fact all relationships intra- or extra-familial are acts of faith.

In this light, I find the narrow definition of biological parents and their children, the "nuclear family", much too limiting, especially at this time of year. My "family" includes, but is not restricted to, my mother, step-father, brothers and sisters. There are other people who have earned a great deal of my faith in them, their trust in me. How can I exclude these from my family, especially in this season of goodwill?

I, then, define my family not only by lineage, but also by faith. the faithful and true friend is as close to me as family. This person is family, and rightly should be. This is the essence of the myth of the virgin birth of Jesus: that God would become a person and engage in familial relationships,interpersonal relationships of faith and trust; that God's message would be heard despite a narrow definition of parentage or lineage; that a bastard son could come into the world and preach a message of hope, of faith, and of love.

- Peter Webster

The Other Letter To Virginia

Yes, Virginia, there is a Scrooge. To be sure, you didn't write asking about him. You wondered about Santa Claus, and some kind old city editor, eyes misted over with the joyous dew of the season, gave you a loquacious answer. Countless little Virginias, Tommies, Janies, Billies, and Sallies have had his letter for you read to them since.

But Virginia, there is another letter you should read. Because of the sweet mood of this season, no one wants to write it to you. More's the shame, because you need to know what it says far more than you needed the assurances of your first letter. You knew all along that there was a Santa Claus. You simply needed to hear a grown person find words for your reassurance. Santa as a phantom of your delight sparkled with truth from your very first encounter with life. You were born to a community of care and concern. A place was made for you. Your needs were provided. The world welcomed you and accepted your newness with the certainty that all life sheds on the mark of its renewal. This acceptance, in its way, is another name for love. Santa's other name is love too. You knew this.

Now Virginia, what you should know - what you need to know - is that there is a Scrooge. Scrooge wears many masks, and in the long days of your becoming, you will find him many times. You must know who he is. Unless you know the masks of Scrooge, unless you know his meaning and can learn to greet him at proper distance, you too can be such as he. You might become a Scrooge, but my story gets ahead of itself.

The Scrooge of fiction is a familiar character of Christmas telling. To cheer and bright greetings, he has but one reply: "Bah Humbug!" He kept his accountant, Bob Cratchit, on a miserly dole. He counted out the coal lumps for the feeble heating stove. His vision of life, and its purpose followed a miserable narrow track - indeed life had no joy and grinding toil was meat enough for any person. Neither did he spare himself. To be sure, as his tale of Christmas unfolds, he has menacing dreams and frightening visions. He awakened a changed and reformed man. But the Scrooge that lives among us, still awaits the healing of visions and dreams.

I pray you recognize the masks of Scrooge. His is the mask of cynicism. He feasts on the sorrow of unrealized dreams and ever seeks to remind you that there is no profit in dreaming. Dreams and expectations of better things, or a better you are foolish fancy. Reality is hard and unrelenting.

Scrooge wears the mask called despair. The frowns of the cynic are graven more deeply. They never give way to smiles. This mask mocks you with certainty that everything good will be worse. The motto on the portals to Dante's Inferno is appropriated for the living venture: "All hope abandon, ye who enter here."

Scrooge wears blinders. This mask is a curtain that keeps you from looking out to the company of others on life's journey. Blinders that keep your purposes narrow, make all dreams private property and deny you the thrill of community achievement and the sharing in another's joy.

Scrooge wears a mirror. This mirror is a mask that tells you that you alone are of value. Purposes end with the fulfilling of yourself. The whole world is your own reflection. The selfish solitary concern of your whole life is your own well-being.

Virginia, your letter telling of Santa was a sweet reminder of the obvious. These words about Scrooge are a warning of the perilous. You need realistic hopes and not just idle dreams. Keep your eyes open. Polish up your stars and visions, but please keep a sharp eye open for Scrooge, that he you not become. Merry Christmas. Much love.

- Richard M. Woodman
from *The Right to Hope*

The Ten Commandments of Christmas

I am the Lord of Christmas, the Word made Flesh in Daring Dream and Winged Hope, who would lead thee out of bondage to the letter into the glorious realm of poetry and song.

Thou shalt have no other gods before me at this season of the year.

Thou shalt not make unto thee any Graven Image or any Idol out of a Mere Fact concerning anything that is in the heaven above or that is in the earth beneath, or that is in the water under the earth. Thou shalt not bow down thyself to them nor serve them. For I, the Lord of Christmas, am a whimsical spirit, visiting the skepticism of the parents upon the children unto the third and fourth generations of them that distrust me, but showing joy and gladness unto thousands that love me and keep my commandments.

Thou shalt not take the name of Christmas in vain, for the Lord of this season wilt not hold any guiltless who say "Merry Christmas" with their lips but does not truly mean it in their heart.

Remember my Festal Day to keep it holy. Six weeks shalt thou run to and fro and do all thine errands, but the night before Christmas thou shalt set aside for the lighting of candles and the singing of carols, and in it thou shalt rejoice together, thou and thy son and thy daughter, thy manservant and thy maidservant, and the stranger that is within thy gates.

Honor the little Children in thy midst that thy day may be a long remembered one, for the least is still the greatest.

Thou shalt not kill their native sense of wonder at the mystery of life.

Thou shalt not corrupt the innocence of their delight in simple things.

Thou shalt not rob them of their rightful heritage of lyric and legend.

Thou shalt not bear false witness against the affirmations of their awakening minds and bodies.

Thou shalt not look back too fondly on the house of thine own childhood, nor yearn for its carefree ways, nor long for its lisping faith, nor covet any of its blessed securities lest the glory of the good that is past should blind thee to the good of the present and the promise of the future.

- David Rhys Williams

A Highway There Be

Long blue shadows . . . The soft call of an altar gong . . .
A yellow man trudges down a dusty road - Confucius

A caravan halts . . . All dismount, heads in the dust,
   hearts toward Mecca . . . .
It is evening in the desert — Mohammed

An Eastern garden . . . . Scent of lotus . . . .
Annunciation . . . . A virgin enrapt — Buddha

A Judean hillside . . . . A star in the East . . . .
Angels proclaiming . . . . Shepherds enfolding their
   flocks — Jesus

White shadows moving in a twilight room . . .
Whiff of ether . . . . A new-born whimper — Your child
   and mine

A highway there be through every race and clime
which ends at last before heaven mirrored in a baby's
eye . . . . Divinity incarnate suckling at the breast of
Eternity

We pause on the highway that is Time — down which
humanity moves — to touch our hearts in greeting,
this blessed Christmas season.

                                    - Elsie Baker Argow

A
CHRISTMAS
TREE IS A TREE
OF HOPE. A CHILD IS
A TREE OF HOPE. A CHILD
WILL GROW AS A TREE WILL GROW,
SWEET AND STRAIGHT AND SKYWARD, IF
THE CLIMATE WILL HAVE IT SO. WITH LIGHT
TO BECKON AND LOVE TO NOURISH, A TREE WILL
FLOURISH, A CHILD WILL FLOURISH. IF ROOTS MAY
FEED ON THE NURTURE OF LOVE, IF THE LIGHT OF HOPE
DRAWS FROM ABOVE, A CHILD WILL GROW AS A TREE
WILL GROW:
SKYWARD

- author unknown

A growing group of person find Christmas to be a time of strain, hurry, and worry. It is for them a season of perfunctory and compulsory, haphazard and prodigal giving. It may become an orgy of eating and drinking, a carnival of sensuous pleasures.

If we balance the commercial dimensions of Christmas with some religious depth, we may become more steadied in our Christmas attitudes. We will come to know it as a season of great and tender thoughtfulness for others; a time when the heart leaps in eagerness to make some return for the gift of life and the miracle that abounds in all creation; an occasion when the fine art of giving wisely and in accordance with one's means is bravely practiced; a period when love's largess may sometimes be only a word, a thought, a greeting; a season when the unfortunate and unblessed, the lonely and the troubled are remembered.

It is a time, for brooding over the wonder and mystery that have caught the imaginations of people in every age, to see in the darkness a light ahead, to see in each child the potential for greatness, to know in ourselves that there is still the potential to realize our unfulfilled dreams.

- Rhys Williams

There Must Be A Christmas

When he was a young man, Bernard Shaw invented a Society for the Abolition of Christmas. On his ninetieth birthday Shaw said he was still the self-elected president of the society and there were no other members. I have had moments of fatigue, and of distaste for commercialism, when I was willing to be the second member of Shaw's iconoclastic society.

But the old enchantment always sweeps away my sullen mood and I say to myself: "There had to be a Christmas. This strangely happy season meets a deep and perennial need in human nature. The goodness in us demands an occasion when it can freely confess itself. Knowing how queer and imperfect we ourselves are, each of us wants to be more charitable towards others.

There must still be a Christmas. Because - even with the frail invincible weapons of unreasoning joy — we fight any black negation of this better side of humanity. We fight against bringing back the dark ages before the Child — helpless and mighty — struck fear into the hearts of tyrants and commanded the homage of wise men.

There had to be a Christmas, and there will be a Christmas to the end of time upon this habitable globe. Much at present seems to cheapen it; but we must not yield to cynicism. Amid perils, troubles and greeds, it is all the more certain that we dare not surrender the true Christmas spirit. "Somewhere, and somewhere, the children unborn are singing, Oh listen!"

The Christmas spirit is the song of what Lincoln called "the angels of our better nature." It is music from the undaunted heart of the world. And somehow at Christmas time we all come home for a little while to what we most really are, which is what we shall be. And suddenly round the corner we come to the unspoiled surprise — to the loveliness and hope and innocent felicity which we so often feared we would never see again.

- Vivian T. Pomeroy

Christmas comes at the darkest time of the year, not just the solar year, but the psychological year as well. Life is a stern challenge. It is hard to live well and with integrity. Christmas comes just a few days before the end of the year when we know how little has been our achievement when viewed from the penetrating light of religious idealism. Yet the Christmas spirit is a light shining in the darkness. It says that within the human spirit, in you and me, there is that which no darkness can extinguish. It says that human history records the lives of some exemplars, men and women like Jesus, who by their lives have lit the world forever with truth and love. It intimates to many that there is a cohesiveness to the forces working for good in the world.

The Christmas spirit tells us also that we must not lose faith in our power to do good nor in our power to transform the world. It tells us also that we must not lose faith in children, in their power, and the power of countless future generations to attain heights of joy and peace, good will and achievement beyond our most fond imaginings.

The spirit of Christmas warms us also, making us remember that there is still a cheer, a laughter and a hope that is part of being alive. When Christmas comes to us we know indeed what a joy it is to give and to receive, what a joy it is to be.

- Paul H. Beattie

Christmas is an invitation to come over on the side of the redeeming forces in human life. The poets have sung the invitation in lines we joy to repeat; the musicians have put it into great melodies that capture our hearts; the artists have presented it in pictures to which we turn again and again to feed on their beauty; writers gifted in story have woven it into such tales as that of Tiny Tim which we recite again and again, the heroes and common folk of earth have acted it out a thousand, thousand times in the substance of their daily lives. Our own hearts prompt us to accept with eagerness and to live in that which is best for humankind.

- E. Burdette Backus

This is the season of the heart. The season when Fantasy and Hope marry one another and their offspring create new visions which become the lighted pathways to tomorrow's possibilities.

This is the season of winter when frigid blasts are no barrier to the inner joy and warmth created by the soul's summer. This is the season when that which is cold, dark and barren is miraculously warmed, illuminated and made fruitful by the human impulse to touch, to share, to create, and to love.

This is the season when human warmth and love thaw the seemingly irreconcilable, temporarily perhaps, but at least long enough to give us each a fresh vision of the possible. When hope seems to take on a dimension of the objective; when happiness is like a thick carpet, and joy is a soft string of light that threads its way into our hearts and binds us as one humanity immersed in love.

This is the season of all people, of all time. The season when the voices we hear are the melodies of the heart's yearning; when the young are never old and the old are as if forever young. This is the season of all people, of all time, when distinctions melt and fade and the children of America are the children of Laplanders, and the Laplanders are the children of Asia and Time.

May our gift to this season and to the Children of Time and Timelessness be an open heart in which no one is ever denied lodging.
-Donald L. Wassmann

We've hung our world this year at Christmas time with shining ornaments of space — for natural moons and suns and stars no longer will suffice. We have the cosmos at our doorstep, and we've decked the planet for our neighbors 'cross the sky. But how about the Prince of Peace we celebrate? Can He mean aught to races on the worlds of other suns? Or might we further ask, for answer to our question:

What is teamwork to the launching of a moon?
Or what is putting bombs aside to travel to the stars?
Or what, again is, the love of each Madonna mother on this globe or on another to her infant child of space and time?

So for myriad friends on earth and, let us trust, on farther shores of light-year seas, this toast:

Here's to a Universal Herald of Peace whose spirit is the only hope, both here and everywhere in space, for life's going on to voyage out among the galaxies!
- Lester Mondale

195

A Reflection on the Gift of a Stuffy Barn

May we join in a moment's relection upon that night so long ago . . .

Think how crowded that barn must have been and how stifling the air: ox and ass, sheep and more sheep and more sheep; wise men, shepherds; townsfolk agape. And all the result of Joseph's poor planning, his failure to make reservations. But then he and Mary would not have been in that predicament in the first place if it hadn't been for the tax collector. What a remarkable story it is! Remarkable not so much for the novelty of its actors' lives as for its echoes of our own.

And yet in the midst of all that yawning chaos a miracle has occurred. Somehow surprise has broken through the dull thread of frustration to disclose a new beginning. Somehow hope has shattered busyness in the interests of the gracious and the old world has earned a second chance. Almost everybody was amazed. Joseph, we know, had been confused for some time since learning of the manner of his beloved's conception. The wise men and the shepherds did not pretend to have a clue to what was really happening. Only Mary understood that the spirit can work wonders.

But then this is the whole point of Christmas: that the gracious comes when it is least expected, when the barn is most crowded and the air most stuffy.

It is not always easy to believe this in July when Christmas is six months behind us; sometimes it is even harder to believe it in December when Christmas is upon us! But there *is* a point to all the chaos just as there was that night so long ago — that surprise must follow consternation to be saving and that the gift of grace can show its face even without good planning.

- William F. Schulz

A Humanist Christmas Exhortation

That there may be love
(I will be loving)
That there may be peace
(I will be peaceful)
That there may be joy
(I will be joyous)
That there may be warmth
(I will be warm)
That there nay be kindness
(I will be kind)
That there may be friendship
(I will be a friend)

When the candle is spent
and the yule log, ash;
and wreath removed
and the tree-stand put away,
I shall keep alive
in my life
love — peace — joy
and
kindness — friendship — and warmth.

(At least I hope that I do,
for if I don't
the season passed me by
without my even *knowing* it.)

- Roger Greeley

This Christmas That Remains

There is a Christmas that remains! Its permanence depends not upon the dictates of custom and convention, or upon tinsel that tarnishes, or upon holly that withers as an old year dies. Its timelessness depends upon an attitude of the heart.

The gifts we give wear out and are forgotten. And yet . . . and yet the wealth of value and meaning they symbolize enriches both those who give and those who receive. Verily, we live not by tangible gifts alone, but by the dearer benefactions of appreciation, kindness, compassion, and affection. To know that others care for us, that there are those who joyously manifest their faith in the power of goodwill to remake the world — ah, this is the Christmas that remains. Like the Bethlehem star, it shines eternally to cheer our hearts, gladden our spirits, and remind us of those things that abide forever.

- W. Waldemar W. Argow

VII. *So hallowed and so gracious is the time*

Some say that ever'gainst that season comes
Wherein our Saviour's birth is celebrated,
The bird of dawning singeth all night long;
And then, they say, no spirit dare stir abroad,
The nights are wholesome, then no planets strike.
No fairy takes nor witch hath power to charm,
So hallow'd and so gracious is the time.
                    William Shakespeare

THE CHRISTMAS CULT

Cults have a strange way of popping up. We're probably all familiar with the so-called "cargo cults"of the South Pacific, for example. Islanders who had never seen airplanes were amazed when these giant birds thundered out of the sky to deposit technological treasures. Presto, a logical development was a cult to woo these creatures to their shores to bestow more blessings.

There's a story about a not dissimilar cult which also arose in the South Pacific during WW II. On a small tropical island an airstrip had been built. The suport personnel, because of the pragmatic and enlightened leadership of their commander, made every effort to both participate with the island natives and to invite the islanders to participate with them.

The chaplain, like all the rest, did so. He participated in their festivals and made a sincere, if slightly chauvinistic, attempt to get the islanders to paticipate in his.

Clearly, there in the South Pacific, so far from home, the Christmas season was particularly difficult for the military personnel. So, the chaplain started earlier than Macy's with Christmas preparation. Including the islanders, who responded enthusiastically, everyone exchanged gifts, sang the old carols, and told the old stories.

Shortly after New Years Day, 1944, the Americans moved on, their airbase no longer being strategically located.

Many years later, in March 1957, that same chaplain made a stopover on his way to the Phillipines. He took a nostalgic tour of the once too familiar island and happened to run into an old woman he had known during the war. She was going to "church" as the officer soon discovered. She was late, but wanted to visit more, so she invited the chaplain to go with her, so that later they could continue their tour together.

The church was an outdoor circle. The singing was "Oh, Come All Ye Faithful," "O Little Town of Bethlehem," and "Silent

Night.'' The ''sermon'' was a recounting of the Christmas story. And the service ended with everyone exchanging gifts. The Christmas Cult!

Every week, more or less — most often more — they celebrated Christmas. That was the only celebration they had learned from the Americans. That's what they thought the American religion was all about. If only it was true . . .

To make the season of sharing, the season of love and hope and ''glad tidings'' live all through the year isn't a bad idea at all. May it be more — more often for us. May we take that spirit of Christmas, the spirit of sharing and love and hope and ''glad tidings'' and make it live. May ours be a Christmas Cult!

- Douglas Gallagher

HOW THE MITTEN TREE BEGAN

For a long, long time, many years, hundreds of years, before any one of us was born and long before Columbus discovered America, even years before the birth of Jesus in Nazareth, people have cut down pine trees and brought them in from the woods and fields to help them celebrate the most special events in their lives.

Trees, in general, have long been very important to them. On the cover of our hymn book there is an engraving of a tree which also appears as a sketch of a tree at the beginning of each section of the book. You may have noticed it, It is there because the hymn, ''The World Tree,'' No. 197, was a favorite of the group of people who dedided what hymns would be in the hymnbook. The music of the hymn was especially written by one of these people so that we might sing the words of Ridgley Torrende's poem, also called ''The World Tree.'' The name of the new tune that we sing is ''Ygdrasil.'' It is a very strange name to us. But is we were Norsemen it would not be strange to us. It would mean a great deal to us. For we would think immediately of the strong, tall oak-like tree which nourishes and supports the earth and sky. The Norsemen believed that there was such a tree and they called it the ''Ygdrasil.''

Do you remember the story of Adam and Eve in the Garden of Eden? The tree is also very important there. The apple which Eve gave Adam to eat was forbidden fruit from the tree of the knowledge of good and evil. And also in the midst of the garden there seens to have been a second, very important, but mysterious tree, the tree of life.

Well, these are a couple of the ways in which trees have been especially important to people in the past. And among the most important trees of all have been the stately evergreens, such as the one which stands in front of us covered with mittens and socks and things

202

this morning. People have supposed that there must be something very special about the tree which managed to grow in so many different places, even where other tree could not grow, and which stayed green with its sticky sap flowing through its trunk and branches all year long, even in the coldest weather. So in Asia Minor, the ancient worshippers of Attis, a god of vegetation, set fire to great pine poles each spring. The Egyptians modeled their chief god, Osiris, out of pine and encased him in a hollowed-out log of pine. The Greeks in the time of Rome waved wands tipped with pine cones in honor of their god of merry-making, Dionysus. And the people of western Europe, the Germans especially, have taken great delight in their evergreen.

The people of the Hartz Mountains in the northwest of Germany tell a favorite story about a poor mining family in which the father, the only one strong enough to work in the mines, became ill so that his wife and children were soon without food for themselves or fuel for their stove. Each morning during her husband's long illness the woman would climb a nearby mountain to pick up as many pine cones as she could carry so that they would have some to burn to keep them warm and enough left over to sell or trade for food to feed them one more day. One day not long before Christmas, just as she entered the woods, a little imp or elf jumped out from a fir tree and said to her, "Take only the cones under this tree, for they are by far the best." She thanked him very much, and as she bent down to pick up the cones there was such a downpout of them from the tree that she was amazed and frightened a little bit. The basket was soon full of cones. And on the way home it became heavier and heavier, so that she could hardly make it to the cottage door. When she emptied the cones from her basket, everyone of them had become pure silver. Her family was no longer cold and hungry. And remembering this story the people of the Hartz Moutains to this day gather fir cones, cover them with a silver-like sulfur paint, and place them in bags to burn and crackle gaily in their Christmas fires.

Among the Germans, there is a story that Martin Luther, the founder of the Lutheran Church, more than 400 years ago, placed an evergreen in his home at Christmas time. He was inspired to do so, they say, while walking through a forest of evergreens at night and seeing the glittering stars between the branches. It was such a wonderful sight that he cut a small tree and stood it up in his house with several lighted candles on the largest branches so that he and his family might be reminded of the delightful view. When Martin Luther did this, he was renewing an old German custom that had nothing to do with the birth of Jesus, and maybe by doing so he meant to say that it was alright for his followers to enjoy the old custom, even if it was not particularly Christian.

There is another traditional German story which tells of two small children who welcomed a little stranger into their home one cold winter night. They gave him food, a choice place near the fire, and their bed. During the night they were awakened by beautiful music, and rushing to the door, they found an evergreen tree bearing on its branches beautiful ripe fruits and golden balls. The little stranger, now revealed to them as the child Jesus mysteriously returned to earth, said, "I was cold and you took me in. I was hungry and you fed me. I was tired and you gave me your bed. From now on, this tree shall delight you each year on my birthday."

Stories and traditions such as these are the reason why we have a Mitten Tree. Not so many years ago in a church much like our own, the people wanted to find a new way of celebrating truly and simply some important things they liked and felt especially at Christmas time.

They wanted to show that they were proud participants in the whole long history of men and women who have tried in ever so many ways to live good lives, not to show that we agree with everything that they have believed and done, but that we are glad to play our part and to pay attention to them. Most of these people thought of themselves as Christians, as followers of Jesus and members of the community created by his followers, but they decided to use the evergreen in the celebration in order to express their feelings of friendship with all who strive to seek the truth and to do the good regardless of their belief.

They also wanted to show that they were glad to be a part of nature, and to show that they value the things of nature not only for their usefulness to us, but also as they are in themselves. So the Mitten Tree is bare at the beginning, just as it is in the outdoors. In a way, it was a shame that they had to cut a tree, and such a large one, too, in order to be able to sense its majesty inside. There was a sadness about having to cut it,* but even the sadness was good. For it was a way of saying that one is glad to be a part of nature as it is, even though we must use it to our own ends.

Then the beginners of the Mitten Tree also wanted to show that they were grateful for the chance to be alive and for the fruits of life that they enjoyed and that they were concerned that others also should enjoy them. So the Mitten Tree became a way of expressing thanks for their own well-being and a sense of responsibility for the well-being of others. The mittens that we place upon the tree are for the good of those who need them, but they are more than that. They are also meant to show our gratitude for what we have and our willingness to be responsible for one another.

And finally, the beginners of the Mitten Tree decided to make a ceremony of it, to decorate the tree with useful and with brightly colored things, and while the tree was being decorated, to sing a lively, joyful song together. For while we seek the truth and do the good it is important also that we should rejoice as beautifully as we can.

Well, there you have it. That's how the Mitten Tree began, and some of what it might mean to those who gather by it at this time of the year. It is a way of saying that we are glad to be alive, that we are confident in life's support and in our creative efforts, and that we rejoice in the responsibility of being caretakers of the earth and lately of the heavens, and of being friends who are concerned for the welfare of one another.

- Robert Reed

*An option would be to have a live tree which is later planted on the church grounds or elsewhere in the community. The planting of the tree could be a continuation of the ceremony. Ed.

A season for children . . .

This is the season when children gather memories, and it is we who determine the memories which they gather and cherish. Let it be a season of warmth in our homes, with the smells of baking Christmas goodies (and always with time to let them help with the mixing, the cutting, the baking, the decorating). Let it be a season of candles with their symbolism of the reviving light of the season, candles wisely and safely placed and watched. Let it be a season of sharing, so that their thoughts are of giving as well as of receiving. Let the charm and fragrance of the Christmas tree be for them a memory of peaceful days, of family pleasures, of family traditions (and each family will have its own).

But let it also be a season when they know that the church is a part of our lives — not an appendage to our days. And above all, let it be a memory of parents with time, not harried with last-minute preparations and the rush of unfinished details. And with starlit nights or softly falling snow, let there be time in this season to enjoy some family excursion to the out-of-doors. The miracle of slowly lengthening days, the beauty of the Christmas myths, the reality of a personal religious faith; these are the ingredients of Christmas we cherish for our children.

- Dorothy Tilden Spoerl

Sharing with chidren deep expressions of the human spirit . . .

Our aim in the liberal church is to help our children understand the deeper meaning of their day-to-day experiences, to discover a spiritual significance in all that goes on about and within them.

No season of the year lends itself more readily to this purpose than Chrismas. Here are all the elements to delight the heart of the youngest child and to provide an outlet for the social idealism of the most mature. There is the symbol of the holy family, a springboard for a more penetrating realization of the miracle of birth and parenthood and the joy of family life. There are all the wondrous decorations — the tree, the star, the holly, the mistletoe, the lights — symbols relating each of us in the here and now to the long ago past of our race and providing opportunity for revealing insights into humanity's struggle for a higher life. There are the age-old customs of the giving and receiving of gifts and concern for the well-being of others — customs that lead into a more moving realization of the ties that bind people to people, of humanity's never-ending need for companion-ship and sympathetic understanding. There is, above all else, the central figure of the festival, Jesus himself, the radiant figure of a human being who realized to an unusual degree the divine potentiality of the human soul, and who lived his life in unwavering devotion to eternal truths. Here is the embodiment of true human greatness, a never-ending vindication of liberalism's faith in the supreme worth of every human personality.

- Wayne Shuttee

What shall we tell our children about Christmas?

Christmas is many things to many people. Our children will find that their friends and teachers have varied feelings about and interpretations of this special season. Parents and grandparents will which to share their own meanings of Christmas with their own children.

What *does* Christmas mean to liberals?

For some of us, the traditional elements of the Christmas story express with warmth and beauty the most profound aspects of human experience, the ideals which represent the highest human hopes. For some of us, the rejection of the religious teachings of our parents, arrived at by painful rebellion, has left its mark and we cringe at the implications of the words we hear and the songs we cannot escape. For some of us, the sentimentality of this "season of good will", blaring from every store and newspaper advertisement, interjected into even the television newscasts, produces real empathy with Scrooge.

Despite our feelings, our children need to find a meaning and interpretation of Christmas. Because literature, art, music, and dance arose as the servants of religion, and because our religious heritage is from the Jew and the Christian (mingled, to be sure, with the Greek and Pagan) our children cannot escape religious tradition; nor would we wish them to. They would miss the rich paintings and sculpture of the Renaissance, the glory of Handel's *Messiah,* the intricate beauty of form which Bach bequeathed us. Many of us want our children to be familiar with the beautiful cadences of the Nativity story, with the carols which , in our darkest hours, have kept alive the flickering hope for "peace on earth, good will to all."

As liberals, however, we are expecially fortunate:

We do not need to attempt to explain or account for the Star of Bethlehem or the song the angels sang. We need only emphasize that this story of the miraculous is a tribute to a life lived in devotion to the truth that love is stronger than hate, a life of courage and commitment. Although we have very little historical data about Jesus, we do know that his life, or what people have believed about his life, has significantly influenced history.

We do not need to explain the visit of the Magi or the adoration of the shepherds. In the gifts of gold and frankincense and myrrh we see the natural desire to give which is shared by all those who love. In the worship of the shepherds we see expressed that reverence for life and awe in the face of the mystery of birth which we also feel. The Holy Family in the stable increases our sensitivity to the joy of family life, the miracle of every birth.

Miraculous stories of the birth of great people are a natural development. Stories about the birth of Buddha and Confucius and of other great religious leaders have in them similar elements of miracles - angels, movement of the stars that were never to be repeated, a birth which was not as others are born, birth of a God rather than human — similar elements of family love and giving. We may wish to tell these stories to our children.

We will not expect to convey all the religious meanings that can be found in the Christmas myth and legend in one year. Rather, we will enjoy the beauty we find in the old tradition and when our children question, we will discuss their questions with them. When our children ask what we believe, we will share (as far as such intangibles can be communicated) the values we have found. We will trust that at maturity our children will give to Christmas not only the meanings we have tried to teach, but also values they have dicovered through their experience in their families.

Our Christmas traditions, however, go back beyond the babe of Bethlehem to the mists of antiquity. When the nights become long and the days the shortest in the year, people always celebrated in order to affirm their faith that light and sunshine would return again, that darkness would not prevail. The Jewish Hanukkah, which Jesus celebrated with his family comes at this very time. The Christmas tree, the mistletoe, and many other Christmas customs go far back in history and are a dramatic indication of our bond with those who lived in far away places and long gone times. These roots, too, we may wish to share with our children.

Parents will wish to reflect upon significant values they find in the celebration of Christmas, and to share these insights with their children.

- Elizabeth H. Baker

Have you heard about the small boy who came home from Church School and reported that the class was beginning to practice singing Christmas carols and that his favorite was a new one called, "When Shepherds Washed Their Socks By Night"?

What about Santa Claus?

What should parents do about Santa Claus? To some people this may sound like a silly question, but to others, it is of considerable importance. For some years now, Santa has been a bone of contention. There has been one prevailing opinion, particularly popular among people who have conscientiously tried to bring up their children in the light of modern theories of education, that you must never tell your children anything which is not true and therefore you are lying to them in telling them the story of Santa Claus. And there is another point of view that you are depriving children of lovely experiences based on belief in Santa if you deny them their few years of this cherished belief. Such a difference in viewpoint is confusing, to say the least. Perhaps a careful look at the facts we have about children may provide the needed information to permit us to draw useful conclusions.

First, there are the many actual incidents cited about children whose faith in their parents has been shattered because, after having been assured of the truth of the Santa Claus story, they learn that it isn't really so.

Second, a different aspect of the problem is epitomized in the comment of the 3½ year old, who, having been told flatly by her older brother that Santa was just a man dressed up in a red and white suit, said with equally vehement forthrightness, "But I want to believe in Santa Claus, so I'm going to!"

Third, consider for a moment, the intimate studies of children which make very plain that children are *never* little adults but do live in a world of their own and only gradually can accept and use adult values and standards. It simply cannot be overemphasized that what is important for adults is *not* important for the young child. On the basis of their limited experience, chidren's interpretation of ideas and events are going to be very different from their parents and older siblings. Children cannot be forced to grow faster than their own rate of development permits, but when they are ready to grow in understanding, they need and want help from their parents in gaining new insights.

What relevance does all of this have for the parent trying to decide what to do about Santa Claus? Just this: It is neither sentimental nor dishonest to tell the Santa Claus myth - or The Three Bears or

Cinderella - to children, for these stories are part of their cultural heritage, part of the poetry of childhood. Not to tell the story of Santa Claus when children become aware of him is a serious deprivation. Little children will not differentiate between a mythical and a real person — both will be real people to them. But at some point in their development - and this may come as early as age three or as late as age five or six - they will begin to ask, "Does Santa Claus really live at the North Pole?" "does he really come down our chimney?" "Why are there so many Santas?" At this point it is easy for adults to make mistakes. They may feel that, because children are still very little, or they have a brother or sister who still "believes" in Santa or for other reasons, that it is better to say "Yes, of course Santa really does live at the North Pole --- comes down our chimney," and so forth. But this is a reply which cannot be condoned, because adults are failing to assume the responsibility they have to help children broaden their understanding at the very moment when children, by their questions, indicate that they are ready to take this step forward.

On the other hand, adults, particularly if they emphasize the practical side of living, may make the mistake of responding to first questions with a brusque "Of course Santa doesn't live at the North Pole. It's just a silly story. Big children don't believe things like that." This kind of reply is too harsh an invasion of children's inner world. It is a real help to children to teach them the difference between fact and wonderful just-pretends which we make up to express our feeling about Christmas, and quite another thing to dismiss the make-believe as unimportant or immature.

The problem about Santa Claus then, does not lie in the telling of stories about him, but the handling of the children's question. Very young children need to be shielded from information which is premature or hard just as they are shielded from bad falls and hot stoves. Older children can be encouraged to allow the little ones their turn at "believing" in Santa Claus. Even so, life being what it is, there will still be a few who are hurt by well-meaning but insensitive people, but if their parents are loving and understanding and keep their integrity as parents, those children will have the courage and the vigor to reply, too "But I want to believe in Santa Claus so I'm going to."

- Aloyse Hume

What is truly important?

We know that the pressure is on for many a parent as the Christmas frenzy approaches. Once again we urge you to consider what is really important for children at this season.

What is truly important for your children?

Not wondrous new experiences, but a happy enjoyment of family traditions.

Not travel far and wide, but a love of home.

Not flight from reality, but full participation in the workings of home and neighborhood and church.

Not constant entertainment, but the habit of doing and making and creating for themselves.

Not widgets and gadgets and ready-made toys, but the ability to make music and paint and mold and build themselves.

Not dancing plastic toys, but encouragement to dance themselves.

Not handed down beliefs, but encouragement in forming their own faith.

Not gold and frankincense and myrrh, but knowledge that they are loveable and that they are loved.

- Felix Danforth Lion

Vocation

We were talking with a man in the Santa Claus racket. He says that the job isn't what it used to be and he is thinking of looking for some other line of work. "You don't get the respect you used to," he said, "I don't know what the younger generation is coming to." He had made a shift this year to this part of the country thinking that he might find a higher class of clientele, but it has been disappointing. "Kids are the same all over," he said. He came up from a place in the South with the idea that kids who lived nearer the North Pole and Santa's traditional home might have a more realistic appreciation of him, but he reports it didn't make much difference.

Kids become more and more exacting. they know just what they want and tend to settle more and more on a few major items. Furthermore, they ask for these with a sinister air that says they better get it, or else! They appear to have copied some manners they have learned from adults, as if they were saying, "This better be a top quality product or you'll get it right back in your face!" Or, "And see it's delivered on time!" Or, "No measly substitutes this year!" He said that it made Santa's cheery "Ho! Ho! Ho!" hollow and it sometimes stuck in his throat. This was especially true when he was fetched up right in the middle of the laugh with a kick on the shins. It made the time on Santa's throne one of apprehension. He spent the time this year in a cold sweat. Because of the costume, one is always in a hot sweat, which is natural enough, but a sweat induced by nervousness has been much too much.

Reflecting on the drift of things, he said, "I got to feel just like a store clerk." As an experienced Santa, he had formerly trained the annual crop of recruits, but he gave this up. "I thought that the reason why it was beginning to seem just like any other sales job was because I was representing store management in training the novice Santas. I thought I ought to get out of this. Maybe I could feel like a real Santa Claus again, with a resounding Ho! Ho! Ho! and a lively interest in each new youngster who came with dreams to invest." He was moody when he said this, and after a respectful silence we inquired, "And it didn't work?" He shook his head sadly to indicate we had got the idea. He said that he could have gone along with the sales pitch attitude required by the department stores, it it hadn't been for the kids. They were way ahead. Their resistance was the match of the sales pressure. One felt caught in the middle of a clash of realists. He suspected for a time that some TV program might be advising, "If you don't get what you want from Santa, kick him in the shins." He could find no one who knew of any such thing going on, and had to conclude that parents were making him a scapegoat. "Isn't it too bad Santa didn't bring you what you wanted! I'd kick him in the shins!" He says that he has always been sentimentally addicted to the notion that there weren't any bad kids, but just bad parents. Yet he had never thought they would be malicious.

He said that he has been thinking of taking up rocketry to help blow the whole thing up, but he is a little short of educational background. There's just not anything left to Santa Clausing. No dreams, nothing. Not even the fellow workers are congenial. Most of them are moonlighters with regular jobs on the side. There's no sense of pride in being the embodiment of the Christmas spirit. There are few dedicated old pros. He is thinking of taking up beachcombing. Anyway it wouldn't be seasonal work.

- Thaddeus B. Clark

T'was the night before Christmas and down in R.E.
Stood the sagging remains of our gay Mitten Tree.
The mittens were bundled for Old Mexico-
Or maybe they went to the cold Eskimo!
The Director was weary - the season was long,
And head was awhirl with story and song.
The candles of Advent, in folk-lore are four -
But being true liberals, we have to have more.

Channukah candles are eight in a row -
The Shamas makes nine - with three Sundays to go.
On Bill of Rights Sunday, we honor all, then
A candle for Eleanor Roosevelt makes ten.
And there's Santa Lucia - the queen of all light,
Her gold crown ablaze with candles so bright.
We celebrate Giving with stories so gay
Of Children in Holland on St.Nicholas Day.

There's the Solstice of Hindus and Druids and Latins-
We can't leave this out of our Christmas-time Matins.
And Buddha, who was born from the heart of a lotus -
"The Man With A Light" - of his birth we take notice.
Then there's one of the wisest and greatest of all
Teachers, who have lived, Confucius the Tall;
And Mithras, the god of the Persian and Roman,
His Heavenly Light was a winter-time omen.

The chapel was quiet, the pews were all bare -
My eyes fell on the Creche and the Babe resting there,
And I heard a voice say, as I put out the light,
"Remember whose birthday we honor tonight."

- Patricia L. Helligas

213

(to be sung to the tune of GOD REST YOU MERRY, GENTLEMEN)

God rest you Unitarians, let nothing you dismay.
Remember there's no evidence there was a Christmas
    Day.
When Christ was born just is not known, no matter
    what they say.
Glad tidings of reason and fact; reason and fact;
Glad tidings of reason and fact.

There was no star of Bethlehem; there was no angel
    song;
There could have been no wise men for the journey
    was too long.
The stories in the Bible are historicallly wrong.
Glad tidings of reason and fact; reason and fact;
Glad tidings of reason and fact.

Much of our Christmas custom comes from Persia and
    from Greece.
From solstice celebrations of the ancient middle
    East.
We know our so-called holiday is but a pagan feast.
Glad tidings of reason and fact; reason and fact;
Glad tidings of reason and fact.

- Christopher Raible
from HYMNS FOR THE
CEREBRATION OF
STRIFE

A persistent UU legend (I might have helped perpetuate it) is that "The Night Before Christmas" was written by a Unitarian. Yet Clement Clarke Moore, son of an Episcopal cleric, Hebrew scholar who helped found New York's General Theological Seminary, had no apparent Unitarian affiliation.

Yet the great Unitarian preacher, A. Powell Davies, declared that the author was a Unitarian (and a guiding principle of my life is always to believe what Unitarian Universalist ministers say). Why did Davies call Moore a Unitarian?

Certainly the original St. Nicholas was no Unitarian. He gave away money, worked miracles, and participated in the Council of Nicea promoting the (there made orthodox) ideas of Christ and God as the same and part of the trinity. He became the patron saint of sailors, pawnbrokers, and Russians (few Unitarians in that lot). With his faithful demonic companion, Black Pete, he rewarded good and carried off bad children (no Unitarian could decide) on the Eve of his Feast Day, December 5. A decade ago, the Pope decided Nicholas was historically questionable and removed his day from the official calendar.

An obscure bishop became a significant saint by a thousand-year process. Pagan winter wonder workers - gnomes, elves, and saturnalian sprites - were as-it-were Christened by St. Nicholas acquiring their stories and duties. (The church excelled at such absorption, hence eggs at Easter, hearts for St. Valentine, and mistletoe at Christmas.)

Moore, with the stroke of a pen, reversed the process (true, he was prodded by works of Washington Irving and others). The Bishop became Santa, exchanging his vestments for sensible fur, acquiring reindeer and sleigh while losing horse and servant, and returning to the solstice celebration where he belonged. Patron saint became pagan sprite, free of all ecclesiastical encrustation, symbol of cheer and charity, without regard to race, creed, or nationality.

Maybe Moore was a Unitarian without knowing it.

- Christopher Raible

Harvard Square, December 22 —

Christmas next year is only 368 days away, so you had better get started with your plans. Don't put it off until the last minute. Avoid the shopping crunch. Mail your packages early. Above all, catch the Christmas spirit early.

I'm quite serious. The Christmas spirit is too precious to be confined to one season of the year. That puts it too much in the same context of the sabbath day worshiper of whom it was said, "He prayed to God on Sunday and preyed on others the rest of the week." Christmas comes but once a year? Bah! Humbug! Let's have it every day of the year.

Alice said something to me yesterday about how strange it seemed that, during a war, there would often be a truce on Christmas day. If they could do it for one day, she wondered, why couldn't they just keep it going. Precisely the point! Why not? If Christ comes as " the prince of peace," surely we could carry the Christmas spirit of peace throughout the entire year. "Joy to the world" on December 25, but don't you dare bring us joy at any other time. What nonsense.

A while back, in one of those years, when Chrismas came on a Saturday, my sermon the next day was entitled "Christmas is Coming!" In the sermon I suggested that there was no reason to send all those lovely Christmas cards and the wishes they express only in the month of December. How nice it would be to get a Christmas card on the fourth of July. For several summers thereafter, one young man in the church faithfully sent me a Christmas card on July 4. Delightful!

But what about all that harried and hectic shopping for gifts, the rat race because we can never quite make it on time? "We should do that all year?" I hear you saying. "Surely you've got to be kidding!" Well, why not spread that out, too? Even if you give them at Christmas time, why not buy them during the entire year? The gifts I most enjoy are those which someone selected because when they saw something it reminded them of me. I must have thrown away a hundred bottles of after-shave lotion in my lifetime, all purchased because I was on someone's gift list. And in February when you see something that jumps out at you and says, "Uncle Charlie would love me," buy it, take it home, and hide it away. Don't look at it again until you're ready to give it to Uncle Charlie.

There are many benefits to my method. (1) Your gifts will be more personal. (2) If you remember what you have purchased you will have

216

the joy of the anticipation of giving the gift. (3) If you don't remember what you have purchased think how much fun it will be when you go to your cache next December and are surprised by all the goodies you have thoughtfully stashed there during the year. (4) You will avoid the pressure of the crunch-crowd shopping. (5) When you have all those plastic card bills staring you in the face in January, think how nice it will be with my system to have them spread throughout the year.

So here's to a Merry Christmas next year - starting now. Don't delay. December will be here before you know it, and then it will be too late. Do it now!

- Edwin A. Lane

Christmas is a time of many things

Lo, Christmas is a time of many things,
A time of being free and young again,
A time of dreaming dreams we thought were lost
And buried in the past of infancy
With teddy bears and 'lectric trains
And wishing things and thinking not of cost.

Lo, Christmas is a time of many things,
Of sheep and shepherds standing in a field
And list'ning raptly to angelic band,
Of seeing wisemen three with humpty back
Meandering dromedaries bearing gifts
Who swiftly chase a star across the sand.

Lo, Christmas is a time of many things,
Of lads and lassies dressed in blue with drum
And bugles blaring forth on city streets
Or ringing bell and opening doors the while
They hope you'll give a coin or two to bring
To some unlucky child a happy smile.

Lo, Christmas is a time of many things,
Of sugar plums — though what they be I can
Not say — I've only heard of them in song;
Of pumpkin pie and mince and apple, too,
Of turkey legs which parcelled out among
Three kids will always, ever come out wrong.

Lo, Christmas is a time of many things,
Of Christmas trees with ornaments
And lights, and needles dropping fast so that
The rug begins to look like fields of grass,
And Christmas cards with sentimental theme
Or comic snowman in a black top-hat.

Lo, Christmas is a time of many things,
Of Santa Claus, that jolly sprite with sled
And reindeer flying through the winter sky
To children bringing fancy packages
With dolls and bikes, and trikes for little ones,
And things that talk or walk or swim or fly.

Yes, Christmas is a time of many things
Which open doors of joy and happy thoughts
Of pleasures sweet, and long-gone memory,
A magic door that leads us back to dreams
Of hope and peace and faith and love; so put
Aside our cares and celebrate with me.

- Adolph W. Weidanz

KEEPING SANE IN DECEMBER

I send out my annual warning against keeping Christmas, following good New England puritan custom of long ago. Perhaps it's a function of aging, a timidity born of depletion of energy reserves, but I believe the problem of keeping sane thru the December holidays cuts across age-group vitalities and calls for a new conservatism in the life-styles of most of us.

Below are 12 rules to be followed faithfully from now thru New Year's day:

1 — Measure out your drinks in a jigger, and keep track of them, and no sloshing over the rim. You may not stay sober but at least you'll remember who's responsible.

2 — Weigh in every morning, the greatest reality-check invented since flu or jail.

3 — Read Euripides' *The Bacchae,* marvelous aversion-therapy for December disciples or frenzied celebration. (I won't give the plot away, but in one part at a party our hero, in a fit of glee, gets his arms torn out of their sockets by his jubilant mother, much to her later distress, and presumably his.)

4 — Be a good listener for all your friends who will fall apart over the next few weeks.

5 — When you wish people Merry Christmas and Happy New Year look them in the eye.

6 — RSVP to December party invitations with a request for a raincheck in February, a month that needs all the help it can get.

7 — Much of Xmas is a mass of cliches, best broken up by fresh collateral reading, for example, the New Testament accounts of the birth of Christ.

8 — Avoid romantic entanglements during December. They are exhausting. And behind the clandestine candle-glow of the season's affair you will discover that your new saviour is as much a slob as your present husband or wife.

9 — The next time you feel impossibly rushed, late with shopping, worried about money, gifts, sending cards, turn on and tune in Bach's Christmas Oratorio, lie back on the couch and disappoint the drug industry and Freudians everywhere.

10 — Permit some Christmas lighting to go far into the night.

11 — When I was a boy scout we were advised in the official manual to take cold hip baths to prevent sex fom rearing its ugly head. It never worked, so I'm modest about offering counsel to those in inner turmoil, sexual or otherwise. But for those of you who get torn apart by holiday depression or anxiety attacks, I commend long walks, looking at Christmas trees and then home for cocoa. Meantime we pray for shut-in who can't walk out at Christmas and pray that they have devised other techniques for beating the devil, the holiday devil who has a genius for raising hell at the worst possible time.

12 — And last, please don't feel too guilty about violating any of the above rules. Merry Christmas, Happy New Year, and a wink at a star in the night's dark sky.

> \- Clarke Dewey Wells
> from SUNSHINE AND
> RAIN AT ONCE

A CHRISTMAS QUIZ

Some of these questions might be tricky, even misleading, but we'll start with a couple of easy (?) ones:

1. Do all the Gospels have a nativity narrative?

2. How many wise men were there?

3. Where were the shepherds when they first saw the star?

4. When and where did the shepherds and the wise men meet?

5. How did the shepherds find the manger?

6. From what direction did the wise men come?

7. How did the wise men find the manger?

8. By whom was the celebration of Christmas considered a punishable offense?

9. Has Christmas always been our most popular holiday?

10. Was Christmas celebrated by the early church?

11. Do all Christian countries celebrate the day by giving and receiving gifts?

12. Is December 25th the real date of his birth? If not, how come it was picked?

Facts are not always important. There are times when we do not need to know the "facts of the case" in order to have an understanding of what is right and good. A person could know all the answers to these questions and have little understanding of the meaning and beauty of Christmas. Fact-finding boards and committees of investigation are all right in their places but many of our social problems and our difficulties in human relations would yield to application of understanding and compassion. An old proverb is worth recalling, "A handful of common sense is worth a bushel of learning".

ANSWERS

1. No. Neither the first one which was written, Mark, nor the last one to be written, John, have nativity narratives.

2. According to Matthew, "There came wisemen", tradition growing out of the three gifts, aided by carols place the number at three and even give their names: Casper, Melchior, and Balthasar. But if one is to adhere to the Biblical accounts, the number and the names are unknown.

3. The shepherds did not at anytime see the star.

4. They did not meet.

5. The angels gave some indefinite directions.

6. The two Biblical quotations giving clues as to the direction of their travel are contradictory. "There came wisemen from the East". "The star which they saw in the East went before them."

7. The wisemen did not go to the manger. "When they were come into the house" is the Biblical statement.

8. The General Court of Massachusetts forbid its celebration under penalty of the stock.

9. It was not until 1850 that Christmas became a generally accepted holiday.

10. No. His physical birth was considered too carnal a matter for celebration. The early Church fathers concentrated upon his baptism - the epiphany - for emphasis.

11. No. In some countries Christmas is a day for special religious observances. New Years is the time for gift giving.

12. Van der Staart Smit, a Catholic scholar whose book received the official nihil obstat, states that the birth took place in August in a grotto. In 601 Pope Gregory set the technique of the Church in dealing with established celebrations.
"Let the shrines of the idols by no means be destroyed . . .
  that the people not seeing their temples destroyed may
  displace error and recognize and adore the true God . . . .
  some celebration should be given in exchange".

Pope Gregory's announcement sealed what was becoming a general custom anyway that the mid-winter festival of the solstice be celebrated as Christmas. What is the point in knowing these oddities and discrepancies about Christmas? We need to know, if we are to make Christmas real, that it is not dependent upon a fact, not an event, not upon an accumulation of custom. Christmas celebrates a need - a real human need. We need to pause in our activity long enough to know that activity without yearning is, as we actually describe it, a rat race. We need to celebrate that transforming birth of hope, joy, and goodwill. We need to break ourselves wide open - giving new birth to all that is in us - responding with budget-stretching generosity and heart-bursting compassion.

- John E. Wood

Christmas Eve At Hull's Cove

Christmas Eve, after eons of waiting and ages of suspense, arrived at last. Invariably it came in calm — windless, certainly cold, but somehow expectant and waiting. There was a pervasive hush, a more than usual stillness. Church, of course, came first. The Christ-child, behind all this yet disassociated from it, must needs be remembered and revered. He expected this, and it seemed reasonable that He do so. God did likewise. Mary and Joseph, and the shepherds, were also deeply involved this night — in fact, the very stillness seemed to bespeak a re-enactment of their arrival in Bethlehem, their search for shelter, and later, the birth in the stable . . .

The going through the door of the church was the best. At any other time of the year, this was a bare austere place. Granite-faced outside, beige-walled and oaken of woodwork within, it was the plainest among the plainer houses of God's worship. Its high, vaulted ceiling had only the barest of varnished roof timbers and crossbeams. Its pews were uncushioned, its kneelers likewise. There were one or two stained glass windows — the one concession to color — but otherwise, only flat, opaque panes. The floors were devoid of carpet. The altar and chancel, gothic in pattern were of the simplest imaginable oak. The eight hanging lamps, converted from oil years before, were of curlecued black wrought-metal . . .

But now! From the doorway, as one first opened it, there burst a wall of evergreen perfume, almost tactile and just short of visible in its intensity and power. Intoxication and resinous, this was a furnace-warmed mix of cedar, ground-pine, spruce and hemlock — clean, pure and sharp. And what garlands of cedar had been looped! From each lamp, great foldup bells of red paper had been hung. More garlands outlined the windows, and in the center of each a beribboned wreath of hemlock and groundpine had been placed. A great frame with three archways had been placed across the chancel and this too dressed in garlands and wreaths.

Even the organ sounded better. Usually reedy and shrill, my brother Lester contrived to make it sound deeper, more substantial, and more dignified as he pedalled away and labored over the keys. It was a transformed and transfigured place now, this church — a place of surpassing and almost painful beauty. Crowded to overflowing, it seemed so right that everyone should be here. It seemed divinely ordained that these mases of evergreen should embrace this place with their fullness and fragrance, and these wondrous lights should glow so exquisitely. Surely this tree, so handsomely clad, was not here by any human forethought. And when over a hundred voices were joined, strong and brave, in "It Came Upon the Midnight Clear," there could not have been a more totally honest or wholesome expression of peace

223

and joy anywhere that seemed more in focus or nearer at hand, and the world was never so right . . .

It was a happy time, this. These uncomplicated, rather rustic people, were quietly reverent here . . . Even those who never entered this church at other times of the year — and there were many — caught here on Christmas Eve a sense of renewed relationship with forces larger than, and beyond, the self. They held this newly-formed identity in their hands for a moment and took comfort from it, knowing a whole year would pass before they would discover it again. They sensed here a promise of hope for humankind and for themselves as human beings. They again found faith in human goodness and worth, and looked upon one another with a clearer and more appeciative eye. They realigned themselves with the old traditions, and drew warmth and joy from being here together, once more. They remembered other Christmases, long past, and loved ones who were gone. Many were moved. A peace and a new resolve came to them in this green-hung, glowing room, filled their hearts, and went with them into the night . . . .

- C. William Chilman

But I still like Christmas

I don't like green apples any more. I used to. I also liked Saturday afternoon movies, collecting match folders, saving tinfoil, playing kick-the-can, gathering horse chestnuts, picking up old spikes along the railroad track, and eating mustard sandwiches. I have no desire to do these things any more. I have outgrown them. I have outgrown so many things!

Happily, there is much I have not outgrown. I still get pleasure both immediate and nostalgic from the acrid odor of beech trees on warm spring days, from the heavy sweetness of a field of buckwheat in blossom, the subtle smell of clean-sawn pine boards, and the saw-sound of a cicada. I still fly kites, make snowballs, catch falling leaves, and read the Sunday comics. I still take delight in knocking down icicles or apples. And I have not outgrown Christmas.

My growing up was in a gabled, turreted, antebellum house in an upstate village cupped in a valley in the high wooded foothills of the Appalachians. It was a village supported by a few small industries that had not yet caused pollution. It was a time when cars were as scarce as money. Kids could play safely in the streets or use vacant lots for games that were one-quarter play and three-quarters argument.

Those were the days before we became affluent and lost the advantages of respectable poverty. It was the time and setting for the perfect picture-card type of Christmas with lots of snow, good cheer, gifts, and jingling bells.

But the waiting! The last leaves, so easily fallen, had been so tediously raked, the last hickory nuts gathered and Indian summer days frozen to drab emptiness before the lasting snow.

Christmas had become a selfish obsession and an elevating dream. In anticipation it was greedier than a birthday, freer than the last day of school, more exciting than the Fourth of July, more loving than Mothers' Day, more delicious than Thanksgiving, and more reverent than Memorial Day. Anticipation gained momentum as the magic month dragged on.

Finally, it arrived in an avalanche of sheer delight. There was the tree, each year "the most beautiful one we've ever had," with ornaments as fragile as memories. And the candy! — warty peanut brittle and mouth-drying peanut-butter fudge, airy divinity and ribbon candy that cut your gums, tooth-locking taffy and stuffed dates that dried out because no one ever ate them. There was the gleam of tinsel and the annual disappointment of those black rubber boots with red tops given by a practical aunt. There was the ever-new sameness of sight and sound and taste that I have not outgrown to this day.

I still hang up my stocking for Santa to fill, though now I know who Santa is. I still want snow for Christmas, and the tinsel trimming is just as beautiful as ever. I have seen Christmas plays performed so many times I almost know the lines. And I like it! Now the trees are not so big, the ornaments so old nor the anticipation quite so magical, but I've never grown too big for Christmas.

- Max Coots

A Personal Reminiscence

I well remember the first Christmas after I became a Unitarian - or perhaps I should say, after I knew I was a Unitarian and acknowledged that fact. It was a time of strangely conflicting feelings. On the one hand, here was a time of festivity, well-nigh universal festivity. One could hardly take kindly to assuming the role of Scrooge and declaring all this to be humbug. One wanted to join in, to be caught up in the spirit of the season. And yet, at the same time, there were the demands of intellectual integrity to be met. The conventional celebrations of Christmas were bound up with theological schemes and pseudohistorical events to which one could no longer give one's assent.

How could one sing about "God and sinners reconciled" if one no longer believed in the scheme of thought which presented Jesus Christ as a unique mediator and saviour? How could one sing about "yon virgin mother and child" if one did not believe the traditional teaching that Jesus had indeed been born of a virgin? How could one sing about choirs of angels if one didn't really believe in angels at all? How could one avoid being a hypocrite without being a spoilsport? These were very real questions; I was not very old at the time and was in any case passing through the teen-age stage of rebellion against the established and traditional way of looking at things.

And so I was a little unhappy and bewildered, perhaps also a little cynical. I made uneasy compromises and got through the season as best I could. I was not very impressed by the efforts of some Unitarians I had met to make the observance a satisfactory one from their point of view by altering a word here and there in the traditional songs and affirmations. However liberal-minded they may have been, they were also literal-minded, "The word made flesh is here made word again," wrote Edwin Muir of his Calvinistic forbears, and Unitarianism had not altogether outgrown this aspect of its Calvinistic ancestry. I myself had certainly not outgrown literal-mindedness at this stage of my religious evolution, but it was still more than one or two particular words that I took issue with. It was the whole pattern of thought they expressed. To the question asked by friends and relatives, "How can Unitarians celebrated Christmas?" I could find no satisfactory answer. Perhaps it was true that Unitarians should join with Jehovah's Witnesses and Christadelphians in refusing to mark Christmas at all.

All that now seems a long time ago. I can honestly say that each Christmas since then has meant more to me than the one before, and I am sure that they have meant more than ever they could have done had I tried to remain within the bounds laid down in the church of my upbringing. It may seem strange to claim that Christmas can mean more to someone not bound down to an exclusive dependence upon the Christian tradition. Yet this is exactly what I do claim.

Why? Because the response of a Unitarian Universalist to the season can include the whole range of its meaning, not confining itself to the one narrow emphasis to be found in the traditional churches. A universal religious festival such as this must appeal to anyone who wants to be inclusive in outlook and sympathy.

- Phillip Hewett

The *Christkind* in Manhattan

As the great day approached, the family gathered at my grandfather's house on Riverside Drive in an atmosphere fragrant with mystery.

The gloomily formal, brocaded, petit-pointed parlor on the second floor was the center of attraction for us children. Heavy curtains had been drawn across the arched doorway. The secrecy was so complete that we never caught so much as an advance glimpse of the tree, which had been smuggled in before our arrival.

Grownups wearing conspiratorial smiles carried packages and cartons through the curtains, but even when there were no sounds of backstage voices or footsteps, we sensed a mysterious presence behind the silent folds. Who was it? Santa Claus? One of his brownie helpers? Kris Kringle? The *Christkind?* The Ghost of Christmas Past? We did not know.

By the afternoon of the twenty-fourth, the tension had become so unbearable that my brother and I were sent to a matinee on Broadway. It was dark when we returned. We bathed, changed into pajamas and bathrobes, and ate our supper on trays in the fifth floor bedroom. Then we waited.

I remember the view from the window overlooking the drive one snowy Christmas Eve. The gently falling flakes flashed white in the glare of street lamps and automobile headlights. Across the Hudson, the yellow bulbs of the Linit sign spelled out their flickering message: THE TIME NOW IS: A moment of blackness, 5:27. At 5:30 exactly, we heard the ringing of the little dinner bell that was the signal.

We thundered down three flights of stairs to where the grownups waited. The curtains had been drawn aside, and the room was in darkness except for the treelights glowing softly in the deep green of the branches. From its place of honor at the top of the tree, the old-fashioned *Christkind* gazed wistfully down at us, while my grandfather, with a smile, a mustache, and a baritone voice that made him seem the embodiment of Santa Claus, led the family, twelve to fifteen strong, in a chorus of "Tannenbaum."

My enchantment was complete, but I never quite succeeded in resolving the dualism between Santa Claus and the *Christkind.* Even after I had learned that *Christkind* meant, literally, "Christ child." It seemed rather, a half-pagan sprite, and elfin Christmas fairy — winged, delicate, beautiful, hovering like a Germanic version of Peter Pan high above the manger, while the dazzling star of Bethlehem on its forehead lighted the night sky.

- Peter B. Putnam

228

Memories of Christmas' Past

Let me drift back in memory and tell you what Christmas meant to me as a child. I don't remember much about going to church then. We listened to a lot of Christmas music, really religious Christmas music, in addition to ''Santa Claus Is Coming'' and that kind of thing. But, I never raced areound any church decorating the tree and laughing, and feeling a part of a group of people in a church who all were friendly with each other.

What we did have was a lot of family and friends and Christmas rituals — many of which I've forgotten and I need to be reminded of them by my older brothers and sisters.

Of first importance was the tree and we would go out to several lots of trees to find the very best one. At least, it looked that way. We probably had only $4 to $6 to spend for the tree and we had to look a long time to get the best our money could buy. One year, my brother, Bill, got a job and decided we would have the finest tree we never could afford — one that cost well over $10. He paid for it himself and so he got to pick it out — a beautiful blue spruce with a heavenly aroma. We were all exceedingly pleased with Bill and happy for him, too, because he was so proud of the tree and having bought it himself. It would have been perfect, except that the fragrance eventually overpowered him. Bill became allergic to the tree. I don't know if we got the tree right out the day after Christmas, or if we just kept Bill down in the coal cellar for the holidays. But I'll never forget that tree.

We had lights and ornaments that had been in the family for many years. Each year it was a joy to open them again, to unwrap these old friends, and restore them to their annual place in our lives. There were tiny houses made in Czechoslovakia, delicate glass birds with feathery tails that we had to pull from inside the body, and a Santa Claus coming out a chimney that we put on the top branches of the tree. I remember the days when we had soft lead icicles, not the kind that slice your fingers with their sharp edges. We used the same icicles year after year, carefully wrapping and unwrapping them to make them last. One night my sister called me to look at the tree lying down. We slid under the tree, as close to the trunk as we could, and looked up through the branches and lights to the ceiling. I was always fantasizing about strange and enchanted worlds. This was another. Of more practical value was the necessity to carefully move all the presents, unwind the sheet, and pour more water into the dish beneath the tree. It was a ritual, but almost as common as doing the dishes or taking out the trash.

On the front pages of the newspaper in December in the early 1940s you could read about the war, and the cities that were being

229

bombed. But, there were also long stories about Santa Claus, about goblins and elves and dwarves. Consequently, I went for the front section of the paper and would read those stories as if they were more real than the war, and for me, perhaps they were.

On Christmas Eve, we lit some old, ivory-colored candles, one in each window. We hung our stockings and knew there would be the inevitable tangerine in them in the morning. It didn't matter that we had crates of fruit every Christmas sent to my father by salesmen who hoped his company would do business with them. Despite the dozens of tangerines stored elsewhere in the house, and the tangerines we had been eating for the past two weeks, that tangerine in the stocking was somehow ours, more precious, something to be peeled with deep appreciation. We could open one present on Christmas Eve. I chose very, very carefully. There was nothing more disappointing then than to open a package and find that your Christmas Eve gift was three pairs of underpants, or four sets of socks. However much I might have needed clothes, I hated to get them when I might have gotten toys or games. I could never understand why I had to have new clothes at Christmas!

Once I was given a hatchet, a metal hatchet. Someone really slipped up and I was dizzy with excitement. And once, I was given a drum. Adults don't make mistakes like that very often. I cherished those gifts. In fact, I think I broke the drum before the month was out. At least, I think I was the one who broke the drum. One year I was given a crystal radio set before I even knew what a wireless was all about. It was a terrible gift. It took a couple of days for my older brothers to put it together and then it didn't work. It was the most special gift I received that year (as far as my parents were concerned). And, though I never understood it, and it never worked , I didn't get any replacement. But, that's O.K. Sometimes, as a kid, I was able to buy presents for other people and would watch their blank stares as they opened my gift to them and tried to figure out why I had gotten it and how to look grateful. It takes a while to learn what and how to give. Chalk it up to experience. My most prized treasure was a stuffed Jiminy Cricket, you remember, that was Pinocchio's conscience. Whether they thought I needed a conscience, or simply knew how much Pinocchio and Jiminy Cricket meant to me, I don't know. But, over the years, after much dragging around, Jiminy Cricket went the way of all stuffed toys, shabby, germ-laden, and battered with age, slipped out of the house by a stealthy adult. I hope he was given a decent burial.

One last thought about my Christmases. I told you that every year my father was given crates of fruits from Florida by salesmen. My father was then a purchasing agent for a large textile mill. He was also given pens and calendars and bottles of whiskey he seldom drank, but which he shared with friends. It was obvious to everyone but my father that these were gifts sent to encourage him to buy the goods of the company they represented. He, however, took it personally. He seemed pleased beyond measure that these friends thought so much of him to send these gifts. Giving to others was, to him, simply a precious and wonderful thing to do. It did not create obligation. It simply enhanced and deepened friendship. He was wrong, naive, and deluded. But, that is what the spirit of Christmas is all about. And, strangely enough, long after my father was retired from business, in no position to help anyone, the salesmen sent cards, occasional gifts, visited, and kept faith with him. On a very deep level. something was more right than wrong with my father's thinking. And, I think that is also true of Christmas.

- Glen H. Turner

VIII. A rejoicing
of the human spirit

Christmas is not a theology;
it is a rejoicing of the human spirit.
It is an accumulation of all the traditions
of hope and gladness from many cultures.
Russell Bletzer

If there were no Advent, we would need to invent it. We human creatures, in spite of all that has happened to us and been done by us, are still hopeful. Something new, something vital, something promising is always coming, and we are always expecting. Thus in Advent candles are lighted to mark the time of preparation, and with each new light our anticipation grows — as it should. We are, after all, a hopeful people, and that hopefulness deserves a festival.

Advent is a time of anticipation and as long as we expect, as long as we hope, someone will light a candle against the prevailing darkness — and neither the winds of hate nor the gales of evil will extinguish it.

- John A. Taylor

Although the nativity or birth of Jesus is the first major holy day of the church year, the year does not begin with Christmas but with the period of preparation — the Advent season. Advent Sunday, the first of four, is the Sunday nearest to the feast of St. Andrew, November 30, and may fall upon any date from November 27 to December 3 inclusively.

The word Advent, meaning "coming," was originally used for the coming of the Christ, and applied to the day of birth only. After the sixth century, its meaning was expanded to include the whole preparatory season in the sense the word is used now. The Advent season marks the beginning of the ecclesiastical year. The orthodox church year is based on the incidents in the life of Jesus with the three great feasts, Christmas, Easter, and Pentecost or Whitsunday, forming the framework of the Christian year. These great feasts of the church are preceded by a period of preparation to enable individuals to meditate and become aware of the significance and spiritual values of the events in the life of Jesus which these feast commemorate.

Advent cannot have for liberals the meaning the season holds for more traditional Christians but it can provide families with an opportunity to become aware of the significance and spiritual values inherent in the winter festival season for them. During this season families can become acquainted with the many Christmas legends, customs, and

235

traditions of our heritage and discover those which are particularly meaningful to them. Out of such experiences come the special family observances so dear to each member of the family and yet so unifying in the effect.

- "Winter Festival and Celebrations" Church of the Larger Fellowship

The Advent Wreath

History

No one knows for sure, but it is a good guess that the Advent Wreath had its beginnings in the pagan fire wheel. The closed circle, wheel, or wreath is symbolic of eternity, and was used by the Christians to symbolize the everlasting flow of time, or a world without end.

The use of an Advent Wreath originated a few hundred years ago among Lutherans in Germany. Made of evergreens, it is either suspended from the ceiling or placed on a table. Fastened to the wreath are holders for four candles representing the four weeks of Advent. On the first Sunday of Advent one candle is lighted and allowed to burn during a ceremony of readings, prayers, and songs. On each succeeding Sunday an additional candle is lighted at the beginning of the service until the fourth Sunday when all are set aglow. On that day, some families light a large candle in the center of the wreath to symbolize Christ, the Light of the World.

Its Traditional Meaning

The Advent wreath is made from greens because they symbolize life. Four candles are said to represent to some the 4000 years of waiting for the birth of a Christ. A purple ribbon is used to decorate the wreath. The coming of Jesus was to Christians the coming of their King, thus the royal color of purple.

Since Jesus was hailed as "the light of the world," lighted candles are most appropriate. Three of the candles are purple (these are sometimes known as the penitential candles). The fourth one is pink, and is traditionally lighted on the fourth Sunday, which is called "Gaudete" or the joyful Sunday of Advent.

Making An Advent Wreath

It is possible to purchase advent wreath frames at most floral supply retailers. They are inexpensive and come complete with candle sockets. The Will and Baumer Candle Co., Inc., Syracuse, N.Y., has provided the following directions for making one:

1. Cross two 12" to 15" flat wood sticks and nail at center.

2. About an inch from each tip nail a candle socket. (Make sockets from 2½'' to 3'' diameter tin can covers. Mark a penny-sized circle in center of each. Snip 6 equally spaced straight cuts from the outer edge of cover to this circle, then bend up every other section to form candle well.

3. Enclose with a hoop or two of coat hanger wire stapled at the ends of the wood strips. Cover the wood that shows in the center of the wreath with aluminum foil.

4. Tie or wire small clusters of evergreen branches laurel, cedar, pine, holly or whatever is readily available to the wire circle. Decorate with purple ribbon.

5. Insert 3 purple candles and one pink in the sockets. Paper collars may be dropped down on candles to protect greens from wax.

Following the last Sunday of Advent, the candles and ribbons may be changed to white for the rest of the Christmas season.

The Advent Wreath at Home

The traditional ceremony is very simple. It takes place on Saturday evenings preceding the four Sundays of Advent. On the first night the wreath is blessed by the head of the household. One purple candle is then lighted and a simple prayer said. Each night of that week the youngest child relights the one candle, which burns throughout the evening meal.

For the second week, the first and second candles are lighted each night by the eldest child, and both burn throughout the meal as before.

During the third week the mother lights the pink as well as the two purple candles, and for the fourth week, the father lights all four candles in proper sequence, each night. Prior to each lighting a prayer is said.

"Let's light an advent candle
A symbol that we care
For those within our family
And all people everywhere."

There is a tale which might even be true that our Advent candle lights began many years ago in a small German village. The people in the village were much too busy with their daily work and lives and the extra burden of preparation for Christmas day so that the season actually menat nothing but labor and distress and Christmas day itself was lost in exhaustion and even resentment.

So the mayor set aside one week for thinking about the meaning of Christmas long before the day itself. The first week the mayor lit a candle to encourage the people to think about the meaning of Christmas. The second week he lit a second candle to encourage the people to do something to further the ideas of Christmas which they had been entertaining. The third week he suggested they now give gifts to somebody other than themselves and their friends in order to make valid and beautiful the thoughts they had been thinking and the things they had been doing. In this way, when they lit the fourth candle on the Sunday before Christmas, they could have great joy within their hearts and within their families and among their friends.

-Duncan Littlefair

A RESPONSIVE READING FOR ADVENT

This is the Christmas season and we are gathered in our church to celebrate the time of the birth of Jesus. For hundreds and hundreds of years all over the world people have gathered in churches and houses of all kinds, indoors and outdoors, to celebrate the birth of Jesus and the glorious Christmas season.

> WE CELEBRATE THE BIRTH OF JESUS AND ALL THAT IT MEANS IN MORE WAYS THAN WE CAN TELL. WE CELEBRATE WITH SONGS AND POEMS AND STORIES AND GIFTS AND PRAYERS.

Our hearts are full of gratitude for all the good and wonderful things we know. We have so many feelings that we cannot expres them all — even in all the ways of Christmas.

> AND SO AT THE CHRISTMAS SEASON WE LIGHT THE ADVENT CANDLES TO SAY ALL THE THINGS WE CANNOT SAY AND TO EXPRESS ALL THE HOPE AND JOY WE FEEL BUT CANNOT DESCRIBE.

Let the first candle we light be the candle of faith, and let it stand for our faith in ourselves and our children and for the good that is in all people. Let it stand for our faith in humanity and our faith in the eternal goodness of God.

> LET THE SECOND CANDLE BE THE CANDLE OF HOPE AND LET IT STAND FOR ALL THE IDEALS AND ASPIRATIONS THAT HAVE GIVEN LIGHT TO PEOPLE IN TIMES OF DARKNESS AND GIVEN STRENGTH AND COURAGE TO US AND ALL PEOPLE IN TIMES OF TROUBLE AND DEFEAT.

Let the third candle be the candle of love. Let it stand for all the tenderness, kindness, affection, forgiveness and glory that we have ever known and still have hopes to know.

> LET THE FOURTH CANDLE BE THE CANDLE OF JOY AND LET IT STAND FOR ALL THE FAITH AND HOPE AND LOVE THAT IS IN US AND WILL BE IN THE LIVES OF OUR CHILDREN. LET THIS CANDLE STAND FOR ALL THE WONDERS UNTOLD OF CHRISTMAS FOR THROUGH SUCH JOY WE SEE THE GLORY OF GOD AND FIND PEACE IN OUR HEARTS AND IN THE WORLD.

- Duncan Littlefair

Small Talk (A talk with the children)
  Lighting the Advent Wreath

Leader: Many times we gather in a circle and place a single candle on a table. Each of us have our own candle. We talk about how the word *light* has different meanings in our lives. It can mean heat, warmth, a beacon for direction; it can mean truth, knowledge, peace or even courage.

After talking about the meaning of light we quietly step forward, one by one to light our candles from the one, single candle. Then we stand for a few moments being very quiet. We try to think about what our candle means for each of us. We try to think of ways it can be a beacon for others in the ways we live our lives.

We all like to see candles burning. Their soft, warm glow gives light to a room in a quiet kind of way. They make us glad that we are indoors and not out in the cold, windy, even wintry night. They can signify that we are happy to be with our families and our friends whom we love and we know love us.

Before you, you see a Christmas wreath with five candles. We call it The Advent Wreath. The word *advent* means "to come". It has always been a pre-Christmas celebration leading up to Christmas itself. It is a time of preparation, of getting ready to celebrate the birth of Jesus. It is also a time of excitement, of expectation, and of learning.

In this service we begin the season of Advent by lighting the first of the five candles on this wreath. Each Sunday through the Christmas season, right up until Christmas Eve and our Candlelight Service, we will light another candle.

These candles on the wreath seem to show how the light in our lives gets brighter as we approach Christmas. Some say that when Jesus was born, "he brought light into the world." He also brought a new way of thinking about things and a new way of sharing and giving. So, we light the candles at Advent to show that the light we make can warm even the darkness of winter and even of the lives of others around us - through the love and the care we show them. "O Little

Town of Bethlehem'' is one of the oldest and most familiar Christmas carols. Let us join in singing it as the candle is lighted.

(As the carol is sung, one child comes forward to light the first candle on the Advent Wreath.)

Leader: Candle, candle,
           burning bright
           on our window
           sill tonight,
           like the shining
           Christmas star
           guiding shepherds
           from afar,
           lead some weary
           travelers here,
           that they may share
           our Christmas cheer.''

                              - Isabel Shaw

Solo or Musical Selection

Closing Words: May the light of this first candle of
                  Advent warm our hearts this day and
                  in the weeks to come. As the candles
                  burn brighter and brighter, may we
                  too, send our light to all who come our way. Amen
                            - Jan Vickery Knost

Hanukkah (Chanukah, Hannukah — it's all phonetic so you takes your choice) comes early enough some years to resist being mixed with Christmas in a well-intentioned but unhistorical spiritual blender. Often it falls so close to Christmas, or, depending on your point of view, Christmas to it, that the urge is irresistible, particularly in UU churches and suburban public schools, to mingle them in awkward, contrived ways. The candles of Christmas and Hanukkah throw independent glows, both warming enough to be celebrated according to their separate integrity.

What the two have in common is a numbered day. Hanukkah's eight days begin on the twenty-fifth of Kislev, third month of the Jewish lunar and solar year. Christmas occurs on the twenty-fifth of December, twelfth month of Pope Gregory XIII's "New Style" calendar. The digits are an interesting coincidence but nothing more. In the Gregorian calendar, Hanukkah and Easter, for similar astral reasons, are moveable feasts. Get it? If not, I'm sorry. Space forbids explaining. To complicate matters further, Yule is something else, fused now beyond extrication with the birth of Jesus.

We celebrate Noel and Yuletide by the best glow that illumines our Unitarian Universalist souls.

We honor Hanukkah, Feast of Lights, in terms of its intrinsic message — dedication to liberty of conscience, freedom of worship, justice, and human rights.

Hanukkah candles will be kindled, songs sung, and words spoken: links between heroisms of the past and reminders of how we in significant ways nurture the human spirit by serving one another.

- Jack Mendelsohn

Hanukkah is often abused by our programs which lump it together with Solstice, Christmas, Divali, and other mid-winter festivals. This is an inaccurate representation. Although it does, way back in unrecorded history, have roots in a mid-winter celebration, by the time of the Maccabees these roots had long died. There are many seasonal and agricultural celebrations in the Jewish calendar. This is *not* one of them.

It was a feast of the re-dediction of the great Temple in Jerusalem to which all Israelites looked for the support of their faith. The events of the Hanukkah story climaxed on that celebration - the search for oil that resulted in the miracle, was a search for the proper cermonial objects to celebrate this traditional festival.

Hanukkah was not celebrated in its present form until well into the Christian era. *Jesus did not play with dreydls!* It is a celebration of freedom from oppression - from the Greeks, and by extension, from all who would try to conquer and enslave. It is all right to include it in a festival of lights program, as long as this distinction is made clear. Not *all* candles represent the sun.

- Mary-Lib Whitney

I am the Hanukkah-Christmas Spirit
That comes with the end of December:
A winter-solstice spell, perhaps,
When people forget to remember —

The drab realities of fact,
The cherished hurt of ancient wrongs,
The lonely comfort of being deaf
To human sighs and angels'songs.

Suddenly, they lose their minds
To heart's demands and beauty's grace;
And deeds extravagant with love
Give glory to the commonplace.

-Anthony F. Perrino

Hanukkah - A Unitarian Universalist Version

About 2150 years ago, Palestine was under the rule of the Syrian Empire. Judah the Maccabee led a revolt against the Syrians. He had a small band of followers which could not confront the Syrian military in conventional warfare, so he used the unusual tactics of guerilla warfare and was successful.

It was largely a fight for religious freedom. The temples of the Jewish people had been desecrated. They were forced to worship Greek gods, to sacrifice what was to them the most unclean of animals (swine), and were forbidden to circumcise their male children.

When Judah defeated the Syrians and re-entered Jerusalem, he ordered the temple cleansed and rededicated. This involved rekindling the eternal flame. Sacred oil had to be prepared as fuel for the flame. But, it would take eight days to prepare the oil.

According to the tradition, a small amount of sacred oil, sufficient for one day, was found hidden in the temple. So the lamp was kindled and, miraculously, it continued to burn for eight days — long enough for a new supply of oil to be prepared. So it is, that the Hanukkah candles are kindled, an additional candle each night, for eight nights. This morning we observe Hanukkah with an adaptation of the traditional Hanukkah candle-lighting.

We begin by lighting the servant candle. It is called the "shamus," which means "to serve." Shamus is the term for one who serves as the sexton in a synagogue and, in popular language, for one who serves you as a private-eye.

As one candle may kindle many others and yet lose none of its own light, so may our religious exploration kindle the light of truth for many people in many times and places. (Light the candles from your left to your right as you face the Menorah.)

The first light is for the first cause, the ultimate ground of existence, the source of our highest values, that which gives meaning to our lives.

The second light is the light of great religious teachers and great scriptures from many lands and many traditions, which illuminate our paths as we search for truth and meaning in our lives.

The third light is the light of justice. No nation can long endure which is unjust to the weak. "Justice, always justice shalt thou pursue," was the teaching of Moses.

The fourth light is the light of mercy. Cruelty hardens our hearts and destroys relationships. "Do justice and love mercy," was the teaching of Micah the prophet.

The fifth light is the light of holiness. When we intentionally live so as to maintain a sense of wonder and respect and act in accordance with those qualities, we can make all of life sacred.

The sixth light is the light of love. "Love does not consist in gazing at each other, but in looking outward together in the same direction. There is no comradeship except through union in the same high effort," wrote the modern-day prophet, Antoine de Sainte-Exupery.

The seventh light is the calm light of patience. Nothing can be achieved in haste. "It is idle, having planted an acorn in the morning, to expect that afternoon to sit in the shade of the oak," wrote Sainte-Exupery.

The eighth light is the light of courage. As Moses said to Joshua, "Be strong and of good courage."

- Paul L'Herrou

The Hanukkah Story

The Christian Festival of Christmas nearly coincides with the Jewish Festival of Hanukkah. Hanukkah is a Festival of Lights. It is the Jewish celebration of religious feedom. In 165 B.C., Judas Maccabeas overcame the Greco-Syrian armies under the leadership of Antiochus IV, who were occupying Palestine. One of the Maccabees' first acts after reconquering Palestine was to rededicate the Temple, particularly the new altar. Their feast of dedication lasted eight days. On the first day, only one candle was lit; on the second, two. On the eighth day, eight candles were lit. This morning we shall light all eight, and, as in the Jewish custom, we light each candle with a special thought.

The first we light in memory of the dedication and the courage of the Maccabees who gave their lives for freedom.

The second we light conscious of the precious gift of family.

The third we light to rededicate ourselves to the study of our traditions, knowing that learning and understanding secures our freedom.

The fourth we light remembering that only through hope is our life illumined and made creative.

The fifth we light with the pledge to share our wealth with those in this world who are starving, who are oppressed, who are sick, who are afflicted by prejudice.

The sixth we light in rededication to the ancient task of securing religious freedom in our world.

The seventh we light in the cause of respect for our fellow human beings in all corners of the globe, in the cause of brotherhood and sisterhood.

The eighth we light in rededication to the search for meaning and the quest for a full life. We trust that throughout the coming year, we may constantly strive for the ideals of freedom, charity, family, study, hope, and fellowship.

May we rise and sing the traditional Hanukkah Hymn, Rock of Ages, HCL #279.

- Will Saunders

246

Hanukkah Celebration — Opening Words and Candlelighting
Ceremony

In the time of darkness, when day gives way to night and mighty
conquerers stride the land demanding that men and women bow down
before the powers of evil, some there be who curse the day they were
born and bow the knee rather than strive for the right. Others know
that the dawn always follows the blackest night, and they seek to find
the slim rays of light that might be a beacon of hope, a sign of the
approaching day.

It is no mere coincidence that so many ot the world's peoples
have chosen the darkest time of the year to observe their celebrations
of light and life. It is a testament to the enduring strength and vision of
the human race that rather than curse the darkness, time and again
some men and women have chosen to light a candle that a way might
be found out of tyranny and oppression and the chill bleakness of the
cold season of the year.

So have we gathered this day in this season of almost winter to
mark the great Jewish festival of Hannukkah, that we might join with
the people of the ages in celebrating our faith that in the world light
does triumph over darkness, good does conquer evil, right does make
might. As Unitarian Universalists we are proud to share in the ancient
tradition of the lighting of candles as a symbol of the light that guides
us through the darkness.

Each candle represents a special light of meaning for us. It is
good that we have come here this day to be reminded of the things that
brighten our lives and give us the sustenance we need to carry on —
however hard the struggle may be, however bleak our circumstances,
however dark the night that wraps its mantle around us.

(Members of the congregation light the candles at the appropriate place, the eight having been chosen to represent different
ages/stages of life from the youngest possible to the oldest member of
the congregation - the shammas or servant candle, in the center of the
Menorah, is lit by the minister at the start of this section of the
ceremony.)

The first candle symbolizes the light of joy, the fact of happiness
that can come with sudden sweetness into our lives and destroy the
gloom that has surrounded us. It reminds us of other times and other
places when men and women have been sunk in ine deepest pits of

247

earthly hell, and yet have retained a sense of wonder at the world, a feeling that at the very heart of the universe there is great gladness.

(Candlelighter):WE LIGHT THIS CANDLE THAT WE MIGHT REMEMBER THE PLACE OF JOY IN OUR LIVES.

The second candle symbolizes the light of truth, the fact that it is possible for us to know the ways and workings of the world in which we live, the fact that we are meant to comprehend things, and that only as we apply our minds to the fullest measure can we understand and by that understanding live fuller, richer lives.

(Candlelighter): WE LIGHT THIS CANDLE THAT WE MIGHT REMEMBER THE IMPORTANCE OF WISDOM AND UNDERSTANDING.

The third candle symbolizes the light of morality, the fact that we do not live in a completely capricious world, but in one in which there are standards of right and wrong that we can know and follow. The light of morality tells us that it is wrong to abuse other people, wrong to sell out to evil for the sake of comfort or security, but right to hold fast to principles of justice and truth for these are the surest realities that can be found.

(Candlelighter): WE LIGHT THIS CANDLE THAT WE MIGHT REMEMBER THE POWER OF MORAL ACTION.

The fourth candle symbolizes the light of courage, the fact that there are times in life when a special strength is needed to persevere in the face of overwhelming odds, moments when only deep reserves of courage enable us to persist in the face of pain and enormous difficulty. Thoreau once said that most people lead lives of quiet desperation. If that be true, then it is even more true to say that most people lead lives of quiet courage as well.

(Candlelighter): WE LIGHT THIS CANDLE THAT WE MIGHT REMEMBER THE NOBILITY OF COURAGE.

The fifth candle symbolizes the light of freedom, that blazing passion within the breasts of men and women down through the centuries that has declared to the world that we are and of right and ought to be free creatures able to direct our own destiny. Freedom demands a constant vigilance against those who would tyrannize and enslave us; it is not for the weak and faint-hearted. Freedom is no easy thing, but part of the peculiar nobility of the human animal, the best way we know of living.

(Candlelighter): WE LIGHT THIS CANDLE THAT WE MIGHT REMEMBER THE DREAM OF FREEDOM.

The sixth candle symbolizes the light of faith, that eternal sense of trust in life itself that enables us to move forward into great challenges, that gives us the strength we need to carry on during times of woe and weakness, that unspoken assumption that ultimately the universe is a good place. as Reinhold Neibuhr taught us, because nothing we do, nothing that is beautiful or true or good, nothing that is ugly or harmful or mystifying, because nothing makes complete sense in any of the immediate contexts of our lives, it is faith alone that saves us and gives our lives an aura of meaningfulness and purpose.

(Candlelighter):WE LIGHT THIS CANDLE THAT WE MIGHT REMEMBER THE STRENGTH IN FAITH.

The seventh candle symbolizes the light of hope, the bright beacon that continues to shine in the midst of the blackest night of discouragement as a far distant vision of life as it might be, that which draws us on in our efforts to make the world better. For the small goals of life hope is not needed, but if our sights are set on grand and glorious things like peace and justice, it is hope that will keep us to the task of working to make these ideals real.

(Candlelighter): WE LIGHT THIS CANDLE THAT WE MIGHT REMEMBER THE VISION OF HOPE.

The eighth candle symbolizes the light of love, without which our lives would dissolve into nightmares of violence and hatred, competition and selfishness. Love is at the center of everything that is good and worthwhile. Love is the reason for every question we ask and the root of every answer we desire. Only as we are able to love and to be loved can we find the deepest meaning of human life.

(Candlelighter):WE LIGHT THIS CANDLE THAT WE MIGHT REMEMBER THE ULTIMATE VALUE OF LOVE.

Eight candles to symbolize the enduring realities by which we live, eight candles that in the Jewish tradition are lit each day of the celebration. But there is also a ninth day, the day after the celebration has ended and we return to the ordinary routines of our lives, the day that stretches on into eternity, the day on which it is seen whether the inspiration of the lighting of the candles has truly lifted up our hearts in a new dedication and a new zeal to overcome every obstacle that stands in the way of our clinging to the best we can know and imagine, the day when we must live the value we say is the highest — to treasure every person we meet as precious and unique and deserving of our respect.

It is good that we set aside a time to remember and a time to celebrate. But what matters most is that we go forward from this time to live our lives in the light of what we have learned, that we work with renewed purpose for that day "which will see all people free, tyrants disappearing," the day when we will hear "happy throngs singing songs, with a mighty sounding."

The following words based on the themes above, are used to close the service:

May the light of joy brighten our lives and the light of truth lead us to new understanding;

May the light of morality teach us the right and the light of courage enable us to do the right;

May the light of freedom burn more purely in our hearts and the light of faith sustain our strength;

May the light of hope give us high vision and the light of love fill our days with meaning and purpose;

May the light of Hanukkah never be extinguished in our lives. Amen

- Kenneth Phifer

The Winter Solstice, the shortest day of the year which falls on December 21, has long been a day around which many pagan celebrations are centered. The word Solstice comes from two Latin words, "sol" meaning sun and "sistere" meaning day. Thus, solstice means "Day of the Sun."

After the Winter Solstice, when it becomes dark at about four-thirty, the days become longer. The ancient people were afraid that the days might just keep getting shorter until finally it was always night. They had celebrations of lights to try to encourage the sun to come back to them.

Later, when they knew a little more, enough to know that the sun would come back after this certain day, they celebrated it with many festivities. But all these celebrations had something to do with fire and the coming back of light to the world.

In Britain, huge bonfires were lighted. These bonfires were kept burning for several days and nights. The people would gather around these fires and dance, sing, and feast . . . . .

In Egypt on this day the High Priest would enter a cave for several hours. When he returned, he bore a torch in one hand and a newborn infant in the other. This he held aloft, crying, "Behold, Horus, the infant sent to us by the Gods to bestow his light upon the world.' . . . . .

In Roman times, the feast of Saturn fell upon this date. His feast was celebrated in Rome by the exchange between friends of lighted wax tapers. When Christianity came into being in Rome, many early Christians were moved by the immense appeal of the joyous pagan celebration. The early Christians held out against such festivities for about four hundred years, till the other celebration was interfering with the conversion of more Christians. So the Christians set this day aside as the birthday of Christ — Christ, the Light of the World.

From the beginning of time, people have celebrated the return of light to earth. No matter whether we celebrate Christmas, Hanukkah, or merely the joyous occasion of the Winter Solstice, we rejoice in the preparation of the earth by the sun for the beginning of new life.

— Christy Thorrat

A TREE BLESSING

From forest to home
From woodlot to church
From wind to warmth,
This tree and these greens are Christmas signals of
    health and beauty.
You have been decked and ribboned in glorious colors.
Innocent as a small child,
Lovely in posture,
fresh to smell,
Bearing needles like a coat of hair,
The history of praise is caught up in your ever-glowing
    green.
May you be for us an abacus of beauty in these days.

                               — Will Saunders

LITURGY FOR TRIMMING OF THE CHRISTMAS TREE

The tree — one of the great biblical metaphors. Symbol of life, hope, fruitfulness. Season by season, gathering within itself the energies of earth and sunlight, in the upward thrust of life; in the season of greening and growth, explosive with ripeness; through the dark season, quietly enduring, as dormant energies await the signal once again to celebrate the spring. Again and again, the great prophets, in the dark seasons of human life, speak of a time when the things that are not, shall be; and in the landscape of the spirit, the earth blossoms, and the trees are heavy with fruit. Thus speaks the prophet Isaiah (may be read by second person if desired):

> I will make the wilderness a pool of water,
> and the dry land springs of water.
> I will put in the wilderness the cedar,
> the acacia, the myrtle, and the olive;
> I will set in the desert the cypress,
> the plane and the pine together;
> that people may see and know
> that the hand of the Lord has done this,
> the Holy One of Israel has created it.

Such visions, indeed, are late-comers on the world scene. The tree-symbol itself is much older than that; its origin is lost in the mists of antiquity, long before the Bible was, long before Israel was. It begins with the evergreen — among all trees, the special symbol of life in the midst of death. During the long months of cold and dark, while nature displays only the dead stalks of yesterday's ripeness, the evergreen lives, fragrant and visible reminder of nature's annual promise.

Thus it was, in ancient times, at the winter solstice, the people decorated the evergreen with fruit and cloth and trinkets — needed reminder, at the darkest moment of the year, of nature's annual pilgrimage back to warmth and light, fertility and fruitfulness. Today the glass balls that we hang on our Christmas trees are reminiscent of these ancient celebrations; and we too, in our family rituals, deck the tree with imitation fruit — in the midst of winter, a sign of summer's eventual return.

And thus came the Christmas tree — pagan symbol adapted to Christian usage, symbol of life in nature transformed into symbol of life in Christ.

And so do we deck the tree, in our homes and churches, that we might remember and celebrate, in deep mid-winter, at the darkest point of the year, Jesus who is warmth to our cold, light to our darkness, life to our death.

Come, then: deck the tree, and let the symbols of faith hang from its boughs, that it might be a worthy reminder of Jesus, who came in the dark season of our lives, bringing light, and the promise of new life, and a new heaven and a new earth!

— Robert W. Gardiner

THE MID—WINTER FESTIVAL

Prelude: A program of carols sung by the choir

Greeting: To you who gather in this hall
In glad mid-winter festival,
We bring this welcome unto you
As ancient custom bids us do.

Now let us turn back to remember
The stories gathered in December
About this holiday most bright,
The birthday of returning light

Carol to be sung by the congregation: *Deck the Hall*

The Rites of Primitive People

Legend: (Note: The legend is historical background
of the various festival celebrations
of human kind. This can be read during the recorded music if desired.)

In very early times and in primitive societies all people have worshipped the sun, and their deities were mainly sun gods. Many of the holy days, the rites and customs of ancient religion have come down to us in our yuletide festivals.

Our forebears depended on the sun for warmth and light, and for the food that grew in the warm sunlight. When, in the fall the sun began to wane, the people were afraid, for the sun, their god, seemed to be weak and ill.

For an offering to their god, the people brought dry cedar to use as wicks, and gathered the fern seed and the mistletoe. Fern, which seemed to bloom like fire at midsummer's eve, was an emanation of the Sungod's spirit. Fire itself was an emanation of the mistletoe, their golden bough, sacred to the sun and all fires.

The people brought wood to feed the fires, which they burned upon the hills. They made crude wheels of dry cedar or pine or willow and rubbed them with resin or fat to make them burn quickly. These they set afire and rolled them up the hills to symbolize the Sungod's ascent.

On Wheel Day morning, resin was burned to his rising. Myrrh would be burned at high noon. To the altar the priest brought emblems of the sun, the image of a hawk, an emblem of the god's ascent to the uppermost regions, a red wheel, with spokes resembling the sun's rays, and a golden cross framed with a halo.

(The children bring in the symbols of the Circle and the Fire Wheel, and the Circles and Cross. They bring wreaths and chains of mistletoe, pinecones, garlands of ivy, and decorate the tree. The lights, which are already on the tree, but unlighted, are turned on.)

Choric Reading: *Hymn to the Sun of the Stone Age*

Great is the shining sun, magnificent among the heavens. Up from the caves of darkness under the world the sun rises in newness of birth. Lord over all the earth, creator of all living things is the sun. Weary from the winter battle with evil and darkness comes the newborn sun.

As a wheel of gold upon the sky, the sun rolls in mightiness. Its heat lies upon the earth, filling it with life, so that the grass and corn will grow from its body, and the fish will gleam in its melted waters, and the rivers of life will flow abundantly.

Have mercy upon us, O Sun, and fill us with your strong fires. Makes us as mighty as the thick-necked bull, and as fleet as the slender-legged antelope, and give us new life even as the snake crawls gleaming out of its old skin.

We light the fires upon our hills in your honor, and bow before you, and beseech you again to stride high in the heavens, and bring your light and warmth to our lands.

Listen to your children, O Shining and Burning One; your fires are
wamth to our lives; when we gaze upon you we are filled with joy.

Now in the time of darkness we light our fires to feed your spirit. We
sacrifice our first-born upon your altars. We are fattening the sacred
bull for your festival of triumph.

Rise again, O Bright Sun, trampling your enemies, burning the gods
of darkness in your fires. Climb the heavens in the morning even as
the goat climbs the mountain. Make all the sky into a sea of your light
and life.

(Recorded Music: ''The Rite of Spring'' - Stravinsky)

Choir: *The Boar's Head Carol*
          The boar's head in hand bear I,
          Bedecked with bays and rosemary.
          And I pray you, my masters, be merry,
          Qui estis in convivio.

Refrain: Caput apri defero,
          Reddens laudes Domino.
           0.The boar's head, I understand,
          The finest dish in all the land.
          Which is thus all bedecked with gay garland,
          Let us service cantico.

Winter Nebutsu in Japan

          (Recorded Music: ''The Japanese Koto''
          The children will bring the symbol of the
          Tori Gate)

Legend:

     Japan and China are lands of many festivals in all the seasons of
the year, and in Japan, on the twenty-third day of the eleventh month
according to the Lunar Calendar, is the anniversary of the death of
Saint Kuya, who built bridges and dug wells in various provinces,
preaching Buddhism, especially in the provinces of Dewa and Mutsu.
From about the thirteenth of November, for forty-eight nights, the
priests and devotees go round beating a kind of drum, chanting the
name of Buddha. In some places they beat a gourd, chanting Buddhist
hymns of the impermanence of things and receiving alms in the gourd
in place of the usual bowl. From this comes the expression ''bowl-
beating''.

Reading: Japaneses Haiku
          The noises that must have mingled
              with it

dies away:
The sound of bowl-beating remains.

A child weeping at night;
We passed that cottage too,
Bowl-beating.

The hand-lanterns, —
Still more pathetic;
Winter nembutsu.

Within the clouds
There are voices:
Winter nembutsu.

The Chinese Winter Festival
(Recorded Music: "Chinese Classical Music"
The children bring the symbol of Yang and Yin.)

Legend:

For at least four thousand years the religion of China saw humans as partners with nature. In ancient China every month had its special meanings and observances.

Winter begins with the Tenth Month. The Son of Heaven, the Emperor, who has made his sacrifice in a different room or in a different direction of the Hall of Light, now occupies the northern halls, the middle one of which was called the Dark, or Somber Hall, facing the gloomy, sunless north. He is robed in black and wears dark jade to aid darkness. He eats his millet and pork in vessels that are wide at the bottom but narrowing at the top, in order to suggest the closing in of nature.

The Spirit of Heaven has ascended on high, the spirit of earth has descended below; Heaven and earth as no longer in contact; all is closed up and winter is made. Winter is the year's end, therefore at this season the mourning regulations are ordered.

And yet during this month there was universal feasting, being the close of the year's harvesting. They made the Great Sacrifice of the bull, ram, and boar, for the host of heaven, the seven rulers of the sky, the sun, the moon, and the five planets.

Reading: *Ode from the Shih King on Sacrificial
and Festal Services*

With correct and reverent deportment, the bulls and rams all pure, we proceed to the winter and autumnal sacrifices.

Some flay; some cook; some arrange; some adjust. The officer of prayer sacrifices inside the temple gate, and all the sacrificial service is complete and brilliant.

Grandly come our ancestors; their spirits happily enjoy the offerings; their faithful descendents receive blessings. The reward will be great happiness, many years, life without end.

They attend to the furnaces with reverence; they prepare the trays which are very large. Those presiding are still and reverent, preparing the smaller dishes.

The guests and visitors present the cup all round. Every form is according to rule.

The ceremonies having been completed, they go in to the private feast. Great and small they bow their heads, saying, "Your sacrifices, all in their seasons, are completely discharged by you. May your children and your grandchildren never fail to perpetuate these services."

Recorded Music: "Hindu Religious Music"

India: Deepavali - Festival of Lights

Legend:

Deepavali is the New Year's Day of India. The word Deepavali means "cluster of lights," and lights are the most important symbols of the day. Effigies are made and burnt. Lamps are lighted on long poles as guides for the souls of departed patriarchs.

Lakshmi, goddess of wealth, is worshipped for prosperity in the coming year. Presents are given to relatives and friends and workers. Pageants of gaily dressed people flock to the fairs, temples, and parks. For children this is a festival of fire-works and sweet-meats. In every town and village there is a great bonfire. Dancing about the fire is the climax of the Festival of Lights.

Reading: ("Hymn to Varuna" - a paraphrase
            from the *Rigveda)*

Praise to Varuna, the god of fire and light, who
shines from within himself, for he is above all
others in mightiness.
Since we have honored you, Varuna, we hope to
receive from you the blessings of fire and light.
We sing of your greatness when in the many dawns the
light breaks over the herds of grazing cattle.
At the work of Varuna the rivers are set flowing,
and are kept in abundance of waters.
the rivers never tire in their journey; the waves

are as swift as the birds upon the air.
Sing a high and majestic song to Varuna, King of
fire and light.
Like the skin of a slain animal, he has spread out
the earth before the sun.
he sets free the air among the trees, makes the cows
heavy with sweet milk, and speeds the hooves of the
horses.
It is Varuna that sets the waters free in the heavens
and on the earth.
the King of the firmament scatters water upon the
world, even as rain falls on a field of barley.
When Varuna is thirsty for milk, his rains wash the
skies and make the earth moist to her deep places.
In the mornings we will wait for the rising sun;
lead us Varuna in all the days we shall live.

Song by Kenneth L. Patton

> Bright light upon our open eyes
> Is life's first moment of Surprise.
> It is the sunlight makes the day,
> And puts the dark of night away.
>
> We fill our lamps when days are long,
> And lighten winter with our song,
> Recall the fullness of the sun
> When months of summer are begun.
>
> So this our festival of lights
> Is set among the longest nights,
> To sing the coming summer's praise
> For briefest nights and longest days.

Recorded Music: "Sacred Music of India
        (the children will bring the symbol of the
        Sacred Jewel of Buddhism.)

Choric Reading: *The Birth of Buddha* (a paraphrase)

In this way was the baby Buddha born:
When her time had come, Queen Maya stood at noon
under a Balsa tree in the palace grounds. The tree
was as straight as the column of a temple, with
glossy leaves and odorous blossoms. The tree bent
down its boughs to make a bower for Queen Maya.
A thousand flowers blossomed suddenly to make a
couch, and a stream flowed from a rock to make a
bath.

Without pain she brought forth her child, a perfect
baby, with thirty-two marks of blessed birth, and
the great news was sent to the Palace.
When they brought the painted palanquin to take him
home, the bearers of the poles were the four Guardians
of the Earth, who had come down from Mount Sumeru.
there was the Angel of the East, whose armies wear
silver robes, with targets of pearl.
The Angel of the South has horsemen who ride blue
steeds, with sapphire shields.
The Angel of the West is followed by Nagas on red
horses, with shields of coral.
The Angel of the North is surrounded by Yakshas, all
in gold, on yellow horses, with golden shields.
But their glory was invisible, and they looked like
ordinary bearers as they took the poles.
On that day the gods walked freely among humans,
although they did not know them.
The sky was filled with gladness for earth's sake,
knowing that the Buddha was born.

Legend:

Beneath all Mid-winter festivals is our dependence upon the
warmth and light of the sun, and fear for the power of the sun in the
short, darkened days of the winter solstice. The sun was one of the
earliest of all the gods. Our first literature comes from ancient
Sumeria and Egypt, and it is to Egypt we turn for this ancient hymn to
the Sun.

Recorded Music: from the Near East
    (The children will bring the Disc of Aton of Egypt)

Reading: *Hymn to the Sun* - Egypt

Thy dawning is beautiful in the horizon of the sky, O
living Aton, beginning of life.
When thou risest in the eastern horizon, thou fillest
every land with thy beauty.
thou are beautiful, great, glittering, high above
every land; thy rays, they encompass the lands, even
all that thou hast made.
thou art far away; thy rays are upon the earth; though
thou art on high, thy footprints are the day.
When thou sendest forth thy rays, the Two Lands are in
daily festivity, awake and standing upon their feet,
when thou hast raised them up.
Their limbs bathed, they take their clothing, their

260

arms uplifted in adoration to thy dawning.
then in all the world they do their work; all cattle
rest upon their pasturage, the trees and the plants
flourish, the birds flutter in their marshes, their
wings uplifted in adoration to thee.
All the sheep dance upon their feet, all winged
things fly, they live when thou hast shone upon them.
Thy rays nourish every garden; when thou risest they
live, they grow by thee; thou madest the seasons in
order to create all thy work.
Thou alone, shining in thy form as living Aton, dawning, glittering, going afar and returning, thou makest
millions of forms through thyself alone, cities, towns
and tribes, highways and rivers.
All eyes see thee before them, for thou art Aton of
the day over the earth.

Hanukkah - The Feast of Lights

Legend:

The Jewish Hanukkah, or the feast of dedication, is celebrated for eight days, beginning on the 25th day of Kislev (December). Tradition tell us that it commemorates the victory of Judah the Maccabee and his followers over the Syrian King Antiochus IV, and their re-dedication of the defiled Temple in Jerusalem in 165 B.C.

Lights are kindled each evening at dusk, starting with one light and adding another on each successive evening. The lighting of the lamps is accompanied by a blessing and the saying that the ceremony commemorates the miracles, deliverance, deeds and power and acts of salvation wrought by God at this season.

The lighting of the lamps probably stems from the ancient pagan custom of lighting candles or kindling fires at the winter solstice as a means of reluming the waning sun. But the Jewish people have related this ancient custom to the re-lighting of the candelabrum in the Temple, and the re-dedication of their holy place.

Recorded Music: Jewish Cantorial Music
(The children will bring the symbol of the
Star of David, and light the candles of
the Hanukkah Menorah.)

Choric Reading: *II Maccabees 10:1-8*

Now Maccabeus and his company, the Lord guiding them, recovered the temple and the city; but the altars which the heathen had built in the open street, and also the chapels, they pulled down. And having cleansed the temple they made another altar, and striking stones they took fire out of them, and offered a sacrifice after two years, and set forth incense, and lights, and shewbread. When that was done, they fell down flat, and besought the Lord that they might come no more into such troubles; but if they sinned any more against him, that he himself would chasten them with mercy, and that they might not be delivered unto the blasphemous and barbarous nations. Now upon the same day that the strangers profaned the temple, on the very same day it was cleansed again, even the five and twentieth day of the same month, which is Kislev. And they kept eight days with gladness, as in the feast of the tabernacles, remembering that not long before they had held the feast of the tabernacles, when as they wandered in the mountains and dens like beasts. Therefore the bare branches, and fair boughs, and palms, and sang psalms unto him that had given them good success in cleansing his place. They ordained also by a common statute and decree, that every year those days would be kept of the whole nation of the Jews.

A Hanukkah Hymn: *Mooz Zur (Rock of Ages)*

The Savior Gods of the Middle East
   (The children will bring the symbol of Mithra)

Legend

   In the Middle East there were many Mid-Winter Festivals, such as the Roman Saturnalia. They celebrated a Hero-God, the god of the earth's vegetation. In the fall the god sickened and died, or was slain, and went to dwell in Hades, the underworld. In the spring he rose from the dead, and the earth became green again.

   He was known by many names, Osiris in Egypt, Adonis, and Dionysus. One of the last was a Persian god, Mithra, also known as the Sun God. His legend tell that he was found one night, a baby, cold and crying in a cave. Shepherds, watching in the fields near by, discovered him and cared for him. He did many things for the people of the land, but after awhile he returned to the sky, travelling daily across the heavens in a flaming chariot.

   Just after midnight as December 25th began, Persian priests, or Magi, led the faithful to a shrine at the mouth of a cave. There a bull was slain and burned as sacrifice. Each worshipper held a torch, and they sang praises to Mithra, the strong, the mighty, god of light and power and truth. They sang, ''Rejoice, a child of heaven has been born.''

The Choir: Two Carols ''Sing We Now Of Christmas''
            ''Now is Born the Divine Christ Child''

262

Recorded Music: Music of the Gothic Period
(The children will bring the symbol of the
Cross of Christianity)

Reading: St. Luke 2: 1-14

The Choir: "Veni Immanuel"

Carols (to be sung by the congregation):
The First Noel and *We Three Kings*

The Hopi Winter Ceremony

Recorded Music: from the American Indians
(The children bring the symbol of the Thunder Bird)

Legend:

Eight days before the winter solstice the Hopi Indians of Arizona start their farewell ceremonies to autumn. Then they welcome winter. The Hopis believe that winter is a very old man. They cheer him and comfort him. Then spring will return.

Many days before the Indians make pahos for gifts, prayer feathers tied to a stick. These signify a blessing to the home. The sacred ceremonial place is called a kiva. It is usually underground, and none but the members of the tribe may enter. Inside the kiva is an altar where offerings are placed, and a special place set aside for colorful sand paintings.

When the morning of the great day arrives, everyone goes to his or her rooftop and watches for the old man. The old man walks up the path to the village and enters the kiva. There he is cared for and refreshed. Now spring will return.

Choric Reading: from a Pawnee ceremony

Now behold; hither comes the ray of our father Sun; it cometh over all the land, passeth in the lodge, touches us, and gives us strength. Now behold where alights the ray of our father Sun; it touches lightly on the rim, the place above the fire, whence the smoke ascends on high. now behold; softly creeps the ray of our father Sun; now over the rim it creeps to us, climbs down within the lodge; climbing down, it comes to us. Now behold; nearer comes the ray of our father Sun; it reaches now the floor and moves within the open space, walking there about the lodge. Now behold; where has passed the ray of our father Sun; around the lodge the ray has passed and left its blessing there, touching us, each one of us. Now behold; softly climbs the ray of our father Sun; it upward climbs, and over the rim it passes from the place whence the smoke ascends on high. Now behold; on the hills the ray

263

of our father Sun; it lingers there as loath to go, while all the plain is dark. Now has gone the ray from us. Now behold; lost to us is the ray of our father Sun; beyond our sight the ray has gone, returning to the place whence it came to bring us strength.

Recorded Music: The Planets - Holst
  (All the lights are turned out, leaving only
  the votive lights on the centers.)

Reader: Now the candles have been lighted at all the shrines of the human family, before the worshipful images of Oceania, Japan, China, Tibet, India, of the Buddhists, of Egypt, Africa, the Moslems, the Jews, the Christians and the American Indians.
  Each man and woman and child has within them the light of their hope and endurance, and each religion has its light, its moral vision, its dreams of a good life, its gods and celebrations.
  We would be poor without the many companions of our race.
  We are enriched by the myths and visions of all religions, from the dawn of human history until now, in every land of earth. So we celebrate our mid-winter fesitval with them.

The Light of the Atom

Light burns everlastingly in every atom of the universe, for matter is energy, and fire is energy incandescent. All the greater fires, from the fires of the stars to the gentler fires in us, are built up from the kindling fires of the atom.

  (The construction of the atom is lighted.)

The Light of the Galaxy

Our sun is only one of many billions of stars. Our true neighborhood in the cosmos is a mighty galaxy of many billions of stars, an island universe among millions of other island universes, clustering the vastness of space.

The great galaxy turns slowly, once in a billion years. This winter solstice marks the end of another turning of the planet earth about its sun. By this our season are marked, and our religious festivals follow the seasons of the earth. For truly, they celebrate the galaxy, the solar system, and the atom, the platforms of our life, and the gods are only other names for the mighty denizens of nature.

  (The galaxy is lighted.)

The Tree of Life
  (The lights of the tree are turned back on.)

264

We have chosen the tree as a symbol of life. Our ancient ancestors adorned the sacred tree that stood before the house of the gods, hanging on it fern seeds and wreaths of mistletoe, garlands of myrtle and ivy, whose spirits manifested fire and life. From the tree's branches they hung small lamps, each with its bowl of fat and cedar wick, and during the long nights the tree was a lovely thing. It served like a hilltop fire, to guide the sun-god back from the abode of darkness.

(The house lights are turned back on.)

Carol (to be sung by the congregation) *O Tannenbaum*

> O mountain pine, O mountain pine,
> On high thou watchest o'er us.
> O mountain pine, O mountain pine,
> On high thou watchest o'er us.
> About thy head the wild winds roar,
> But firm thou standest everymore.
> O mountain pine, O mountain pine,
> On high thou watchest o'er us.
>
> O mountain pine, O mountain pine,
> How faithful thou art ever.
> O mountain pine, O mountain pine,
> How faithful thou art ever.
> Thou art as green in winter snow
> As in the summer's richest glow.
> O mountain pine, O mountain pine,
> How faithful thou art ever.

Choir: *Angels Now In Heaven Are Singing*

Closing Sentences:
This is our hope: that many lights will be lighted, until the light of one lamp overlaps the other, and the hall of the earth becomes a glory and a festival of light. We will kindle the fires of understanding and appreciation, until all people are within one family, one nation, one human commonwealth.

— Kenneth L. Patton

I pray that when the pressures start building up, when I begin to feel fragmented and "unreal," when life seems too complicated and hopeless, I will be able to see again in my mind's eye those many softly-lit faces filling our church on Christmas Eve, each one holding a small flame within their hand — a flame so small that it barely lights up each person's face with a soft glow and a shimmering halo that makes each person look angelic, holy, divine! When I feel that dull, aching pain of despair may I hear once again our voices blending together in songs of hope and joy and solemnity, drifting on the dark wave of night. When I become worried about the future of our planet may I see again our candlelit church surrounded by the quiet of night and the falling snow piercing the darkness with its glow. And may I feel once again the overpowering joy and the depths of hope that filled my being on that glorious night.

— Michael McGee

As the winter solstice turns our earth and early twilight closes down the day, while all about December snowfall covers our streets and walks with its frosty garment, we come together as people have done from earliest times to celebrate with flame the waning winter and rejoice that our globe now swings once more toward the light. As our burning candles bespeak this ancient faith, so may it express our prayer that the power that directs our planet in its path will set such a solstice for our hopes for our future. From the dark hours of perversity and wrath, we pray that sad humanity may be guided in the path of peace, that like our earth we may emerge from darkness to a brighter day.

— Paul Carnes

With the profound joy of one who has traveled far and finally come home again, we find ourselves once more upon the threshold of Christmas. The charm, the beauty of these few brief hours touches our hearts and cheers and warms us. As did our forebears of ages long ago, we light our lights and strive again to press back the darkness that ever encroaches upon our lives. In this anxious age we are keenly aware of the intensity of that darkness, and the fears that haunt us are no less real than those the ancients knew.

Sometimes we look about us, and, like them, wonder if another circling year may bring the full defeat of light. But we are gathered here because we have a faith - a faith that responsiveness to good lies somewhere within the heart of every person — waiting, sometime, to be called forth by deeds of loving kindness all too long withheld.

Nor is this faith an idle fancy. Christmas ever calls us back to see, to think upon, to cherish and adore, a history of good and noble deeds that truly did take place, and do today. We see the Christmas gifts of love, of kindliness, of sacrifice, of service, not alone in the figure of the Man of Galilee whose birth we mark today, but also in the thoughts and deeds of countless persons, great and small, who have, for some brief moment, or perhaps for a whole lifetime, lived the Way which, universalized, would truly save the world.

May we, with fitting humility, remember that we, too, have known those moments of our own when, rising above the shallow, the thoughtless, the pointless, we have felt ourselves commanded by and given to those ways of love and thoughtfulness and service which a soul-sick world so desperately needs. May these festive days bring home to us the knowledge that could we but capture for a longer day than Christmas, the warmth and graciousness which that day imparts to us, the world might soon swing out beyond its haunting shadow to a daylight truly full of Peace on Earth, Goodwill to All. To the joyous task of carrying forth into all the days of our years, a more generous portion of the Christmas spirit than ever before, let us dedicate this quiet hour.

— William D. Hammond

Christmas Eve is a time for candlelight.
It is a time when one desires nothing more than family and soft music.
Who can say what passes through our hearts on Christmas Eve?
Strange thoughts, undefinable emotions, and sudden tears —
All this and more, unbidden, come without reason.
>   And we burn our candles
>   For this is Christmas Eve.

Christmas Eve is not a time to be merry, but quietly glad.
It is the proper time to wish upon a star.
It is the time to watch children with excited, happy eyes troop off to bed to await the miracle of dawn.
It is a time of wonder, of thankfulness that life is still being created anew out of darkness.
It is a time of quiet awakening to beauty that still lives on through the strife of a war-torn world.
>   And we burn our candles
>   For this is Christmas Eve.

Christmas eve is a time of heartbreak,
When those who are not at their own fireside are most missed.
Christmas Eve is a time of blessing
When all the heartbroken world give thanks
For the quiet beauty of rest.
When one is closest to one's companions
And is not then enemy to any person.
>   And we burn our candles
>   For this is Christmas Eve.

Christmas Eve is a time of memory,
When one remembers past happiness and love
And often sighs for the good that might have been.
Peace on earth, and now comes the memory of the story of the first Christmas
So old, and yet so new.
We lose ourselves in legend, and dream of storybook people; Tiny Tim and the Other Wise Man
Live again in the memory of human hearts.
>   And we burn our candles
>   For this is Christmas Eve.

— Tracy Pullman

We are here this Christmas Eve to be together,
To feel the warmth of human bodies —
A reassurance against the cold of this winter night.
We come to fill our eye with the light of candles,
To fill our ears with the sounds of music,
To fill our hearts with the wonder of new hope —
Hope for the love of one another,
Hope for peace on earth with good will toward all.
Give us this night that inner peace which comes
    from the knowledge that we are not alone
But that we are here, together,
    sharing common hopes,
    common dreams,
    common resolves.
Give us this night the joy and wonder which fill our souls with the
knowledge
That we are a part of the interweaving patterns of the human and
divine —

Each of us a spark of light in the Universe
Together, a brilliance which calls forth the promise of Bethlehem
Together, may we find the courage to realize that promise.
                  So Be It.
                      — Sydney Wilde-Nugent

We are joined this evening by the light of candles. From light we have
the symbol of warmth, of sharing, of newness of life, of enlighten-
ment and hope in a world of tragedy and darkness.

For Christians the light in the sky represents the birth of a new
world religion by Jesus of Nazareth almost 2000 years ago. He moved
people's hearts in ages past and he moves people today.

For others light can symbolize a new life ahead — a new
relationship, a marriage, the birth of a child. It can even be a reminder
of the significant persons that have died in this or other years.

For all of us it can be a symbol of hope for a struggling world,
health where there has been sickness. It can mean new insight, fresh
beginnings, a new commitment to peace. For all these reasons we
come together this evening, alone and together to share in the joy of
the light.
                      — Morris W. Hudgins

This is my prayer for tonight.

> I pray that I shall find and hold onto the joy, the hope, the
> love and the peace that is associated with this very special
> night.

I pray that I shall capture the very special magic of which the story of
the Christ child and the birth of every child reminds us

> That special magic that lightens these dark days
> As they did the dark days so long ago.

I pray that I shall experience at least some of this joy, some of this
hope, some of this love and - some of this special magic - On all the
days of my life.

— Judy Deutsch

O Light of Christmas Eve, moments of nearest total poetry in our
lives, grow brighter and steadier in our hearts as the years go by.

> Midnight services and gatherings of every kind, bring moments
of highest joy, on this enchanted night, to hearts and sanctuaries.

> Light which lighteth every one who cometh into the world, may
thy transforming grace assure that our failure to realise our love will
not forever be earth's greatest defeat.

> When darkness descends, this side of sunset's fires, and the tree
tops dance wild dances in the wind, when the visitor at the door can
hardly be heard above the swirling snow, then, on this icy solstice
night, glows the magic of human spirit, in homes never brighter,
warmer, more aromatic and music-filled.

> Even if we are grasping and selfish and most prone only to
receive, thy Light would always say: "You must give! Give gifts
wisely, delightful, and needful."

> Though some can not receive because in giving they are proving
something to themselves, thy Light reproves, saying: "In receiving,
you give pleasure that you owe to those who love you."

> Light of Christmas Eve, through all such lowly human ways, we
know thou comest from the Great Spirit, Whose will for us is righteousness, Whose desires for us is our growth and Whose promise to us
is our fulfillment.

— Gaston M. Carrier

Thou Love informing all our loves, fill our hearts with thy care for all the world. Slowly we awaken from our dream of sleep, to be centered on ourselves alone no longer. We have swollen in time with many desires, and these images have crowded out every one: mother, father, child, friend. Too late we awaken to take up our watch in the enclosing dark, the nighttime we fear.

Allow us this night before Christmas a fresh start. Only allow us and we will find our own way in freedom. Inform our love anew, and we shall see ourselves in images of innocence no longer, but see it straight, with our own eyes: that we have been cradled receivers of good, thanks be to thee, and know that, come the morning, Christmas is for giving.

— George K. Beach

Once again we come together, young and old, on a winter night, following a Star. We come to seek and to celebrate Christmas. We do this every year. But the winter night, the shining star, and the newborn babe - these remain three mysteries.

In ages past, our primitive ancestors feared the winter. For, as the sun diminished, life diminished. As the sun slowly withdrew its life-giving rays, all nature shriveled and died, or seemed to die. Shivering in the biting cold and the long darkness of the nights, people believed they were being punished. They prayed that the sun might return, and dead things come to life again.

And the sun always did return, and people rejoiced and gave thanks. They celebrated its return every year with a festival of joy, a festival that has lasted through the centuries, even to our own days.

The sun's going away is no longer a mystery. We know why it seems to go away each year. And we know that even now it has turned, and has started on its long journey back. This is not a mystery to us. But, just the same, there remains the mystery of our own need, the winter drafts about the heart, and the question that has always been asked and has never been answered: "Why are we here, on this beautiful ball, turning through the vastness of space?" We all of us share this kind of winter, and our eyes still search through the darkness of the night for a sign.

— Robert Killam

271

O Thou Immanuel! God-With-Us and God-Within-Us! This is our meditation on a midwinter's night, addressed to that listening Inner Self who knows us better than we can dream. We praise the coming of unutterable serenity, peace and love into a world that knows it not. "The people that walked in darkness have seen a great light." Truly the light is here, brought to us by the great souls of many times and places. Now in unwinking, star-cold, sweet-singing night, we hope for another Christmas miracle. May we truly find it in children's eyes no longer hungry or afraid. May we find it in justice for all people, no longer trapped in ghettos which we have helped to build. May we find it in families closer-knit in mutual respect and uncloying affection. May we find it in councils of peace and cooperation among the nations. May we find it at last inside ourselves: "surprised by joy," quietly accepting our bright brief destiny. On the eve of Christmas in the winter solstice season, we praise the dayspring from on high that makes bright our star and enriches our lives, that sings a lasting music in the heart.

— Charles Grady

It is not by accident that the religious calendar closely matches the celestial calendar, for our very bones and breath are tied into the movement of the spheres, the waxing and waning of the seasons. Seen in this light, the winter solstice is the bravest holiday of all. Those of us who live in the northern hemisphere have watched as the sun traveled farther and farther away. Her light has gone from us, and the days grow cold. Yet even now, as the sun all but fails us, we light a candle against the darkness as a symbol of hope - as a symbol of faith - that the light will come again.

— Eileen B. Karpeles

Blessed are the stars of the wintry night that sprinkle the floor of heaven with their lustrous and far-shining light.

> Blessed is the moon that seems like a lovely maiden walking in the fields of sky, clothed with raiment of wondrous golden light.

Blessed is the sun with its great brightness, circling the seasons and bringing the benediction of ever renewed life to the earth.

> Blessed are the hearth-fires, the lamps and tapers that hallow our homes and make a glow of beauty within the surrounding shadows.

All these are wondrous fair.

> But blessed beyond all these is the light that lighteth every one that cometh into the world . . . the imperishable flame of the human spirit touched into being by the Eternal One . . .

> > O fire of reason
> > O fire of leaping thought
> > O fire of compassion and pity
> > O fire of friendship
> > O insatiable burning of the hunger for beauty
> > O divine glow from on high kindled in the

human heart, strangely and deathlessly!

> Thou art the illumined glory by which we of earth fashion our visions and our dreams of sweeter life and nobler realms!

Thou art the sacred flame discerned in every age . . . by Persian and Jew, by Hindu and Christian, by scientist and prophet, by sage and child.

We see the holy fire flaming this night in the manger-cradle, and it signifies hope and promise to lift against the darkness of the night. Many there have been in other centuries and other years who have been guardians of this flame . . . they have carried it to the shadowed regions of the world . . . they have dispelled ignorance and superstition and cruelty and injustice . . . they have been way-showers and lightbearers . . . they have thrown back the frontiers of darkness and planted the sacred torches boldy in far and perilous places.

Now it is our watch. Now the light will move from the manger cradle to the silent and saddened and songless streets of the world only if our hearts carry it, and our hands shield it from the blasts of the wintry selfishness.

> Many are the windows of the world that will stay darkened unless we light them. It is our watch now!

273

Come then . . . apostles . . . come great-hearts . . . come dreamers and singers and poets . . . come builders . . . come healers . . . come those of the soil and those who command the might of machines . . . carry the Sacred Flame to make light the windows of the world . . .

It is we who must be keepers of the flame . . .

It is we who must carry the imperishable fire.

It is our watch now.

- Max A Kapp

Beatitudes of Christmastide

On this blessed day let us worship at the altar of joy, for to miss the joy of Christmas is to miss its holiest secret.

Let us enter into the spiritual delights which are the natural heritage of child-like hearts.

Let us withdraw from the cold and barren world of prosaic fact if only for a season.

That we may warm ourselves by the fireside of fancy, and take cousel of the wisdom of poetry and legend.

Blessed are they who have vision enough to behold a guiding star in the dark mystery which girdles the earth;

Blessed are they who have imagination enough to detect the music of celestial voices in the midnight hours of life;

Blessed are they who have faith enough to contemplate a world of peace and justice in the midst of present wrongs and strife.

Blessed are they who have greatness enough to become at times as a little child;

Blessed are they who have zest enough to take delight in simple things;

Blessed are they who have wisdom enough to know that the kingdom of heaven is very close at hand, and that all may enter in who have eyes to see and ears to hear and hearts to understand.

— David Rhys Williams

274

We have come here seeking Christmas,
   searching outside ourselves for what can be found
   only within.
We will not find Christmas here unless we have
   brought it with us.

Christmas is
      a season of the spirit,
      a habit of the heart,
      not reserved for designated days in December,
      But available all days, all year,
      lighting our way through the darkness and the
            dullness of the winters of our souls to the
            Bethlehem that dwells in each of us.
There a star shines in spite of ourselves and the
   absurdities and the ironies of our existence.

We need to be reminded, now and then, of that star's
   abiding presence and persistence in each one of us.

Her we pause, if only for a moment, in the midst of holiday madness,
to listen for the angel voices that sound softly inside each of us,
proclaiming the truth of Christmas that lies beneath all the ribbon and
paper, the tinsel and glitter of getting and spending, the ho ho hos that
quickly become, for many of us, bah humbugs!

   As we pause here on this winter's eve, let us listen quietly
   to those whispers of Christmas truth . . . of the gifts of
   Christmas that cannot be got or bought or sold but can only
   be freely received and gladly given — shared — with
   ourselves and others.
                                          — Patricia Bowen

A Stop on the Way

All praise, all love, all honor to thee, newborn son!
Nestling within your mother's arms 2000 years away,
Your radiant name lights up our winter dark
Into a blazing festival of light!

No one before or since your birth has given, in his
    one life, such ever verdant testament of good.
To Jesus, man and myth, we dedicate this hour
And reverently relight the flame of Christmas,
Christmas — which is enduring —
And we — who pass — are one this night.

There is a kind of immortality in this:
All Christmases that went before and all that are to
    come
Are joined tonight by this one hour.
There is a kind of immortality in this:
To be alive tonight;
To share here the immortal feast of Christmas;
To watch once more the candles glow;
To hear retold the ancient tale;
To hear and sing the ageless Christmas songs.

Rejoice that we are here, together once again.
Rejoice that we can worship love and life.
Rejoice that one — one soul can be a bright, clear
    star for centuries
Rejoice! In Jesus' name, rejoice!

— Ann Foster

Down thru the years, candles have said many things to many people; they have been one of our most enduring symbols.

We think of the light of reason, and truth that is wisdom, the spark of inspiration and of beauty; the warm glow of safety and salvation from whatever dangers beset us.

We fan the flame of friendship, and seek to brighten that flame into love. We candlelight the dining table, and in its soft glow the ties of family feel close and strong.

Life itself is compared with a flame and that same glow stands for the quest for meaning in existence.

— W. Bradford Greeley

The Careless Candle

A candle is a careless thing, God wot. See how it is always stretching up and reaching out.

It gives its substance without murmur or complaint to the flame that is consuming it. It doesn't even seem to care into what corner the flame flings its light; whither the corner is clean or dirty, pretty or ugly, far or near, high or low, deserving or forgotten, useful or neglected. Apparently, too it doesn't care to whom it sends its warmth; whether to the outer chill, a lonely heart, a child's delight, a bore or a lout.

A candle that tries to conserve its substance is poor company on a dark night. It was pleasant to look at in the daytime. It was slender, smoothly appealing. But any candle that does not give itself away is a disappointment in the deepening shadows of a long evening. Some friends are like that. Good fun in days of play; poor company in the hours of dusk and trouble.

A candle must give itself away. In the giving, in the spending, the spreading, the sending, it finds itself.

There is a proverb, "The human spirit is the candle of the Lord." In the worship of my church, let me learn to spend myself. Amen.

— John Wood

Three hundred years ago in Moravia a group of Protestant worshippers, known as the Moravian Brethen, held a candlelight service at midnight on Christmas Eve. Since that time, each Christmas Day has been ushered in to the music of carols echoing through the still Moravian countryside.

The worshippers entered their darkened churches to light their small candles from a large candle at the altar — symbol of the Eternal Light that lighteth every person that cometh into the world. For an hour or more in the light of the blazing candles, they sang their timeless traditional carols, concluding with the resounding "Gloria in Excelsis."

As the worshippers returned home they carried the lighted candles and placed them in their windows so that all who passed might know that in those homes there had come a special Christmas blessing.

— Tracy Pullman

Let us light the Christmas candles we hold so dear —
Candles of joy wherein sadness disappears
Candles of hope where despair hangs heavy with tears,
Candles of courage to lighten all our fears
Candles of peace to calm the tempest of the years,
Candles of love to ease the burden of our cares
Candles to enflame the heart with the grace and
    radiance of Christmas comfort and cheer.

                        — Richard M. Fewkes
                        (Free   adaptation   after
                        Howard Thurman)

Candles have been lighted for centuries as symbols
    To brighten the darkness of winter days
And bring hope and courage to our minds
    To lend warmth to the coldness of winter days
And warm our hearts with love and understanding.

There is a magic in candlelight. The magic that
    one candle can kindle a flame in many others,
    yet not be diminished in its light.

And the magic of warmth as well as brightness in its
    light.

We will each of us have our candle lighted from this
    one candle; as you receive its light, pass it to
    another.

Take your candles home from this Christmas place and
    light them again this evening.

Think of the warmth and light we can share with others
    and not diminish our own.

Think of the warmth and light we share with others
which makes our own light glow a little brighter.

                        — Ellen Fay

As I look at this lighted candle, I think of all the people I've read about who lit up the world with their love. I think of Jesus and Buddha, St. Francis and Schweitzer, Clara Barton and Martin Luther King, Jr. And I know in my heart that I can light up the world with my love, too.

As I look at this glowing candle, I think of all the people I have known in my life who lit up my world with their love. Parents who gave me birth; teachers who taught me in schools; people who walked with me for a while. And I know in my heart that I can light up the world with my love, too.

As I look at this bright candle, I think of all the people I know now who light up my world with their love. My spouse and my children; my colleagues and my friends, people in this parish who are standing with me tonight: others absent, but with us just the same. And I know in my heart that I can light up the world with my love, too.

Loved ones, friends, and you who are strangers, I pass this flame to you. Take it, and let it brighten up the darkness of this house. Let its glow sparkle against our eyes and lighten up our faces. And know that by sharing our love - even in little ways - we touch others with our light and our world becomes brighter. It all began so many years ago when one light lit up the midnight sky. But it's been passed on to us by saints and prophets, parents, teachers, and poets, and all the friends and lovers of humankind. Take it, pass it on — tonight, tomorrow, and whenever you see a shadow or dark place your love can lighten. No one is ever too old. No one is too young. Each of us can touch someone by our love and inspire then with our light.

Little light; little light;
Come shine upon us tonight.
Quiet peace in darkness sing;
Sharing love, a light we'll bring.

— Charles A. Gaines

This flame from my candle is so very small. It's but a speck in the darkness of this house. But soon, something spectacular is going to happen. I shall pass this flame to the ushers. They, in turn, will pass it to you. Slowly and quietly, the flame from this small candle will spread to a hundred candles and more. And with all candles lit, this house will seem warmed by our light. Every dark corner will be brighter, every face will reflect a glow, and together, we shall have shared the light.

And that is what I believe the Christmas message is about. We each have a light - an inner light that is revealed when we share it. That light is called wisdom. It's called kindness. It's called love. It's called idealism. It's called hope. And when we share this light - just as when we pass the flame from this candle from one to another, we help to brighten up our world. Perhaps we can just be there when someone is in pain or is alone or afraid. Perhaps we can just simply tell the truth or deal honestly with our friends, business associates, merchants and tax collectors. Perhaps we can give a helping hand when someone needs one. Perhaps we can face our own difficulties with courage and dignity, providing others with an example of how to live. Perhaps we can be quiet when others are noisy; or loving when others are hateful, or sympathetic when others ridicule. Whatever the way, we all have something to share, some inner light to give — and that's what Christmas is about. The birth of a child of light — every child — each of us — as saviors in the world. You and I can't do every thing. Our lights are small and the darkness is great. But together we can do more than we realize. For when we share, all dreams are possible.

I pass this flame to you. Let its light brighten your life this Christmas Eve as you touch one another with the passing flame. It all begins with one light, one child, or one grownup — with you and me.

> Little light, little light,
> Come shine upon us, tonight.
> Quiet peace in darkness bring,
> Share love, of joy we'll sing.

> — Charles A. Gaines

May each of us carry into the
world through out own lives
and deeds the light of this church —
a flame of the endless
search for truth,
a flame of the endless
quest for peace,
a flame of the endless
love of and faith in humanity.

   (light candles)

Let the flame from this church
light our hearts and our lives.

   (candlelighters light)

Light of warmth,
Light of truth,
Light of love,
Light our path this night,
Light our way now and
   onward forever more.

— Robert Edward Green

May the love that is the
   doctrine of this
   universal church
   prevail in this time
   of joy.
May our Christmas be
   marked by the sharing
   that is the enactment
   of our love.
May the fellowship of this
   season be our memory
   throughout the year
   that is to come.
May peace on the earth,
   good will to all be our
   song and the song of
   all the world's people.
And thus may it be,
   as now we part,
   "A Merry Christmas to
   all — and to all a
   good night."

— Robert Edward Green

May the peace of Christmas bring you comfort and the wonder of Christmas fill your hearts with joy.

May you feel the special love that is the meaning of Christmas and know that sense of warmth and belonging that is the endless story of Christmas.

May kindness and sharing and laughter be part of your celebration in this moment, through the hours of tomorrow, and in all the days thereafter.

To each of you, those who are visiting with us and those who are dear friends: Merry Christmas . . . Merry Christmas . . . Merry Christmas!

— Kenneth Phifer

Miracle

This snow that falls so silently tonight,
As though the earth had need of such a thing,
By dawn will work a miracle in white,
In clean-cut distances these winters bring.
Now all the lonely lines against the sky
Of fields and trees left barren here will go,
Softly to disappear and softly lie
Under the benediction of the snow.

So falls the Christmas spirit in our year;
To cleanse the wound and heal the bitter scar,
And stir the soul and still the darkling fear
With ancient dreams that cannot be — and are.
Oh, I have seen a miracle tonight.
Of winter snow and shining Christmas light!

— Waldemar Argow

Now we take our leave from one another,
going out into the night-lit streets to find our
    homes, and make them warm and bright with love,
that we may ever be ready to welcome and receive the
    stranger and the sojourner,
whether coming to us as a stable-born child,
or as a neighbor,
or as a lost and half-forgotten part of our own lives.
May we go in peace. Amen

                     — Libbie Stoddard

Reach out to carry your light of faith as we leave for our widely scattered homes. Let us be one, this Christmas Eve, knowing that the gift of life belongs to all.

With us are the long remembered years, the quiet hopes that flood the borders of our dreams, the love of life which is needed everywhere. Here is where the angels of our better selves must sing; here, the heavenly host of human care. Here, now, is joy for us who nothing were before our birth! Rejoice! Reach out, with a Merry Christmas!

                     — Robert Zoerheide

The light which shines
Is the light of this season,
Which comes to us from the past,
Which shines here now,
Which we shall give to the future.

In a moment this light
Will be shared with all of us.
The room will be darkened.
Two candlelighters will come forward
To have their candle lit.

At that point you are asked to rise
And come forward down the center aisle
To have your candle lit by them.
Those of you in the side aisles and the balcony
Are asked to go to the back of the church
And come forward down the center aisle.

When your candle is lit
You are asked to help form
One large circle 'round the church.

Will you please not speak
But stand and move in silence.
Fire is bright - but it also burns
So please watch your candles carefully.

When all our candles are lit
And the circle is formed,
We will be given the musical cue
To sing softly a stanza of "Silent Night"
And then hum it through again together.

A spoken closing will end the service.
You are invited to take your candle
Home with you - to light again
At some appropriate time
During your own holiday celebration,
Thus carrying the light from here
Out into the world.

— Christopher Raible

CANDLELIGHTING CEREMONY

Would our candlebearers now please come forward. (Leaders light their candles; they light congregants candles.)

We have come together from our many homes to join in this celebration of rebirth and joy. We have come together out of the cold and the dark to fill this sanctuary with songs, stories and poetry - and the warmth of people willing to share of themselves during this glorious season. My hope is that:

Here, we have found light,
Here, we have found a measure of peace,
And here, we have found a bit of the happiness
and strength we all need to carry on
in our lives.

Let us share, then, the light of these candles, as we dedicate ourselves to sharing with one another and with all the others of this world.

Our candles lit, I will ask you, then, to join in singing the loveliest of all Christmas carols, "Silent Night."

— David Sammons

(These words are spoken as the candlelighters proceed down the aisles, lighting the candles of those at the end, who then light the candles of those sitting next to them, and so on.)

Receive the light.

It is not easy to receive light. Our candle must be held in a certain way. The wick must be exposed and the wax capable of melting.

Receive the light.

Love and comradeship spreads. Though there be darkness, we are not alone. Three hundred flames announce our faith. The darkest hour has past, the sun has begun its ascendency. Hope is valid, hope is eternal.

Receive the light.

Pass on the light.

It is not easy to pass on light. Our candle must be held in a certain way. The wick must be burning and our wax melting.

Pass on the light.

In sharing, we find our candle does not go out, it flares. In sharing, not only does our path become brighter, we become a beacon for others.

Pass on the light.

To those we know, to those unseen and unknown, share what you have with those who have not.

Pass on the light.
(unison closing)

  With our breath we blow upon the flame.
  The smoke rises
  As flame is light
  As breath is life
  As smoke is spirit
  So our life conjoins with light
  Releasing spirit.

  We rejoice in the spirit of life.

— Charles S. Slap

(After the prelude, a silent processional, each member carrying a candle, led by minister, who lights candelabra, turns and says:)

In the midst of darkness, we light a candle.

In the midst of fear and despair, we call forth hope.

The long nights of winter are upon us, and the sun has wandered far from our land. Only we, through our own acts of affirmation, can bring it back again. Only we together — the tribe, the clan, the family — can change the course of the sun, which for so many weeks has moved farther and farther away from us. Not for ourselves, but for one another, do we pour forth our gifts of love and light. Only for this will the sun pause in its travels, to look at our twinkling lights, and hear our gladsome song, and smell our savory feasts. Only then will the sun bring its warmth to us once more.

(In closing, once again the light are extinguished, one by one, except for a single candle, held by the minister, who says:)

From time out of mind, the candle has been the symbol of hope, the flame that welcomes the lost child, or the stranger in from the storm. It is the fragile spark that survives, when all else is gone, ready to rekindle warmth and love in a cold and lonely world.

(Two ushers approach and light their candles from the minister's candle. As they pass the light to the person nearest the aisle in each row, who in turn passes it on down the row, the minister continues.)

From a single fragile flame, another spark is ignited — and from it, another, and another. That which we give to one another has power to banish darkness. To love is an act of courage. To one another we give hope — the hope which conquers fear. To one another we give love — the love that frees us to act courageously. Together we unlock the doors of darkness, and shatter our separate cells. We are one people, and we have come home again.

(Silent processional to the patio - or social hall or lawn — where everyone puts their candles in the center of the area — bunched close together — and steps back to join a circle around the candles. They give off not only a surprising amount of light but even heat! When all are present, we join hands and sing the first verse of "Silent Night")

Minister: This, then, is the miracle of Christmas:

That from one light we kindle many flames.
That darkness will flee before the gift of love.
That every death is only a beginning.
Morning will come — and with it, a new birth.
Each from our separate homes, we bring a candle.
One candle has little power for warmth or light.
But when one candle is added to another, together we have the power
to light up the world . . . It is in this spirit that we wish to one another a
Christmas full of joy, and wonder, and love.

(Sing two verses of "We Wish You a Merry Christmas," changing
the last line of verse two to "and a glass of good cheer.") And now we
invite friend and stranger alike to join us in the gifts of food which we
have brought to share with you and a glass of good cheer.

— Eileen B. Karpeles

CHRISTMAS EVE

Prelude

Opening Words

Hymn: O Come All Ye Faithful

The Meaning of Christmas I
Christmas as a Festival of Midwinter

Since the dawn of time, people have celebrated the longest night of the year with light and fire and thanksgiving, for they have learned that the darkest and longest night marks the turn of the year, the time when the sun, giver of warmth and light, turns back from death, and grows strong again. The turning of the year is a promise of renewing life. The sun will climb the heavens again, and the darkness will be pushed back each day. People will walk upon the greening earth. The green shoots will burst from the seed and the young will be brought forth from the womb. In the midst of winter, the promise is given of the summer season. In the midst of darkness comes the assurance of the light.

The Lighting of the First Candle of Christmas

In this time when days grow short, the time of the long night, and the darkness and the cold,

Light in our hearts the light of faith.

We have faced, each one, our own times of darkness; we have been discouraged and lonely; we have been afraid.

Yet we trust that we, too, will find light for our darkness, and turn again to life with courage and with faith.

(Candle is lighted in silence)

Hymn: The First Nowell

The Meaning of Christmas II
Christmas as a Festival of the Birthday of Jesus

Reading: Luke 2:1-14

No one knows at what time of the year Jesus was born, but when long after his death, stories of his birth were collected and written down, and the growing Christian Church wanted to celebrate his birthday, the church fathers wisely decreed that it should be at the time of the most beloved and universal festival in the experience of people the world over — the Mid-winter celebrations — the festivals of light.

So to the old festivals were added all the new celebrations which centered around the Christmas story, of the child born in a manger, whom the wisest men visited, and about whom all the hosts of heaven sang. Stories gathered from many times and many places, and told and re-told in story, and song, and in poetry, each adding its magic to the meanings of Christmas.

289

Each year, at this time, we turn again to hope in a time of darkness, to the old hope of people in a world of terror and tumult for peace on earth, in some far day, to people of good will, and of the importance and promise of every child who is born into the world.

Lighting the Second Candle of Christmas
Christmas has come once more to the earth.
Light in our hearts the light of hope.
Let us remember that the great and holy may sometimes be found in unlikely and unaccustomed places, and that from the most humble beginning children come who carry within them the seeds of greatness and a great light.

May we remember that in each one of us burns an unquenchable and eternal light within which every person who comes into the world.
(Light second candle in silence)

Anthem: There Is No Rose

The Meanings of Christmas III
Christmas as a Festival of Giving and Sharing
Christmas is a festival of giving and sharing. It is a time of secrets and surprises, of gifts chosen with loving care and shared with joy. The child in Bethlehem was himself a gift — to his parents, and to the world, which is a better place because he has lived. The gifts of Christmas are the gifts of life itself, and of love, which makes life possible. They are the gifts of song, of grace, of beauty, the gifts of sharing the best we have to give with those we love.

Lighting the Third Candle of Christmas
At this time of the giving of gifts lovingly made and carefully chosen, at this time of the sharing with one another that which is deepest and dearest to us,
Light in our hearts the light of love.
Heal in our hearts the wounds of misunderstanding, mistakes, and regrets; help us to reach out with joy and grace for the gifts which life and love offer us, and sustain our hopes and labors together for that time when all people shall come into the circle of peace and world fellowship.

May we share, this Christmas, the best of who we are with
those we love. Together may our hearts share peace.
(Light the third candle in silence)

Hymn: Joy to the World

The Meaning of Christmas IV
Christmas as a Festival of Joy
Christmas is a festival of joy. It is a time of feasting and fun, of singing and visit, of friends and family reunited, of glittering trees and lighted houses, of stocking and presents, of fires and candles, of stories of a

tiny child in a manger — all the bright heritage which has come down to us as members of a large human family. The joy of Christmas belongs to those who have vision enough to seek a guiding star in the dark mystery which girdles the earth. the joy of Christmas belongs to those who, in the midst of the darkness, have lighted candles in the night.

Lighting the Fourth Christmas Candle
>   In this happy season, light in our hearts the light of joy.
>   To miss the joy of Christmas is to miss its
>   holiest secret.

Let each of us build into our Christmas all that is bright and warm and joyful, the holiest and most precious of human qualities.
>   Let there come into our hearts the wisdom to be for a little
>   time as a little child; to warm ourselves by the fire of
>   imagination; to learn the abiding wisdom in poetry, and
>   legend and in song.

Let this be the season, where wisdom enough and time, are ours for the seeking and the asking.
>   And where joy may abound.
>   (Light the fourth candle in silence)

Pastoral Meditation: ''The Light Shineth''

Litany of Light
>   Candlelighters will light the candles of those on the aisle
>   seats, these people will light the candle of those next to
>   them and that person in turn will light the next person's
>   candle. When all the candles are lighted we will join in
>   singing ''Silent Night''

Hymn: Silent Night

After a moment of silence, candles will be blown out.

Postlude: Silent Night, echoed by piano
— Deborah Pope-Lance

A CELEBRATION OF THE SOURCES OF CHRISTMAS WITH CANDLELIGHT AND CAROLS ON CHRISTMAS EVE

Setting: The Great Hall is decorated with wreaths and banners of the season. A small stage is set in front of the Great Window. An undecorated fir tree is to the left. An unlighted candelabra is to the right. Center is a simple bench. Off right: pulpit

Lighting: House lights are on. Spot lights are set (1) on the tree, (2) on the candelabra, (3) on the bench, (4) on the pulpit.

Musicians: At piano and organ are playing carols and other music of the season as the people come by.

Ushers: Dressed in colorful tunics, they hand programs to the people wishing them a Merry Christmas, sending them to the tree.

Seating: The room is full of chairs with smaller chairs set nearest to the stage.

Congregation (as they enter), go to the tree with their decorations and their mittens while ushers and adult helpers assist in arranging the tree attractively. A step ladder is available to arrange the higher places. As the people settle down and are seated they are called to order by:

Minister:

For unto us a child is born, unto us a son is given; and the government shall be upon his shoulder; and his name shall be called Wonderful, Counsellor, the mighty God, the everlasting Father, the Prince of Peace. Of the increase of his government and peace there shall be no end, upon the throne of David, and upon his kingdom, to

292

order it, and to establish it with judgement and with justice from
henceforth even for ever. (Issiah 9: 6-7)

All sing:　　　　　O Come All Ye Faithful
(spots out, ladder away)

Minister:
　　　Welcome! We are gathered here on this night of nights as family
and friends, young and old, to celebrate this richest of our holidays.
For Christmas comes to us from many places and many times and
there is no way of telling all the sources of this night. Yet we will tell
what we can in this brief hour of how these traditions came to be —
how they enrich our lives — how they give us the goose bumps of
holiday — how they get us doing things we never do at any other
season of the year — and how they get us singing.
　　　To do this and give form to the celebration of the Christmas night
we shall light the lights of this candlestick — this menorah of
Hanukkah — this candelabrum which has come to us from the eye of
the artist and the hand of the craftsman and is ours to keep for many
celebrations yet to come — we shall light each light in fond recognition of some parts of the traditions that bind our hearts to this house.
　　　The first and central light that we shall light is in appreciation for
the gift of Hanukkah:

Candlelighter: (comes forward and with a taper lights the central
　　　　　　　candle. As s/he lights the candle the Spot #1 comes
　　　　　　　up. S/he stands by the candelabra while the people
　　　　　　　listen to:)

First Reader:
　　　　　　　Our Jewish friends have given us the tradition of
　　　　　　　the nine branch candlestick from their celebration of
　　　　　　　the eight days of Hanukkah. This central light is called
　　　　　　　the "Servant Candle" as it serves throughout this
　　　　　　　holiday as the servant to light the other eight.
　　　　　　　Hanukkah is the Feast of Dedication for the Jews
　　　　　　　celebrating the liberation of Jerusalem from the
　　　　　　　Syrians almost 200 years before the time of Jesus.
　　　　　　　Judas Maccabaeus was their hero who with a tiny
　　　　　　　band drove out the occupation army. The Syrians had
　　　　　　　desecrated the Temple with pagan rites. After the
　　　　　　　Temple was restored, the Jews held festivals for eight
　　　　　　　days, rededicating the Temple.
　　　　　　　Hanukkah this year began on December — . In
　　　　　　　Jewish homes a candle is lit each night and children
　　　　　　　are often given a present on each of the eight days.
　　　　　　　In recognition of their tradition at this holiday
　　　　　　　time of year, let us join in singing the Hanukkah
　　　　　　　Hymn.

293

All Sing: Hanukkah Hymn (HCL #279)

Minister:

The second light we light tonight we light for all the greens of Christmas. The trees, the holly and the ivy, the wreaths in windows and on doors, and the gladness that they all do bring.

Candlelighter: (comes forward with an unlighted taper and, taking a flame from the "Servant" candle, lights a second one.)

Second Reader:

Did you know that our New England ancestors didn't celebrate Christmas? They just didn't think it was right to take anything away from the celebration of each Sunday as the holiest day of all. They didn't allow any celebrations that were fun: no carols, no instrumental music, and no decorations.

It was our sister Universalist Church, now in West Hartford, that held the first church celebration of Christmas in Connecticut and that was just a little over 100 years ago. Why, in Boston, as late as 1870 a child who stayed home from school on Christmas Day could be expelled.

So, having trees and wreaths and such things in these parts is relatively new. But the custom was very old in Europe before Puritan times. We think the Christmas tree comes to us from Germany. There are a lot of stories about it and one is that it is symbolic of the tree from the Garden of Eden. The balls we tie on the tree now symbolize the apple which tempted Adam and Eve. The greens may come from the ancient Roman celebration of the Saturnalia when homes were decorated with green boughs and lighted candles — there were big dinners, visiting, good luck greetings and general merry-making. Let's sing!

294

All Sing: O Christmas Tree
(Spot #1 on full)

Minister:
We light our third candle for mistletoe — for touching and hugging — for kissing — and for love.

Candlelighter (comes forward with baskets of mistletoe passing them back and forth among the congregation for distribution)

Second Reader:
(continuing) We give you mistletoe to take home tonight to use at home, or if you dare, to sneak a kiss right now. It was a sacred plant among the Druids in Britain and was supposed to have all sorts of miraculous powers. So great was its power that enemies coming upon each other beneath the mistletoe in the forest would lay down their arms, exchange greetings and maintain a truce for a day. Placing mistletoe over the door of a home became a symbol of welcome and peace to all who entered. It became associated with Christmas strangely enough, because it was banned from the church because it was pagan. But one priest defied the ban and put a large bundle on the altar at Christmas declaring its healing power symbolized Christ's healing ministry. So, let's sing for all the green that decorate our Day!

All Sing: Deck the Hall

Minister:
We light our fourth candle for the gift of giving, for this is certainly a time of presents and baubles and stockings and things.

Candlelighter (comes forward as the others)

Third Reader:
The custom of giving gifts comes from at least two sources. In Spanish speaking countries especially the tradition of gifts from the Christ child is still followed. In other countries they celebrate the story of Saint Nicholas, a bishop who lived over 1500 years ago. He was rich and used his wealth to help the poor without leaving his name. Once three girls were about to be sold as slaves because their father had no money for a dowry. According to the legend, to avoid being seen, Bishop Nicholas dropped three bags of gold, one for each daughter, down their chimney where they landed in the daughter's shoes which had been left on the hearth to dry from the wet snow. that is supposed to account for the orange or tangerines or gold-covered chocolate coins in the foot of your stocking.
The names Kris Kringle and Santa Claus reflect these two traditions. The name used for ''Christ Child'' in Germany is *Christkindel*. And in Holland the Dutch for Saint Nicholas is *Sinter Klaas*.

One thing for sure, Christmas means great joy for all the children. So, let's sing the carol of great joy!

All Sing: Joy to the World

Minister:

Let us light our fifth candle for the sounds of Christmas — the laughter of young voices, the carols that we sing, and the bells, the many bells that peal forth our Yuletide cheer.

Sound Effect (bells pealing play over sound system as:)

Candlelighter (comes forward as the others.)
(As the pealing stops:)

All Sing: I Heard the Bells on Christmas Day

Minister:

We light this sixth candle for part of the story of the birth of Jesus. This is the story as it is found in the Book of Matthew.

Fourth Reader:

Now in the days of Herod the King, behold, wise men from the east came to Jerusalem, saying, Where is he that is born King of the Jews? for we saw his star in the east, and are come to worship him. And when Herod the king had heard it, he was troubled, and all Jerusalem with him. And gathering together all the chief priests and scribes of the people, he inquired of them where the Christ should be born. And they said unto him, In Bethlehem of Judea; for thus it is written by the prophet:

And thou Bethlehem, land of Judah,
Art in no wise least among the princes of Judah;
For out of thee shall come forth a governor,
Who shall be shepherd of my people Israel.

Then Herod privily called the wise men, and learned of them carefully what time the star appeared. And he sent them to Bethlehem, and said, Go and search out carefully concerning the young child; and when ye have found him, bring me word, that I also may come and worship him.

And they, having heard the king, went their way, and lo, the star, which they saw in the east, went before them, till it came and stood over where the young child was. And when they saw the star, they rejoiced with exceeding great joy. And they came into the house and saw the young child with Mary his mother; and they fell down and worshipped him; and opening their treasures, they offered him gifts, gold and frankincense and myrrh. And being warned of God in a dream that they should not return to Herod, they departed into their own country another way.

Matthew II

296

All Sing: We Three Kings of Orient Are

Minister:

So let us light our seventh light for all the lights of Christmas. The star that led those wise men in the east, the lights in store windows bringing trade to the merchants who clothe us and bring good things into our lives. Let us light the light for our hearths and windows and the light that shines in the branches of our trees the light of peace in the places of those we love and in the countenance of God.

Candlelighter (comes forward to do this as the rest;
                  at the same time)

Soloist: O Holy Night

Minister:

Our eighth light is for the shepherds — humble and nameless and poor — who heard the voices of angels on that night of nights.

Candlelighter (comes forward as:)

Fifth Reader:

Now there were in the same country shepherds in the field, and keeping watch over their flock by night. And an angel of the Lord stood by them, and the glory of the Lord shone round about them: and they were sore afraid. And the angel said unto them:

Fear not; for behold, I bring you good tidings of great joy
which shall be to all people:
For unto you is born this day in the City of David a
Saviour, which is Christ the Lord.
And this is the sign unto you:
Ye shall find a babe wrapped in swaddling clothes and
lying in a manger.

And suddenly there was with the angel a multitude of the heavenly host praising God, and saying:

Glory to God in the highest,
And on earth peace, good will toward all.

Minister:

Our last candle is lit for the infant Jesus. It is lit for all the children of the earth. It is lit for Moslem and Jew, Protestant and Catholic, black and white. It is lit for all the children and for men and women, young and old. It is lit for each one of us with a prayer for peace.

(All lights off)

Candlelighter (leads mother and child to the bench and
                  after they are seated)

A group of Children sing "Away in a Manger" while

Candlelighter (lights the last candle, slowly)

All Sing: Silent Night, Holy Night
                 verse 1, to guitar; soloist
                 sings verse 2 and all sing
                 verse 3.
(lights up gradually)

All Rise   (joining hands and saying)

Closing Words May faith in the human spirit
                 And hope for the human
                    community
                 And love of human freedom
                    Be ours, now,
                 And in all the days to come.

Minister:
         Just before we go let's just wish everyone
         A Merry Christmas

Piano Players   strike up "We Wish You a Merry
                 Christmas" and then "Jingle Bells"
                 whereupon emerges

Santa Claus with tangerines and bedlam ensues!

(This script was devised by a committee of children and their parents at Unitarian Universalist Society, East Manchester, CT. The text was written by Arnold Westwood. The material about some of the candle stories was gathered from a sermon by Ed Lane preached in Westport, December 24, 1967.)

LITANY FOR JOINING FOUR SIGNS ON CHRISTMAS EVE

earth

We light the brown candle this night for earth who gives us life. Ours be it to feel with the west people among us; they know her. Ours be it to not listen to the whispers of the taming people who would rend and pollute our Mother for gain.

We smell soft pines and snow patches on her flanks. We hear her soft sighing as she moves. We are reminded by her holy mountain west. We feel her, we live at her bosom.

air

We light the light blue candle this night for air, breath of life and sign of heaven come down to earth.

Ours be it to see with the east people among us who vision luna as she enters aquarius, for love. Ours be it to seek the Christ energy. For love, he came down from heaven. We shall press hearts and bodies close, for love. With each inbreathing we shall be vitalized, healed, by love.

We vision the dawn star rising in the light blue air, sign of love come down from heaven. We smell something new in this night's wind.

water

We light the dark green candle for water who gives new beings life.

Listen to the north people, few amongst us, who meditate by the waters and sky the new children and new beings coming to us. Ours be it to channel blessing to the new souls as they come from the One Soul. Ours be it to name them.

Listen to my heart's song as we name them, just given light. Be the holy warmed water touching them. Smell with them the corn meal that gives them their spirit name. Hold them by the waters of mystery through the long night of sweetness and dark velvet joy.

fire

We light the red orange candle for fire who gives us strength.

May we feel the warmth in our church family this night. Warmth flows from hand to hand and heart to heart. May each child of earth be warmed by our fire this holy night. May the old power of evil which beats about our stone walls tonight be driven off by our flames.

Feel with the south people tonight, for they teach us to dance and love with warm hearts. Look to their promise of Sol returned and days grown light again. Listen to their runes. We shall light our candles in hope!

— Forrest Whitman

299

CHRISTMAS EVE SERVICE

Prelude

Ringing the Bell

Narrator:

We are children of the light. Without the light of the sun, nothing would have come to life on this globe, and we would never have been. Our lives follow the pattern of night and day; we have made lights for ourselves to brighten the dark, and we stand in wonder at the beauty of the lights of stars and moon. We have now reached the turn of the year, when the days - grown very short - have started to grow longer once more. Like our forebears through many ages, we light candles to celebrate the turning of the year.

Song: Watchman, Tell Us of the Night

All people acknowledge the power of the sun. Indians danced to the sun, invoking its power to help them. One chief said, "When a person does a piece of work which is admired by all we say that it is wonderful; but when we see the changes of the day and night, the sun, moon and stars in the sky, and the changing seasons upon the earth, with their ripening fruits, anyone must realize that it is the work of someone more powerful than us. Greatest of all is the sun, without which we could not live."

People have thought of darkness as a symbol for ignorance and sin; they have made light the symbol of knowledge, hope, and salvation. The coming of a long-hoped-for Messiah had to be heralded by a magnificent and other-worldly light, one which was glorious beyond the possibilities of the everyday. And so the story was born, of how the shepherd heard the angels' song in the fields above Bethlehem, and "glory shone around."

Song: While Shepherds Watched Their Flocks By Night

The Greeks told the story of Prometheus, the Titan, who stole fire from the gods to bring it ito earth for people. The courage of Prometheus was surely needed when some shivering person drew near to the embers of a lightening-struck tree, and the skill of a Prometheus went into learning how to make fire anew when the embers died. Fire was a new light;it protected against enemies and the winter's cold. It stayed bright when the sun went down, and around it people could gather in the dark hours for the telling of stories that were passed down from generation to generation.

Even today, when our heat comes from coal and gas and oil, and our light from electricity, a fire on the hearth is the symbol of home, of family, of friends gathered for companionship. These days we appreciate the natural gifts of warmth and light more than usual, as our

300

resources are depleted and cost us more. Still, however the light and warmth may be made, we will always gather around them when the winds are chill and the snow lies on the ground.

Song: Joy to the World

We celebrate at this time of year a festival of light and of freedom, Hanukkah. The story is told, that when the Jews, under the leadership of the Maccabees, defeated the Syrian tyrant who had desecrated their Temple, a miracle of light occurred. The holy light which was to burn eternally in the Temple had been put out, and there was only one day's supply of oil. The miracle that Hanukkah recalls is that the oil lasted for eight days, until more could be obtained.

Menorah Lighter: Fresh oil have I prepared
And festal lamps have flared,
Come tell me what my lighting
means to me:

I have made a holy flame
Which reminds me of the name
Of the glorious and gallant
Maccabee.

Blessed art Thou, Lord our God, Ruler of the Universe, Thou hast sanctified with Thy commandments and ordained that we kindle the Hanukkah light. (Shammas candle is lighted.)

Blessed art Thou, Lord our God, Ruler of the Universe, that Thou hast given us life and sustenance and brought us to this happy season. (First candle is lighted.) (Remaining candles are lighted as narrator says:)

These lights we kindle to mark the marvelous liberation, and the wonders which Thou didst perform for our ancestors through Thy holy priests. Wherefore these lights are sacred all the eight days of Hannukkah, and we are not permitted to make profane use of them, but only to look at them so as to give thanks to Thee for Thy miraculous saving providence.

Menorah Lighter: Chilly winds may blow outside,
But my lamps with me abide.
Down, down with evil winds
wherever they be!

With my little oil prepared,
All my sacred lamps have flared
To the glory of the glorious
Maccabee!

301

Trumpet Solo (or #279 "Hanukkah Hymn")

In the day, the sun fills the skies. At night, there are other lights, not as bright, but lovely. For centuries people have been curious about the moon and the stars. Humans may have walked on the moon, and we may know much about the stars, yet we still look at them in wonder, and marvel at their beauty. Sara Teasdale wrote about stars -

> Stars over snow,
> > And in the western planet
> Swinging below a star -
> > Look for a lovely thing and
> > you will find it,
> It is not far,
> > It never will be far.

Legend tells that on this night, long ago, three wise men travelled by the light of one brilliant star to the place where a special child was born. they had studied the lore of the heavens, and to them this marvelous star meant that marvelous events were taking place. Sure enough, "swinging below a star" they found a "lovely thing," a babe as lovely as all babies ought to be.

Song: We Three Kings, verses 1-3

Through all of human history, mothers have sung to their babes by the light of whatever lights they had. Eskimo mothers sang by the light of whale oil lamps; mothers in early America watched over cradles lit by flames of candles they had dipped themselves. By whatever lights, mothers have given birth, have sung to their babes and cared for them. The story of Jesus' birth tell that the wondrous star lighted the stable. And perhaps his mother sang him a lullaby, as so many other mothers have done; if she did, she was unaware that, many years later, people would sing beautiful songs about the birth of this one child, and would call them "Christmas Carols."

Song: It Came Upon A Midnight Clear

The lights in the sky and the lights on the earth have meant more to us than light to see by and heat to warm our bodies. Light is a symbol of all the hopes of our kind. We know that we walk in the darkness of ignorance and evil and the fear of death; if we would go forward we need many more lights. As the sun is the symbol and source of physical light and energy, so the enlightened heart and mind are the sources of spiritual light. This light burning here is a symbol of the light that shines in the human heart. These persons who come bearing unlighted tapers come to take light from the heart of humanity and so spread it abroad in the world.

First Candle Bearer: This is the light of Love. With love we reach out to people near us, and then to people far away, people we have never seen. Loving and helping others makes us feel good, too.

Second Candle Bearer: This is the light of Peace. When there is anger and war, people are hurt and die, their homes are destroyed, their countries laid waste. When people understand and care for one another, they will live happily and peacefully together.

Third Candle Bearer: This is the light of Hope. Hope keeps us going when we're feeling low; hope keeps us believing that a time will come when there will be no taking of hostages and no fighting among nations - a time when all people will be friends.

Fourth Candle Bearer: This is the light of Freedom. It reminds us that many people in many lands are not free, because they live under tyranny. It reminds us too that freedom is more than freedom from that tyranny; it is freedom to learn and to think, freedom to be and become the best of which we are capable.

Over the face of the ancient earth, weary and torn with strife, the passing generations have come and are gone, and we have not yet seen the triumph of good will among people. May we here dedicate ourselves to the task of bringing our lights, our gifts of light, so that Life will turn bright in this world.

(Children with candles go down the aisles and light end candles in each row. All light candles from one another's. Sing first verse of "Silent Night" and hum next two. Then lights are put on in chancel and candles extinguished.

Song: Silent Night

Benediction:
    May the blessing of Christmas, which is peace of mind and heart, be with us all, and with it may there be fulfilled the words: "Peace on Earth, Good Will Towards All." amen
                                                    — Maryell Cleary

Note: This service is partly original and partly put together from other UU materials — some from WACH, some from REACH packets. Maryell Cleary varies it a little each year, but the basics remain the same. An older child who can memorize does the lighting of the menorah candles. Younger children may read their verses on the meaning of the candles.

CHRISTMAS EVENSONG

This service was prepared by Mark Belletini for the Starr King Unitarian Church, Hayward, CA. It is the custom here to have a potluck dinner on Christmas Eve (with the minister preparing the soup). Since handheld candles are against local fire regulations, several racks of candles are placed in the front of the Meeting Hall. A menorah is also present and a water-filled green glass chalice with a candle standing in the water. This serves as the chalice which is always lit at the beginning of the services in Hayward, and as a source of water and fire for the blessing of the child with the Four Elements. The renditions (translations) of the gospel narratives are by Mark Belletini. This liturgy, "The Lessons and Carols," is done the same each year, with different music and a small change in wording only. The basic order is in the hands of the assembly.

Gathering: with table talk and supper and greeting and a bit of chaos as we get ready to celebrate Yule

Preparing: with the bellsound comes silence, movement and music. We clean and move chairs and center ourselves around the menorah and the Naming Table: as we do all this, the music of William Mathias: "AVE REX: A Carol Sequence"

Beginning: The bellsound strikes and we enter into the spirit of things:

President: We are here

Assembly: TO GREET THE CHILD IN US THAT DESIRES NAUGHT BUT PEACE.

President: How beautiful upon the mountains are the feet of them that bring good news, that cry

Assembly: Peace! Peace!

President: and that bring tidings of the good, and that publish the coming of a healthy holiness!

Assembly: LET THE ROSE OF CHRISTMAS UNFOLD IN OUR HEARTS; LET THE NEW SUN RISE INSIDE US!

President: and may the star of Reason and the angel-song of Passion keep us true to ourselves, true to each other, and true to our vision of what we can become . . .

Kindling: here the chalice of our heritage is kindled in silence

Invoking:	a meditation on the chalice and the flame for Christmas
First Invocation:	By the lighting of these candles we signify the bursting forth of light in the midst of the shadows of winter,
	By the lighting of the flaming chalice we signify even more; the steadfastness of the light of truth, the universality of the light of choice, the brilliance of the light of courage shining in our history.
	By this symbol we affirm that the cup of salvation belongs to everyone, and that this our faith survives even the heat of fire because it is true. We invoke our future as well as our past with this present symbol. For the truth is ever victorious. amen
Quieting:	silence for a time, ended by the bellsound
Naming:	At the Christmastide it is the custom to celebrate parenting and to bless the babes: the order for the Rite of Naming: Statement to the parents, Queries to the parents, a gift of poetry, statement to the godparents, query to the godparents, blessing of the child with the four elements: earth, air, fire and water, blessing the child with names, closing through. And let us say AMEN.
Moving:	at the bellsound we move toward the candles, which we light, one at a time, each of us. (adults will aid the children, please) when you have lit a candle, please set up a chair. The music (again, Mathias) will help us make the transition to the lessons and carols.
Kindling:	the candle and a bit of frankincense
Invoking:	a meditation on the incense
Second Invocation:	(there is a single candle on the table with the bowl for frankincense, the banks of candles are flanking the table)
	By the lighting of this candle we signify the bursting forth of light in the midst of the human individual.
	By the lighting of these candles we signify the bursting forth of light in the human community.

305

By the kindling of this incense, we invoke the senses, those gifts by which we affirm this world, even in the midst of the long winter night. We praise the pungency of frankincense on our tongues, the sweetness of it in the air, the warmth of its haze against our skins, the crackling sound of it melting in the fire, the splendor of its swirling fronds of smoke dancing in the rich darkness. May we celebrate the winter holidays with all of our senses; with moderation in our bearing, with relief from our working, with joy in our heart of hearts. amen.

Caroling: Adeste Fideles (in Latin)

Reading: The first Story, a pause, a reflection

First Story: From Matthew's gospelbook

This is the story of the birth of Jesus. A young woman named Mary is engaged to a man named Joseph. But sometime before the wedding ceremony, he discovers that she is pregnant. Now Joseph is a good and kind individual, and knows that Mary will be disgraced if he were to publically accuse her of infidelity; so he resolves to keep the whole thing to himself, and break off the engagement "for private reasons" so that Mary will be free to marry the presumed father of the child.

However, on the very night that he has worked out this plan, a divine messenger speaks in his dreams: Joseph, descendant of King David, do not fret about marrying your fiancee, Mary; for it is through divine influence that she is to become a mother. The child born to her you shall name Jesus, and he will show the people a way that shall end the error of their ways.

And so Joseph continues his engagement with Mary, and takes care of her, but he does refuse to sleep with her until after she has given birth to her son.

First Lesson: By this lesson I learn that the world may indeed be different from what my reason tells me; and I learn that experience of that world is wide enough to embrace my dreams, and that love can learn much from a good and honest sense of honour.

Caroling: Lo, How A Rose E'er Blooming

Reading: The second Story, a pause, a reflection

306

Second Story:
And so, it comes around that the Roman Emperor, Octavian Augustus, issues an order calling for a census of the entire inhabited world for purposes of fair taxing. This census, the first of its kind anywhere, is mandated in the East by Suspicius Quinrinius, the Governor of Syria, who orders that all persons return to the town or city where they had been born.

So Joseph, who lives in the jurisdiction of Quinrinius, leaves the city of Nazara up north, and travels down south, to Bethlehem, his ancestral town; and along with him rides his fiancee, Mary. Mary is pregnant, and her term is almost over. It comes as no surprise then to find out that she gives birth to her first-born there in Bethlehem; she wraps him up tight so he can't move, according to custom, and his first crib turns out to be the cattle-trough in the yard, for there is no privacy for the young family in the teeming lodge.

Second Lesson: By this lesson I learn that the one called Almighty by the orthodox is actually as powerless as a babe; I learn that privacy and solitude are necessary if I am to give birth to anything worthwhile in my life; and yet I also learn that the good to which we give birth will not be able to move or grow lest we remove the swaddling clothes of hesitation and blind custom we tighten around it.

Caroling: O Little Town of Bethlehem

Quieting: silence for a time

Reading: the third lesson, a pause, a reflection

Third Story:
Now in the area around Bethlehem are many sheep herders; and some of these are keeping a nightwatch on their flocks the evening that Mary gives birth. So there, in the open fields, a messenger of God appears to them, and the earth around them is lit with a powerful light, and to-the-last, the sheepherders are frightened out of their wits.

But a voice from the messenger comforts them: Do not be afraid! Please! For I am bringing you news of great import which will bring joy to all people. For today, over in Bethlehem a Messiah has been born, one who shall mean more than the whole world to you; you will find this child easily; he is the one lying swaddled . . . in a cattle-trough!

Suddenly there appeared with the messenger a whole sky-born

choir praising God: GLORY TO GOD IN THE HEAVENS AND ON THE EARTH! PEACE TO HUMANITY, WHOM GOD FAVORS WITH LOVE!

When the choir vanishes, the sheepherders decide to look for the child. And so they hurry off to Bethlehem, and they find Mary and Joseph and the babe lying in the feeding-trough. They begin to tell the astonished parents what happened to them. Mary does not understand, but nonetheless will continue to think about the strange story the rest of her life. After a while, the sheepherders return to their tasks, singing songs and praises to God for the wonderful things that had happened to them that night. After a few days, Mary and Joseph have a Naming Ceremony and a Circumcision Rite performed: and they name the baby Jesus, just as the messenger had asked them to.

Third Lesson:	By this lesson, I learn that only those who keep watch steadfastly in the pitch of nighttime and the cold of winter will receive the good news of light; and I learn that song is very close to what the mystics mean when they speak of the eternal, and that some things in this world I shall never understand, but neither shall I forget their wonder, either.
Caroling:	Angels We Have Heard On High
Reading:	the fourth and last lesson, a pause, a reflection

Fourth Story:

Now, after Jesus had been born in Bethlehem of Judea, in the days of King Herod the Great, a party of astrologers from Iran arrives in Jerusalem, and begins to ask amongst the citizens: Where can we find the young prince who shall inherit the throne of Israel? We have seen the Star of Royalty appear in the constellations of Jewry at sunrise; and so we have come to pay all due respect to the new-born prince of the Jews.

Now King Herod is livid when he hears about the query of the astrologers, for he knows that he has not recently sired a son. So he calls a counsel of fact-finders and experts to advise him on the matter. And these search the scriptures and say to Herod: The star-gazers must be sent to Bethlehem, for listen to what Malachi says:

And you, Oh Bethlehem of the South! You are the last but you are not the least; oh no!
For it's from you that the leader of my people Israel shall come, and nowhere else!

So Herod invites the astrologers for an audience, privately; he finds out from them the exact date when they began to notice the Star

308

of Royalty. Then he tells them about the verse from Malachi, and says: Go to Bethlehem now, and find out all you can about this child, and then, come back and tell me about him so that I can find him myself to pay all due respect.

So the astrologers agree to Herod's request, and they set off to Bethlehem, the Star of Royalty shining before them the whole way, indeed, seeming to rest upon the house where the child is to be found. They enter the house, see Mary and the babe, and immediately genuflect, as before a king; then they proffer their gifts: royal gold, priestly incense, healthful myrrh. The astrologers are warned in a dream not to keep their word with King Herod, and so they return to Iran by another route.

Last Lesson:	By this lesson I learn that from the humblest oft comes the greatest; I learn that jealousy is a sin that leads to careless wrath and the sundering of the peace, and that the stars above us can serve as wondrous lights and guide us at last till the rosy sun doth rise and make the whole world light.
Caroling:	We Three Kings
Blessing:	The proper for the day AMEN
	Joan Baez carols send us quietly and safely into the night.

AMEN AND HAPPY HOLIDAYS

Blessing:

Let us go in peace, the peace which haunts our imaginations and Christmastide, and dogs our tracks all year, which burns as a thousand candles beneath the gloom and pall of history, burning forth, bursting forth, like the sun in January, like a child from a womb, great and humble, great and humble. And let us not be afraid, and let the child be born at last, and the whole world give back the song which now the angels sing. Amen and Amen.

— Mark Belletini

LIGHT-BRINGERS

Prelude: Herald Angels, Mendelsohn
                     Jesus Who Didst Ever Guide, Bach
                     Cantique de Noel, Adam

Introit: Angels We Have Heard On High

Prologue: *Unheralded, Save By A Song*

The new arrival, now as before
Is unknown, unacclaimed once more,
Unheralded — save by a song
The heart may hear that listens long.

For music out of stillness breaking,
The ancient Word again awaking
That only love will yet fulfill:
On earth peace, to all good will.
                          — Anon.

Carol: O Come All Ye Faithful

Reading: Angels and Shepherds, Luke 2:8-16

Antiphonal Carol: Whence, O Shepherd Maiden
                     #160, *We Sing of Life*

Reading: *Wonder of Wonders* by David Rhys Williams

Wonder of wonders
Is the mystery
Enshrining the birth of every Christ-child!

Brave Akhnaton, prophet of purified religion,
Zoroaster, heroic champion of righteousness,
Meek Moses, divine leader of revolt —
Compassionate Gautama,
Uncompromising Socrates,
Confucius, the wise and wonderful counselor,
Mystical Francis, gentle brother to both man and beast,
Imperious Mohammed, welder of wild hordes,
And lowly Jesus, Prince of Peace,
And herald of heaven on earth.

Whence came these Saviors?
Whence these embodiments of Moral Genius?
What Mystic Spirit sired them?

What Cosmic Womb conceived them?
What spiritual Omen presaged their advent?
Were they not Sons of Giant Meteors,
Progeny of the Milky Way,
Sparks from far-off Suns and Stars
Come to illumine Earth's Spiritual Night?

Who sent them here?
What brought them here:
We wonder!
We will never cease to wonder!

Carol: O Little Town of Bethlehem

Reading: *A Frontier Nativity* by Carl Sandburg from
                     The Prairie Years Vol. I, page 529

Carol: Little Jesus, Sweetly Sleep
                     (#159, *We Sing of Life*)

Episode: The Light Bringers (led by minister from desk; with six 6-8 graders, each representing a Light-Bringer. They were seated individually throughout congregation. Each stood to read, facing as many people as possible; then sat down)

"Aunt, take him, he'll never come to much," So said young Dennis Hanks, handing to Betsy Sparrow, kindly relative, the newborn baby whom all the world would know as Abraham Lincoln. Though he was born in a house with only one door and one window, he would come to know many doors, many windows, he would read many riddles and doors and windows.

Every child newborn is both an unlikely and a likely child: Jesus around whose birth our Christmas stories are gathered, Lincoln, with an early laughing child prophecy that he would never come to much, and every other child loved, neglected — those born to be remembered by a few or by a multitude — those born to be unknown or little known — those born to take, each one, a special part in the world's life and work — among them all the babies who, when grown, would be humanity's light-bringers of many countries and of different eras.

There was the child whose very name has been forgotten, born in Palestine some centuries before the time of Jesus, whose written word, twice embodied in the Hebrew scriptures, has never been forgotten, never entirely fulfilled:
    And they shall beat their swords into plowshares, and their spears into pruning hooks; nation shall not lift up

sword against nation, neither shall they learn war any more.

Many centuries before the coming of that nameless light-bringer there was born in Egypt a child destined to be Emperor. Who could have known that from the shining of the sun upon all people of the world that child would later recognize the oneness of all? As Emperor he chose the name Akhnaton. Of the one god symbolized by the sun with its helpful rays, he said:

> Thou alone, shining in thy form as living Aton, Dawning, glittering, going afar and returning. Thou makest millions of forms through thyself alone; cities and tribes, highways and rivers.

In ancient Greece was born a baby named Socrates, who when grown kept asking questions, challenging people then and ever since to think for themselves. According to his great disciple Plato, this was a prayer of Socrates:

> Give me beauty in the inward soul; and may the outward and the inward person be at one.

Gathered around the birth of Gautama of India a century or so before the birth of Socrates, are birth stories like the birth stories of Jesus. Gautama, known also as the Buddha — the enlightened one — told, as did other teachers of humanity, of a light within:

> Be ye lamps unto yourselves; be your own confidence; hold to the truth within yourselves as to the only lamp.

A baby born in China at about that time, known as Confucius, became the most greatly revered of all Chinese, and one of humanity's great teachers. Among the things he taught was this:

> Within the four seas all are brothers and sisters.

Of Jesus, whose birth is celebrated every Christmas, it is written, "In him was life; and the life was the light of all." When he grew to maturity, Jesus said as he was teaching:

> Ye are the light of the world. A city that is set on a hill cannot be hid. Neither do we light a candle, and put it under a bushel, but on a candlestick, and it giveth light unto all that are in the house.

These and many others, of many countries, Light-Bringers to the world, came into the world as babies, each with wonderful potentialities, but, like other babies, each with an unknown future.

312

As we celebrate the birth of Jesus let us recognize with deep gratitude the wonderful potentialities of every baby, the commonwealth of all the people of the earth, and the truth and understanding we may learn from the world's light-bringers.

Anthem:	Break Forth, O Beauteous Heavenly Light, Schop-Bach
Episode	*A Christmas Eve Choral,* by Bliss Carmen

(This lovely reading may be found in "Christ in the Poetry of Today," by Elvira Slack, p. 21) A speech choir, "Mary" and "Joseph" can read this poem antiphonally.

Carol:	Silent Night
White Gifts:	(canned goods and other staples)

We bring White Gifts, thinking of other people, and also remembering that it is blessed to receive ourselves, the gifts that show the thoughtfulness and love of those who care for us. We bring White Gifts not knowing exactly who will receive them, yet in a spirit of friendliness, and hoping that the various things we bring will add something to the happiness of people like ourselves. We bring as our White Gifts the kinds of things that we ourselves find good, hoping that whoever it is who may receive them will also find them good — hoping that the people who receive these gifts will have us in their kind thoughts this Christmas time. And we are remembering that to give and to receive are good at any time when giving and receiving mean that people have kind thoughts for one another.

— Vincent Silliman

Carol:	Ring Bells Ring (#147, *We Sing of Life*)

Benediction (adapted from Karl Chworowsky)

The joy that abides, the love that never fails, and the peace of God that passeth understanding be with you, and with people everwhere.

Response:	Peace on Earth, Wilson
Postlude:	Joy to the World, Handel

— Vincent B. Silliman

The Christmas season is a natural time to hold child-naming services or dedication services. Not only because part of the Christmas celebration centers around December 25 the symbolic birthday of Jesus, but also because this is a time when many family members are home for the holidays. Grandparents, aunts and uncles who might not be available at other times, can join in the celebration.

Some combine the naming ceremony with candlelighting. One congregation, for instance, has older brothers and sisters light candles in honor of their new siblings. Other congregations vary the dedication services by seasonal references. Some congregations combine both of the above elements. A sampling of some of these services follows.

The center and core of the Christmas festival, the Holy Family, long antedates the Christian era. People have worshipped before the shrine of the Madonna and Child from time immemorial for the simple reason that it symbolizes one of the sacred realities, one of the supreme mysteries of life — the miracle of birth and motherhood. The wise men do well to bow before the cradle; it is inconceivable that an event so fraught with significance should not be clothed in the garments of sacredness, the robes of religion. The value of the Christmas story lies not in its recital of the birth of one marvelous child, but in that it takes up the common experience of parents, their joy and wonder over the miracle they have wrought, their tender love toward this helpless creature, their fond dreams for its future, and weaves them into a myth that seeks to express their inherent sacredness. All families are potentially Holy Families.

— E. Burdette Backus

Christmas is the season when we celebrate the birth of the little Jewish baby, Jesus. It should be the season when we celebrate the birth of *all* babies. To every parent their child is a very special child, its birth is a very special birth, and divine possibilities are there. James Oppenheim said of every newborn child:

"You may be Christ or Shakespeare, little child,
A Saviour or a sun to our lost world,
There is no babe born but may carry furled
Strength to make bloom the earth's disastrous wild."

This year we are celebrating Christmas with an added ceremony — a ceremony of welcome to every new baby born to a family of our church since last Christmas. As a sign of our loving welcome, we shall light a candle as each child's name is read:

(Read each name and date of birth — a candle is lighted for each one.)

One of the candles on the Communion Table, we now light in commemoration of the little baby's birth so long, long ago — the baby who grew up and became the one who said among other things, "Suffer the little children to come unto me, and forbid them not; for of such is the kingdom of God. Verily, I say unto you, whosoever shall not receive the kingdom of God as a little child, shall not enter therein." And he took them up in his arms, put his hands upon them, and blessed them.

The other candle on the Communion Table, we now light in commemoration of another little baby's birth years ago this Christmas, the baby girl who grew to womenhood and ministered unto people, binding up wounds bringing light and love and comfort; and founded the American Red Cross — Clara Barton — Universalist, humanitarian, lover of humanity.

On Christmas Eve, you may light a candle in your own home, place it in your window so that all who pass may know that at Christmas, light came into the world through Clara Barton, Jesus, and oh, so many other babies.

— Lawrence W. Abbott

315

NAMING AT CHRISTMAS

As is our custom, we set aside time at this special season of hope to celebrate the births — the Christmases we have had within our midst this past year. It is not a sacrilege to say that somewhere any given day there is another Christmas — as Sophia Fahs has said, "Each night a child is born is a holy night . . ."

READING: Sophia Fahs: "For so the children come . . ."

Will the families of the children whose births we are celebrating now please bring them forward?

We celebrate these births with lighted candles to symbolize the new lives that have begun — in a universal recognition of the awe and wonder we all feel at the creation of life, our feeling of obligation to be worthy of this great gift of life, and our acceptance of these new lives into our society.

Will the older brothers and sisters (or parents) of the children born this past year come now and light the candles in their brother's and sister's names. (As each person lights a candle, the name of the child is spoken loudly along with the birth date.)

The lighting of these candles affirms that the gift of life is a good gift, and we all re-affirm this now by reading together:

> AS WE CONTEMPLATE THE MIRACLE OF BIRTH, AS WE RENEW IN OUR HEARTS THE SENSE OF WONDER AND JOY, MAY WE BE STIRRED TO A FRESH AWARENESS OF THE SACREDNESS OF LIFE AND OF THE DIVINE PROMISE OF CHILD-HOOD. MAY WE SO LIVE THAT OUR CHILDREN WILL BE ABLE TO ACQUIRE OUR BEST VIRTUES AND TO LEAVE BEHIND OUR WORST FAILINGS. MAY WE PASS ON THE LIGHT OF COURAGE AND COMPASSION, AND THE QUESTING SPIRIT; AND MAY THAT LIGHT BURN MORE BRIGHTLY IN THESE CHILDREN THAN IT HAS IN US.

And so we welcome (repeat name of each child and acknowledge each one individually) into our circle of light and life and love — we time-worn folk renew ourselves at your enchanted spring, as though we are begun again in you. Welcome!

READING: Edward Ericson: "We Stand With Eyes Toward The East"

— Patricia Bowen

Christmas Eve Child Welcoming Ceremony

A tradition of our faith speaks of a child born in a rude stable two thousand years ago. It is written that great and humble came to view the babe and then departed, never again to renew the promise they felt in that event.

So does legend convey the oft sad truth of promises broken and unfulfilled.

Tonight we come to keep faith with a promise — the promise of the young life before us. For these children need the love, the understanding, the continuous guidance, which only we as their friends and teachers can give.

Therefore do we covenant together in a solemn yet joyous service of welcoming.

Charge to the Parents

By bringing your children to this ceremony you have said that their lives are sacred to you and to the members of this congregation.

You have also said that you will do your best to encourage these children throughout their growing years to gain an ever deeper sense of their own potentiality and of how they may make of this world one community of love.

Do you now reaffirm these intentions?

(The parents will answer: We do.)

The Congregation's Promise

As members of this congregation it is our task to strengthen each other in every high resolve.

This must apply to the infant, the child, and the youth as well as to the adult.

Therefore, we will do our best to make of this meeting house a home wherein these children may learn that love, patience, honesty, courage, beauty, joy, and service to humanity are real values shared and sought after by real people. And that our hearts will always be open to these persons in their failures as well as their triumphs.

Thus do we covenant with these children and their parents.

Act of Welcoming

(To the parents) Please tell us your child's full name.

_____, with a rose and water, ancient symbols of love and purity, it is my joyous privilege to welcome you into the guardian fellowship of this church.

— David Hicks MacPherson

The Seeker of the Water Sign — for Christmas Eve Blessing of Children

I am the seeker of the sign of water.
The deeps of the soul, sisters and brothers; it is the deep places in you I seek. The great ocean of memory, myth, song, and dream is my seeking ground, and north is my direction.

Children are given us out of this mystery. Out of the firmament of the waters above the heavens they come to us as precious gifts. And, each year, the north people in our church tell their names. Always the same they are given light. There is the breaking of the waters and the long patient giving of the mothers while the fathers of our people care beside. Holy and beautiful is the night a child is born. Lovely the gifts from the women's group, always including the blue corn. And mysterious too is this night! Each time one soul comes forth from the One Soul is a night of mystery. Here are some puzzles: Why did this child choose us? Why does the honor of blessing come to us tonight? Where will we dance in the long way of work, and care, and sorrow ahead? The answers are in the deep places, in the waters. (The ceremony of blessing children — with water — and naming them with their new middle name and using blue corn meal grown near takes place.)

THE CONGREGATION RESPONDS: THESE CHILDREN ARE A SIGN TO US. WE SHALL CARE WITH THEM, ASSIST THEM TO KNOW THE WISDOM OF RELIGION, THE LIFE OF FAITH. TOGETHER WE LEARN MORE OF OUR TRUE NAMES.

I announce to you, my church family, that the sign of the waters is in our midst and that this night the new age dawns! The dark green candle I light is for the sign of waters.

— Forrest Whitman

The New Year is before us, like morning-fresh untrodden snow, unmarked by human tracks.

As we walk the days ahead, may our paths be straight and clear, widening into highways fair.

Where we pause and have dealings with others, may homes of fellowship arise.

May streets and market places echo with gladness; may we build a city of tomorrow, peopled with understanding and rich with peace.

The New Year is like a new day unlived; a tomorrow yet to dawn; without life, empty.

We shall fill the coming year with our daily living; it is ours to make or mar.

May our dreams and hopes be worthy of the best within us, and our lives be worthy of our dreams.

— Sydney H. Knight

Lord, take the moments of our lives, the good and the bad, the happy and the sad, and turn them into timeless memoria in the making of our souls, that we may reach beyond things temporal to truths eternal, wherein the holiness and wholeness of life is known and celebrated in all its pain and glory, and whence all beginnings and endings begin and end in Thee.

New stars
New hope
New friends
And friendship ever true
New food for soul and body
New love
And love ever to renew
New days
For a new year
Of life —
Gratitude ever fresh
With the o'ercoming
Of strife.
A new you
And a new me
To better serve one another
And to worship Thee.

— Richard M. Fewkes

TO BEGIN A NEW YEAR

The troubles in sailing are most likely to occur at full sail, running before the wind.

The dangers of a nation are greatest when its luxury and power make the going easy. The difficulty is that people begin to trust in their luxury rather than in those values that are necessary to sustain them generation after generation.

Over and over in history this point has been discussed. It is one of those old truisms that is often neglected because we think we know it well enough to forget it. Reading the other day in a work of history, I came to this sentence: "The Carthaginians had wealth beyond the dreams of avarice together with a commerce which made them masters of the Mediterranean, yet, in the sequel, they became the mere puppets of a soulless splendor, and ultimately they were crushed beneath their weight of golden circumstance." (Tsanoff, *The Moral Ideals of Civilization*).

"Puppets of a soulless splendor" — that is perhaps the danger of every nation in full sail before the wind; "crushed beneath the weight of golden circumstance" — that is a danger of every affluent nation. At what point does a nation slip from its spirit, unable to use its wealth for great ends, not ready and willing to pursue ideals — at what point does it slip into that state where the personage is visible but the person has decayed? The question must ever be in our minds, especially at the beginning of a New Year.

We need not be Jeremiahs announcing, as do scores of writers in our time, that our national past was golden good and that we are now the degenerate sons and daughters of our forebears. Such is not the case at all, for in many areas we have a much higher moral concept than did they. Surely our concern for the sick and maimed, the mentally ill, the displaced persons of our culture, and for those who in one way or another have been shortchanged in life, is greater today than formerly. We are more tolerant of differences, more understanding of deviations, and have a fair-mindedness that did not characterize much of our past. Still our concern as we face the New Year must be that we uphold certain public standards.

320

We need honesty in public officials so that graft does not figure so prominently in most public work projects; we need a citizenry who realize that there are lasting values money can't buy; we need people in every human calling who are interested in doing a good job, to make a contribution, and to serve humanity; we need men and women who have an internal authority to match the material grandeur of our day.

With such citizens in our land in great numbers we'll know when to heave to and head up wind.

— Ralph N. Helverson

We cannot enter the New Year clean and pure as the shiny babes pictured in illustrations of New Years Eve. Neither we nor the world work that way. We enter a new year bearing the encrustations of our time-worn past.

I know it's always a shock to parents when they see their new and perfect children for the first time cut open by accident or injury — the shock of recognizing a permanent blemishing, the beloved scarred forever. We collect over a lifetime scores of scars and no amount of New Year celebrating or cosmetic surgery can conceal them.

We get permanently bruised from falls out of our cribs, at play, in barns and fields and kitchen, from collisions and escapades, illnesses and war. We collect scars on our thumbs, fingers, hands, around the eyes (oh blessed eyebrows so punished to save our sight), and vaccination scars, acne scars, appendectomy scars, a lifetime of lesions on the back, belly, our knees, necks, ankles.

The world's history is engraved with scars, from a plague of pox to a felon's branded cheek, to a sight I'll never forget in college after football practice, in the shower, an ex-Commando who'd got hit in the chest by a flamethrower at Dieppe. Our carcasses get battered, even the luckiest ones, and these significations carry into every future history.

But if our marked hides testify to our vulnerability and fragility, they also tell of our durability — the transfiguring into the toughest of tissues this baklava of our skin. Amidst the brutalities of life our scars witness to the persistent, countermanding mysteries of healing, re-knitting, re-joining, re-covering, as miraculous as any birth.

On Crispin Crispian anniversaries Henry's veterans of Agincourt would strip their sleeves, show their scars, and proudly stand a tip-top. We cannot enter the New Year smooth as babes, but we do enter as survivors, often enriched, tougher, wiser, and, seasoned by life's struggles, readier for the time to come. Our scars signal more than lamentation; not injury but renewal, not grief but reconciliation, not ruin but restoration, not the old year's accumulation of woe, but the new year's reality of healing, strength, and hope.

Standing a tip-toe, let us greet one another this Holiday time. Happy New Year.

— Clarke Dewey Wells

A NEW YEAR MEDITATION

This moment of silence
    we have dedicated to listening
    in silence . . .

It represents stillness:
    the stillness of repose, beyond our striving;
    the stillness of peace which we seek in God
    or miss achingly in this torn world;
    the stillness of an ultimate peace and
    perhaps a healing
    which we seek beyond our days.

It represents fullness:
    for silence is not emptiness but fullness;
    the fullness of potentiality before the deed;
    the fullness of possibility before the thought;
    the fullness of the Divine Life before Creation.

And, at last, our silence represents:
    all that we cannot say,
    the words which we often cannot find
    in our praying
    or in our groping thought upon
    the ultimate things.

Our silence represents astonishment
    at the Miraculous Fact,
    after which there is nothing to say.

It means receiving, not giving;
    waiting, not doing;
    hoping, not knowing;
    resting, not strife;
    and peace.

Silence, too, is prayer and meditation
    acceptable to God.

After we have thrown into the void our folly and our
    noise, after we have instructed divinity in the
    ways of divinity or sought to entice personal
    favors,
    God waits for us in silence
    which will be filled.

Silence is often the better prayer.

                           — Ernest C. Werner

WATCHNIGHT SERVICE: NEW YEAR'S EVE

Prelude   "Rememberance"
                     "The Horseman"
                     "Northern Song"
                     "New Year Song"
                         from *Album for the Young*
                         Op. 68 Robt. Schumann

Opening Reading   *The Loom of Years* by Alfred Noyes

Carol   Tune: Nos Galan (Welsh traditional)
                     See *The Oxford Book of Carols*
                         #50 for text and tune.

Reading   *Ithaca* by C.P. Cavafy

Unison Reading   #501 HCL by Walt Whitman

Music   "Wintertime" Op. 68, No. 38
     Robt. Schumann

Fire Communion

You are invited to write on the slips provided some happening of the past year you would be glad to be rid of and forget - something about which you are regretful, ashamed, or unhappy. These papers will be collected and incinerated unread as part of our service.

Carol   Tune: Deus Tuorum Militum
                     Words: Tennyson (adapted)

Ring out, wild bells, to the wild sky,
The flying cloud, the frosty light:
The year is dying in the night;
Ring out, wild bells, and let it die.

Ring out the old, ring in the new,
Ring, happy bells, across the snow:
The year is going, let it go;
Ring out the false, ring in the true.

Ring out false pride in place and blood,
The civic slander and the spite;
Ring in the love of truth and right,
Ring in the common love of good.

Ring in the spirit broad and free,
The larger heart, the kindlier hand;
Ring out the darkness of the land;
Ring in the light that is to be.

Silent Meditation

Bells at Midnight

Reaffirmation of Fellowship #160 HCL
Shalom, havayreem!
— Phillip Hewett

THE TIME OF DYING AND BORNING - A New Year
Celebration

The Time of Dying

No one can say when humans first knew that their lives would
come to an end. Somewhere back near the beginning people may have
believed that deaths were due to accidents or to some offense committed against the gods. Eventually, however, it became apparent that
death would be the final portion of all. Then came the time of
supposings:

Suppose we had a medicine to heal all ills.

Suppose we had a god to forgive all sins.

Suppose there were no volcanos, no mammoths, nor swamps,
and just suppose we were not stupid, evil or even human - then we
might live forever!

Religions have made much of such supposings; such seekings to
banish death forever. That's natural. In fact it has been just about the
only hope for millions of this world's oppressed.

Yet in our day when death has come in such massive forms and
numbers there is a deep need for us to come to terms with it; to stop
pushing it away; to admit its presence; to accept its call to us. Perhaps
if we do enfold it we may end its age-long terror, and in the bargain
cease to misuse its power through wars, pogroms, and famines.

In such a hope, this New Year's Eve, we celebrate our endings as
well as our beginnings. We say, Goodbye to all of those who in this
past year have died; those known to us, and those many millions more
unknown.

How many millions have died I cannot say, nor can I pin-point the manner of all their endings.

I am certain that some have died quite unawares, satisfied in their years and their deeds; loved and mourned by their families and friends.

I know that others died far, far too young; died hard and sure or soft and full of fear; while others were swept along by the winds of passionate patriotism.

I realize that hundreds of thousands more, even millions, of all ages, died as the earth called them in its periodic harvests of drought, famine, and disease.

And I am aware of those who cried for help, or screamed in anger as they ended their own lives.

Most of us knew one or more of these. What can we now say to them?

To those who lived fully, whether briefly or long, we salute you, and give thanks that you walked and shared among us!

To those who lived meanly, by a mixture of self or other's choice, we salute you in sorrow. May you, the perpetrators and the victims, rest now forever.

To those whose deaths were the tragedy of a humanity which cannot yet bestir itself to embrace its whole being, we salute you in repentance. We will try again to make this a universalist world. Do not let us rest.

(The lighting of the candles)

To pierce the darkness, but not to dispel it, we will light some candles. May their flames serve to honor those who gave this universe a consciousness by their coming and going.

First, for those members of this church who died during this past year: (at this point the full name of the deceased person is called out and then a candle is lit. Softly in the background the pianist/organist is playing the tune of the hymn, "Rank By Rank.")

Second, for the relatives of our members who died this past year: (Members and friends of the church family whose relatives have died in the past year are asked to stand. The hymn continues.)

Third, for all our brothers and sisters in the body of humanity: (The remainder of the congregation is asked to rise while John Donne's poem is read. The hymn continues.)

No one is an island, entire of themselves;
Every person is a piece of the continent,
A part of the main;
If a clod be washed away by the sea,
Europe is the less,
As well as if a promontory were
As well as if a manor of thy friends
Or of thine own were;
Any person's death diminishes me,
Because I am involved in humanity;
And therefore
Never send to know for whom the bell tolls;
It tolls for thee.

(The whole congregation shall then join in singing the hymn, "Rank By Rank," #258 HCL.)

After the congregation is reseated:

The Time of Borning

Since we last celebrated the New Year something like seventy million infants have been born into this world - and lived. I do not know how many more died in their first year. Whatever the lands of their births, the tongues of their parents, the colors of their skins, or even the amount of time they will spend on this planet, the fact of their coming is at once our hope and our dread.

They are our hope, because through them humanity renews itself. We try again to fulfill the ideals to which in the past we have been but partially equal. So with a slowly awakening consciousness of our place in the family of humankind, to all these children we say, "Happy Birthday!"

You do not have to show us your credentials. You are here and that is enough for us. We are, to borrow a promise from our religious past, your godparents. Your fate is increasingly our responsibility, as is our future in your hands. And that is why we also dread your coming.

Our intertwining fate forces us to admit how baby-like we still remain; how helpless we are that with all our knowledge, with all the power at our command, we have not yet made this world a safe and exciting place for you to grow. So not only in joy, but in deep, deep humility we cry out our greetings to you: Again, - "Happy Birthday!"

(The lighting of the candles)

(Now the pianist/organist begins softly the hymn, "Now I Recall My Childhood" - #82 HCL.)

First, for the children born into our church family during this past year: (at this point the full name of each child is called out as each candle is lit, and members of their family are asked to stand.)

Second, for all the children born into the body of humanity; as you grow may the flame of freedom, love, and justice grow within you, that you may know peace and be a blessing to the generation you will bring forth. (Now the whole congregation is asked to rise and join in the singing of "Now I Recall My Childhood." At the close of the hymn the following dedication is spoken:)

These candles will not burn very long. In a few minutes we will leave this meeting house and go our separate ways. But in another sense these candles need never go out. For by our lighting them we have committed to our memories the hopes they symbolize, which no winds can extinguish. Let us then live in the bright promise they hold forth in the year before us all. amen

— David Hicks MacPherson

JANUARY TWELFTH NIGHT CELEBRATION

Purpose: This celebration was conceived in order to provide UU families and individuals of all ages with a communal experience to consciously end the winter holiday season as part of the larger ''calendar life'' of each year; and in a related fashion to commemorate the birth of Michael Servetus, a martyred forerunner of what came to be the Unitarian movement.

The similarity in name to the traditional ''Twelfth Night'' is intentional both for seasonal flavor and because its inclusion of the date January Twelfth can thus impress minds of all ages with ready reference to Servetus and to the date of his birth in the year 1511. Overall the occasion can be a valuable teaching tool in regard to cultural practices and traditions and for enhancing UU religious identification with an outstanding historical figure and the important events which surrounded him.

The initial potluck and gift-sharing are not incidental or expendable: their purpose is to insure a strong group closeness that is essential to the Undecorating of the Tree, the Renewal of Resolve, the Burning of the Tree, and the Honoring of Servetus. Any activities substituted for the supper and sharing should have the same purpose.

The activities in this Celebration also have an intentional flow: beginning with the sharing and mutual support symbolized in the potluck; direct interaction of all ages in gift-sharing; review and perspective of the holiday season past and its cyclical recurrence by undecorating the tree; introspective awareness through personal resolution; the sacral nature of sacrifice in bearing of the tree to the burning area outdoors; the honoring of Servetus; and to final expressions of spiritual unity as the embers fade and all depart.

The church Christmas Tree had remained decorated and in the main foyer as a means of continuity till January Twelfth.

This celebration was conceived and led in performance by the Rev. John Burgiaga and Ms. Caroline Fenderson, respectively the minister and professional Director of Religious Education of the UU Church of Clearwater, Florida, on January 12, 1981. Participating were 50 persons affiliated with that congregation. All had gathered in response to previous announcement of a "January Twelfth Night" Celebration to bid farewell to the Winter holidays and to commemorate the birth of Michael Servetus. (Note: check local fire laws before burning your tree.)

Order of Activities

Potluck Supper (social and communal, symbolizing mutual sharing, caring, support)

Gift-Sharing (All have brought inexpensive, wrapped gifts, placed under the tree on entering. After the supper, each child and adult takes a number which indicates order of selection for the gift of their choice. Successive selectors may exchange their gifts, on demand, with a previous selector. Good-natured interchange is thus created between all ages. This is enhanced by adult seating in a large circle with tree at top of circle; children tend to assume the open space within and in front of the tree.)

Undecorating of Tree (All gather in family groups, or in friendship clusters):

Minister: The tree is the great symbol around which cluster all the meanings of the great winter festival we have enjoyed. Its lights and decorations symbolize bright hopes and the joys of celebration; the gifts beneath were symbols of our expectations and of the feelings we come to know when good things come to us.

Trees have been part of countless human celebrations. They are living things that we borrow to dress and adore in our winter holidays; but they also shelter us from their places in the ground, and they give their bodies for our warmth in the hearth-fire. We bless this tree for the life it yielded to our need for bright hope in the midst of winter.

Minister of Education: Christmas is the season of love. And the family unit is where love is created, nurtured, and shared. So one at a time, let's celebrate our family bonds by each family coming forth and each family take one ornament off the tree. We'll continue, taking as many turns as necessary until the tree is all undressed except for its lights. (Then added): (Minister, by name), I would like to ask you to remove the lights, as a symbol of how you held our lights to shine and to connect with each other.

Renewal of Resolve (All received pieces of white paper, and pencils at this time)

Minister of Education: On your clean, new, white piece of paper, write a New Year's Resolution that will help you to renew your

330

life for the New Year . . . something that will bring you new strength, purpose and meaning. Keep this piece of paper in your hand after you have written on it and focus on how it will feel to have what you have written a part of your life this coming year.

Bearing of Tree to the Place of Burning (While still indoors):

Minister: This tree was sacred to us this season; that is, it was special to our deepest meanings. Now it becomes even more so for we shall commemorate the life and sacrifice of Michael Servetus by committing this tree to the fire, knowing that the hope it gave to us at Christmas is eternal, though the tree ceases to live — just as the death of Servetus could not diminish the truth he gave to us.

Now, as the Native Americans always bore their ceremonial tree aloft from its earth-home to the ritual lodge, our young people will bear this tree from its stand here, carefully and lovingly to the fire area. (The tree is borne outdoors.)

Burning of the Tree (outdoors)

Minister: Michael Servetus was a forerunner of Unitarianism because he taught a truer Biblical meaning of the nature of God and of the great human prophet, Jesus of Nazareth. But Michael said his truth at a time when some persons did not wish to hear it. Some religious leaders, being fearful and insecure in their own minds, thought their idea of the truth could not stand in the presence of Michael's.

So Michael's life was taken from him by fire. But his truth would not die. Michael died but his truth lived on because it has helped us to see even greater truths: that whatever we know of God was not only in Jesus but in all of us. Miguel Serveto: as we light this fire, it is in memory of the bright hope you gave us when you died for your truth.

Minister of Education: As you hold this piece of paper in your hand, meditate for a moment on the meaning your resolution will bring to your life . . . And now, think, too, that this piece of paper came from a tree which gave its life, just as this tree lying here before us gave its light so we could have joy this Christmas. Just as Servetus sacrificed his life for something bigger than life to him, so we too will have to sacrifice in order to give life to our resolutions. For everything important, we pay a price. And so, as you add your papers to the fire now to be lit, in silence let each of us think of the price we will be willing to pay for our own growth."

(The fire is lit and each one's written resolve added to it.)

(The group then sang these songs together:
  Tis a Gift To Be Simple
  O Tannenbaum
  Listen, Listen, Listen to My Heart's Song)

331

Benediction (as the embers diminish)

Minister: An old custom was to keep part of the Yule Log from burning so that it could be used to light the next year's log. As this tree burns away, let its memory and this moment live in us till, next winter, we gather again to celebrate a season of joy. Let us go now with hearts warmed and the glow of family and friends ever within us.

— John E. Burciaga
— Caroline Fenderson

IX. *Before us goes the star*

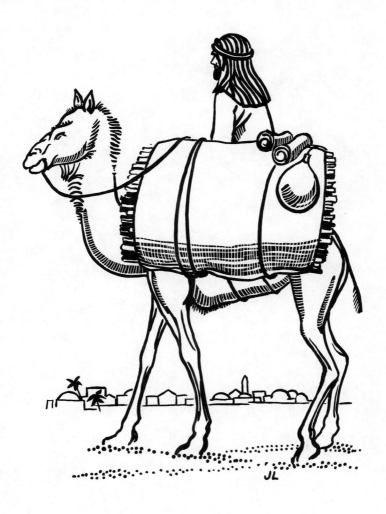

Before us goes the star
That leads us on to holier births
And life diviner far.
        Frederick Lucian Hosmer

A NOTE ON THE CAROLS

We love many of the traditional holiday carols and Christmas hymns. They have the feeling of being old friends known from childhood. Their melodies tumble out of us almost spontaneously, and many of us can sing verse after verse from memory.

We in liberal congregations also seek new artistic expressions that use music to capture today's meanings and hopes as we reconsider the messages the holidays hold for us in the modern era.

So, this collection gathers texts, mostly by poets in our own religious household, and it sets them to tunes that will be mostly unfamiliar to us. In some the harmonies will be in more contemporary musical modes than our traditional hymnals. A few have words that are old favorites or tunes that are, but you'll find some surprising combinations and varieties.

The settings are intentionally straightforward, and primarily for use with piano. Most, if not all, are adaptable to organ. Chord symbols for guitar, autoharp, or chord organ accompaniment are indicated in several pieces - capital letters for major chord, lower case for minor.

Specific adaptations of this music to individual congregational needs, and elaborations thereupon for choir or special use are to be encouraged, and thus left to local taste and requirements. For fuller harmonizing, the hymn tunes may be sung in the parts given; in others, it is hoped that the implied harmony will be sufficient.

Some editorial markings for tempo, dynamics, and phrasing are indicated. Our effort, however, has been towards finding that melody which lifts the text into song. Should this be felt to be so, then the particular sense of the words themselves will suggest the essential expression of the music.

To aid congregations and others in making the best use of these new carols, we are issuing simultaneously with the publication of this book a cassette tape entitled *Celebrating Christmas in Song*. the tape captures the melodies, moods, messages, and tempos of the carols. We hope that the tape will provide a new teaching aid as well as a pleasant introduction to our new Christmas carols.

Leo Collins
Eugene Navias
Carl Seaburg

335

THE HOLIDAYS ARE HERE AGAIN

Rebecca

John I. Daniel

Leo Collins

With a lilt (♩ =c. 88)

mf The Ho-li-days are here a - gain, To lift the dark'-ning year,
And Ha-nuk-ka is free-dom's shrine For all,'neath ty - ran - ny,

And ce - le-brate the feast of lights 'Mid glow of Christ-mas cheer.
The lamps are lit with - in our hearts For faith to make all free.

For not a-lone was Je-sus sought By wise men from a - far,
Joy to the world, these fes-tive days, No - where may hope grow dim,

The joy of oth - er hal-low'd births Shines with the won-drous star.
And, as the glad-some sea-son glows, Sing, ca - rol, song and hymn!

336

PAGEANTRY AND POETRY

Shout On

Katherine Wensberg

American Folk Hymn

1. The manger bed, the shepherd's fear, As lighted heavens sing, The star that draws the wise men east To kneel before a king; Such pageantry and poetry are universal art; They start a tide of Christmas joy That overflows the heart.

2. Sing "peace on earth; goodwill to all," And question not the way Those blessed words first came to us; What matters that today? For Christmas, heart time that it is, Must use a poem's art, Revealing truth in ancient ways To mind by way of heart.

3. Remember, too, the deeper truth That Christmas would not be Did not the core of Christmas prose Inspire the poetry; For fact it is that Jesus liv'd, And we will never cease To thank our Maker for each life That teaches ways of peace.

4. Accept the poetry, adore A wondrous child at birth, (p) But oh, keep Christmas all your life As Jesus liv'd on earth: Prose at the heart of poetry Affirming without fear The mystery and miracle Of God reveal'd right here.

337

I HEARD THE BELLS

Houghton

Henry Wadsworth Longfellow

Leo Collins

With a swing (♩.=c. 56)

1. I heard the bells on Christ - mas day Their
2. And thought how, as the day had come, The
3. And in des - pair I bow'd my head; "There
4. Then peal'd the bells more loud and deep: "God

old, fa - mil - iar car - ols play, And
bel - fries of all Christ - en - dom Had
is no peace on earth" I said, For
is not dead; nor doth God sleep!" The

wild and sweet the words re - peat Of
roll'd a - long th'un - bro - ken song Of
hate is strong and mocks the song Of
wrong shall fail, the right pre - vail, With

"Peace on earth, good will to all."

338

YULE FIRES

Greensleeves

John G. MacKinnon

English Traditional

In an-cient days— the folk of old,— when chill'd with fright— by win-ter's cold, Did
So we, whose minds now sense a chill— of dan - ger in —— the ev - il will, The

kin - dle up—— a great Yule fire,— With leap - ing flames— in its great pyre;
hu - man con - flict, hate and strife, Which hold a men - ace ov - er life;

So to en-tice—— the wan - ing sun— to rise a- gain,—and wi - der run;
Would kin-dle up—— a flame of love— that we with-in —— our hearts may move,

A fier - y course— a-cross the sky,— To warm— them so —— they need not die.
In yule-tide joy, —— to love our race,— And thus a - bide —— in peace and grace.

339

A CHRISTMAS CAROL FOR THESE TIMES

Salzburg (adapted)

Edwin T. Buehrer

Jacob Hintze, 1678

Enthusiastically (♩ = c. 152)

f

1. Po - ets, tell the an - cient sto - ry, sing the un - i -
2. Calm the an - gry pride of na - tions, stay the threat of
3. Pro - phets, speak with great - er pow - er; lead - ers, mark your

ver - sal song; Take from war its cru - el glo - ry,
ho - lo - caust. Let all peo - ples' lift - ed voi - ces
mis - sion clear, Match the chal - lenge of this ho - ur,

speed love's tri - umph ov - er wrong. Hate be - lies it,
call for peace, lest earth be lost. Fear re - jects it,
rid the world of hate and fear. Faith be - lieves it,

doubt de - nies it ___
hope ex - pects it ___ PEACE ON EARTH, GOOD-WILL TO ALL!
Love a - chieves it ___

340

AROUND THE CRIB

Hilariter

John A. Storey

Cologne, Kirchengesang, 1623

With spirit (♩=c.160)

p 1. A - round the crib all peo - ples throng In
mf 2. In pi - ous hearts Christ lives a - gain As
f 3. This Christ - mas - tide let us re - joice And

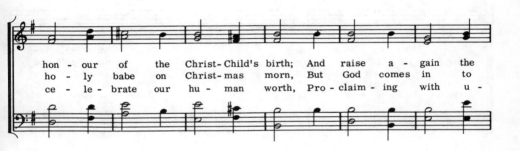

hon - our of the Christ-Child's birth; And raise a - gain the
ho - ly babe on Christ-mas morn, But God comes in to
ce - le - brate our hu - man worth, Pro - claim - ing with u -

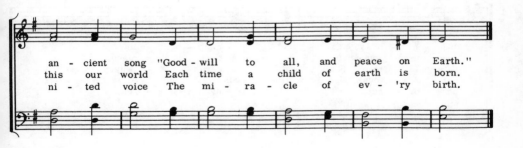

an - cient song "Good - will to all, and peace on Earth."
this our world Each time a child of earth is born.
ni - ted voice The mi - ra - cle of ev - 'ry birth.

341

CHRISTMAS JOY

Willdavi

John G. MacKinnon

Leo Collins

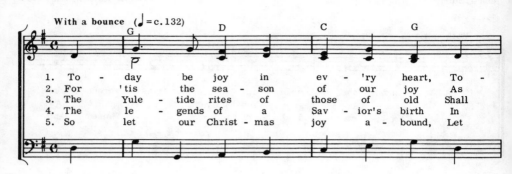

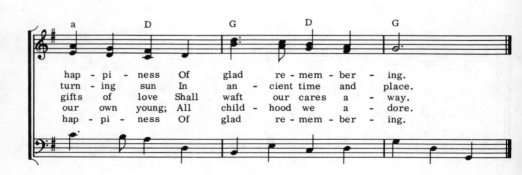

1. To - day be joy in ev - 'ry heart, To -
2. For 'tis the sea - son of our joy As
3. The Yule - tide rites of those of old Shall
4. The le - gends of a Sav - ior's birth In
5. So let our Christ - mas joy a - bound, Let

day let voi - ces sing, To - day let spread the
long liv'd as our race, When peo - ple watch'd the
warm our hearts to - day, The glad ex - change of
Beth - le - hem of yore En - rich our love for
Christ - mas ca - rols ring. To day let spread the

hap - pi - ness Of glad re - mem - ber - ing.
turn - ing sun In an - cient time and place.
gifts of love Shall waft our cares a - way.
our own young; All child - hood we a - dore.
hap - pi - ness Of glad re - mem - ber - ing.

ONCE IN ROYAL DAVID'S CITY

Irby

Carl Seaburg (based on a phrase of
Mrs. C. F. Alexander)

H. J. Gauntlett

Stately (♩=c.72)

1. Once in roy-al Dav-id's ci-ty stood a low-ly cat-tle
2. Shep-herds came to see this won-der, And to kneel in ho-ly
3. From a-far three wise men jour-ney'd To that sta-ble rude and
4. In that hap-py Christ-mas spir-it, Hear the an-gels from on

shed, Where a moth-er laid her ba-by In a
awe, At that low-ly sta-ble man-ger Where the
bare, To pay hom-age to the in-fant, Off'-ring
high Sing their an-cient sal-u-ta-tion: Joy's a

man-ger for his bed; So may we when life turns
in-fant lay on straw; So may we this hap-py
gifts both rich and rare; So may we our gifts be-
gift you can-not buy. So may we, with heart that

hard Find in love our stay and guard.
morn Hon-or ev'-ry child that's born.
stow, Whe-ther we be high or low.
sings, Share the truth this sea-son brings.

O BETHLEHEM TOWN

Lynne

John Haynes Holmes

Leo Collins

Tenderly (♩.=c. 54)

1. The Beth-le-hem stars are dim_to-night, The Beth-le-hem skies are still,____ The
2. The Beth-le-hem streets are dark_to-night, The Beth-le-hem winds are cold;____ A
3. O Beth-le-hem town, our hearts_to-night Are fill'd with a dream of thee;____ Hast

wea - ry shep - herds sleep_ a-mong Their flocks_ up-on the hill;____ But
hun - gry jack - al howls_ its pain Out on__ the emp-ty wold;____ But
thou no song_ for us__ to hear, No star__ for us to see?____ Must

Cae - sar's le - gions guard_ the gate, His trum-pets wait__ the morn;____ Why
Cae - sar's ban-ners flaunt_ their wings A - thwart the torch - es' glare____ On
Cae - sar's trum-pets cry__ the doom Of God's dread Judg - ment Day,____ Or

come not an - gels,____ to pro-claim The Prince of Peace is born?____
sol - diers in a ____ sta - ble - yard Why comes not Ma - ry there?____
shall we find thy ____ peace a - gain, And at a man - ger pray?____

rall.

PEACE

Glasgow

Mary A. R. Livermore

Thos. Moore's "Psalm Singer's Pocket Companion" c 1756

Affirmatively (♩=c.112)

1. No war - like sounds a - woke the night, An-
2. Not in the war - rior's ar - mor mail'd Was
3. But meek and low - ly was his life, The
4. Then let the war - cry ne'er be rung Be-
5. But let the bliss - ful pe - riod haste, When,

nounc - ing Je - sus' birth, But an - gels borne on
Je - sus ev - er found; Not striv - ing, when by
gen - tle Prince of Peace, Whose law con - demns the
neath the smil - ing sky, Nor to the clouds the
hush'd the can - non's roar, The sword shall cease our

wings of light, Who chant - ed "Peace on earth!"
wrath as - sail'd, Not with the lau - rel crown'd.
hos - tile strife, And bids dis - sen - sions cease.
ban - ner flung That tells of vic - to - ry.
lives to waste, And war shall be no more.

345

MUSIC O'ER THE WORLD

Deck the Halls

W. Waldemar W. Argow,
adapted

English Traditional

Joyously (♩ = c. 72)

Mu - sic o'er the world is break-ing, Mak-ing hearts in joy and glad-ness lift;
Chil-dren of the na - tions call us Bit - ter strife and an -gry war to cease,
Join us in our Christ-mas cho - rus, Sing-ing out the might-y song of peace;

An - cient words a - gain a-wak-ing In the ce-le-bra - tion of the gift.
Pov - er - ty and want to con-quer, Bring in - to the world a song of peace;
Peace trans-lat-ed in - to act-ion, So that hate and war for - ev - er cease.

Sym-bols from all lands and peo - ples; Mis-tle-toe, hol-ly wreath, Christ-mas tree-
At the fes - ti - val of Christ-mas, May our hope and our work ev - er be
Lift - ing up re - joic - ing voi - ces, March-ing on to this goal ea - ger - ly;

Man - i - fest the hap - py sto - ry, Fill-ing all the world with mel - o - dy.
That the child-ren of all na - tions Al-ways may be gen - tle, kind and free.
Join hu-man-i - ty in seek-ing Un - i - ver-sal love and un - i - ty.

346

AWAY IN A MANGER

Waverly

Traditional Text,
adapted

Gustav Mahler,
adapted by Leo Collins

Gently (♩ = c. 88)

(ding, dong, ding, dong)

1. A - way— in a man - ger, no
2. The cat - tle are low - ing, the
3. The sweet ba - by Je - sus a

crib for a bed, The lit - tle ba-by Je - sus laid down his sweet head. The
ba - by a - wakes, But lit - tle ba-by Je - sus no cry - ing he makes. They
teach-er will be, To show us how to love, and from en - vy be free. May

stars— in the bright sky look'd down — where he lay, The
love — ba - by Je - sus, all those — kneel - ing by, They
each — lit - tle child here re - ceive — ten - der care, Pre -

lit - tle ba - by Je - sus, a - sleep on the hay.
stay be - side his cra - dle, 'til morn - ing be nigh.
par - ing them for ser - vice in life, ev - 'ry - where.

HANUKKAH/SATURNALIA/ADVENT HYMN

Toplady (adapted)

L. Stein, et al, adapted
by F. Forrester Church

Thomas Hastings, 1830

Firmly (♩ = c. 116)

Rock of a - ges, let our song, Praise thy good and
Rock of a - ges, star of dawn, Break up - on our
Rock of a - ges, prince of peace, May thy glo - ri -

sav - ing pow'r. Thou, a - midst the rag - ing foes,
dark' - ning year. Touch thy lamp to our dis - tress
ous re - frain Pub - lish tid - ings of good will,

Wast our shel - ter and our tow'r. Mad with fu - ry
With the rad - iance of thy cheer. Ring the hea - vens,
Dance with - in our hearts a - gain. Rock of A - ges,

they as - sail'd, But thine arm it did a - vail.
bless our sight, Pledge thy gift, per - fect - ing light.
child or king, As thy gifts, our - selves we bring.

348

X. Grateful for
small miracles

LANGAN

We gather in the early blackness and deep cold
of winter solstice, finding warmth from each
other, turning darkness to a time of light,
nourishing hope where reason fails.
Grateful for small miracles, we rejoice in
the wonder of making light out of darkness
and the daring of hope.
Chanukah, Congregation BETH EL
of the Sudbury River Valley
Vetaher Libenu Siddur

SOME ADDITIONAL RESOURCES

It was not the intent of this collection to range beyond denominational inspiration, but these pieces can be heartily recommended to Christmas celebrants.

Copyrighted Poetry about Christmas

Conrad Aiken, *Christmas Eve*

W. H. Auden, *For The Time Being*

Joseph Ausland, *Christmas*

Robert Bridges, *Noel: Christmas Eve, 1913*

James Broughton, *Nativity 1956*

G. K. Chesterton, *The Feast of the Snow*
The House of Christmas

John Ciardi, *A Sentiment for December 25*
Christmas Eve

Grace Noll Crowell, *Leisure*

e. e. cummings, *little tree*
love is the only god

John Drinkwater, *Christmas Eve*

Richard Eberhart, *The Incomparable Light*

T. S. Eliot, *Journey of the Magi*

Robert Frost, *Christmas Trees*

Thomas Hardy, *The Oxen*

Robinson Jeffers, *Two Christmas Cards*

Robert Lowell, *Christmas Eve Under Hooker's Statue*

Archibald MacLeish, *Pole Star For This Year*

John Masefield, *Christmas at Sea*

Phyllis McGinley, *Mince Pie and Mistletoe*
To A Modernistic Christmas Tree
New England
The Ballad of Befanna
The Victorian Years
The Western Country
Virginia

Thomas Merton, *Carol*

Edna St. Vincent Millay, *To Jesus on His Birthday*

A. A. Milne, *King John's Christmas*

Odgen Nash, *The Boy Who Laughed at Santa Claus*
Merry Christmas Nearly Everybody
A Carol for Children
April Yule, Daddy!
Heil, Heilige Nacht!

Dorothy Parker, *The Maidservant at the Inn*
Prayer for a New Mother

Boris Pasternack, *Star of the Nativity*

Kenneth Patchen, *I Have Lighted the Candles, Mary*

Rainer Maria Rilke, *Birth of Christ*
Annunication Over the Shepherds
Before Christmas 1914

Edwin Arlington Robinson, *The Gift of God*

W. R. Rodgers, *White Christmas*

Carl Sandburg, *Silver Star*
Special Starlight

May Sarton, *Winter Grace*
The Birthday
Christmas 1974

Karl Shapiro, *Christmas Eve: Australia*
Christmas Tree

Odell Shepard, *The Gifts*

Allen Tate, *Sonnets at Christmas*

Sara Teasdale, *Christmas Carol*

Nancy Byrd Turner, *The Christmas Star*
                   God Is With Us

Louis Untermeyer, *For Another Birth*

Mark Van Doren, *Dialogue in December*

William Carlos Williams, *The Gift*
                         Burning the Christmas Greens

William Yeats, *The Second Coming*

SELECTED BIBLIOGRAPHY

Stories and Anthologies

A Christmas Treasury
     Jack Newcombe, ed.
     New York: Viking Press, Inc., 1982

Four Christmas Stories
     W. Edward Harris
     Urbana, IL: 1980

Behold That Star
     The Society of Brothers, eds.
     Ripton, N.Y.: Plough Publishing House, 1966

Once Upon A Christmas
     Pearl S. Buck, ed.
     New York: John Day Co., Inc., 1972

Told Under the Christmas Tree
     Association for Childhood Education
     New York: Macmillan Publishing Co., Inc., 1962

The Fireside Book of Christmas Stories
     Edward Wagenknecht, ed.
     New York: Bobbs-Merrill Co., Inc., 1943

A Christmas Feast: Poems, Sayings, Greetings and Wishes
     Edna Barth
     Boston: Houghton Mifflin Co., 1979

Joy to the World
     Ruth Sawyer
     Boston: Little, Brown & Co., 1966

Christmas Observed
     Owen Dudley Edwards and Graham Richardson
     New York: St. Martin's Press, Inc., 1982

We Believe In Christmas
David and Beverly Bumbaugh
Alexandria, VA: 1982

Music

The Oxford Book of Carols (1)
Percy Dearmer, R. Vaughan Williams and Martin Shaw, eds.
London: Oxford University Press, Inc., 1928

Carols for Choirs (2)
David Willcocks and John Rutter, eds.
London: Oxford University Press, Inc., 1970

Carols for Choirs (3)
David Willcocks and John Rutter, eds.
London: Oxford University Press, Inc., 1978

A Treasury of Christmas Songs and Carols
Henry W. Simson, ed.
Boston: Houghton Mifflin Co., 1955

We Sing of Life
Vincent Silliman, ed.
Boston: Beacon Press, Inc., 1955
(25 seasonal songs here)

American Songs for Christmas
Ruth Crawford Seeger
New York: Doubleday & Co., Inc., 1953

Celebrations

Hinge of the Year
Leonard Mason
London: Lindsey Press, 1967

Channukah
Mary-Lib Whitney
New York, 1981

Winter Festivals and Celebrations
Meredith U. Anderson, ed.
Boston: Church of the Larger Fellowship, 1982

A Book of Advent
V. Beck and P. Lindberg
Rock Island, IL: Augustana College Library, 1958

Celebrate While We Wait
St. Louis: Concordia Publishing House, 1977

Customs

The Christmas Tree
Daniel Foley
New York: Chilton & Co., 1960

The Book of Christmas Folklore
Tristam P. Coffin
New York: Seabury Press, Inc., 1973

The Jewish Holiday Book
Wendy Lazar
New York: Doubleday & Co., Inc., 1977

Seasons of Our Joy: A Celebration of Modern Jewish Renewal
Arthur Waskow
New York: Bantam, 1982

The Winter Solstice
Shirley Toulson
London: Jill Norman & Hobhouse, 1981

Seasonal Feasts and Festivals
E. O. James
New York: Barnes & Noble Books, 1961

The Trees of Christmas
Edna Metcalfe, ed.
Nashville, TN: Abingdon Press, 1969

Holidays Around the World
Joseph Gaer
Boston: Little, Brown & Co., 1953

Christmas Everywhere
Elizabeth H. Sechrist
Philadelphia: Macrae Smith Co., 1962

The History of the Christmas Carol
George Buday
London: Rockliff, 1954

Celebrating Christmas Around the World
Herbert H. Wernecke
Philadelphia: Westminster Press, 1962

Food

John Clancy's Christmas Cookbook
New York: Hearst Books, 1982

Christmas Cookbook
  Susan Purdy
  New York: Franklin Watts, Inc., 1976

Betty Crocker's Christmas Cookbook
  Racine, WI: Golden Press, 1982

Crafts

Treasury of Christmas Crafts and Foods
  New York: Better Homes & Gardens Books, 1982

A New Look at Christmas Decorations
  M. Gratia Listaite and Norbert A. Hildebrand
  Milwaukee: Bruce, 1957

Christmas Crafts
  Carolyn Meyer
  New York: Harper & Row Publishers, Inc., 1974

Christmas Gifts for You to Make
  Susan Purdy
  New York: J. B. Lippincott Co., 1976

A Complete Christmas Book
  Franklin Watts, ed.
  New York: Franklin Watts, Inc., 1958

Eight pieces by Howard Thurman had been chosen for this book but were unavailable because of copyright restrictions. Attention is called to a forthcoming anthology of Dr. Thurman's work to be published by Harcourt, Brace, Jovanovich, *The Thurman Reader*. Readers may also wish to consult *The Mood of Christmas* by Dr. Thurman (Harper & Row, 1973) for additional items.

Index of Authors

357

358

When nothing is left of the merry-making but withered holly and faded mistletoe and the few red embers that still shine among the hickory ashes of the Christmas backlog, we rejoice that we are spared to pause and wonder over that strange miracle we call life.
— Julia Peterkin